GERMANY AND ISRAEL

'A well-researched and impressive book, revealing a historical chapter unknown to many, yet which shaped modern history in several ways. Marwecki's erudite scholarship shows that Germany's unconditional support to Israel was based on cynical strategic considerations which had little to do with genuine guilt.'
— Ilan Pappé

'Describes ... moral absolution of a ... still profoundly antisemitic Germany in return for cash and weapons.'
— *London Review of Books*

'Unconditional solidarity with Israel is rapidly destroying the immense moral prestige Germany built in the decades after the Shoah. Marwecki demonstrates in eye-opening and deeply discomfiting detail how Germany first came to possess this moral prestige. Everyone interested in Germany's past and concerned about its future should read it.'
— Pankaj Mishra

'In its balance and erudition, [this] analysis ... has much to recommend it.'
— *Asian Affairs*

'The most important and insightful historical analysis of German-Israeli relations since the establishment of both countries. Marwecki's clear-eyed, hard-hitting assessment of two nations that still cling to each other for all the wrong reasons is an unsparing must-read.'
— David de Jong, author of *Nazi Billionaires*

'A sober, thoughtful and valuable history of a strange relationship. Much academic and official discourse assumes that it was driven by moral concerns, yet Marwecki shows clearly and compellingly that it was driven by interests on both sides.'
— Hans Kundnani, author of *Eurowhiteness and The Paradox of German Power*

'Using foreign office archives, cabinet protocols, parliamentary debates and expert interviews, Marwecki provides completely new insights into why postwar Germany supported Israel and why, despite Nazis remaining in German power, Israel accepted this assistance. This fascinating account not only sheds light on historical developments, but helps makes sense of the present moment.'

— Neve Gordon, Professor of International Law,
Queen Mary University of London,
and author of *Human Shields*

'A fascinating study providing detailed perspectives into the evolution of German-Israeli relations. Covering sixty years of interaction at all levels of state and society, Marwecki impressively captures how the two have remained strategically intertwined.'

— Alexander Clarkson, Lecturer in German and European and International Studies, King's College London

'A carefully researched, forcefully argued and clearly written account of Germany's political relationship with Israel through the logic of the 1952 reparation agreement. An important contribution to scholarship, and a critical corrective to the official representation of this special relationship.'

— Felix Berenskötter, Senior Lecturer in International Relations, SOAS University of London

DANIEL MARWECKI

Germany and Israel

Whitewashing and Statebuilding

HURST & COMPANY, LONDON

First published in the United Kingdom in 2020 by
C. Hurst & Co. (Publishers) Ltd.,
41 Great Russell Street, London, WC1B 3PL

This paperback edition first published in 2025 by
C. Hurst & Co. (Publishers) Ltd.,
New Wing, Somerset House, Strand,
London, WC2R 1LA

A Cataloguing-in-Publication data record for this book
is available from the British Library.

ISBN: 9781805264484

www.hurstpublishers.com

CONTENTS

ACKNOWLEDGEMENTS

Writing a book has been on my personal bucket list since I was about eight years old. I am grateful to Hurst Publishers for enabling me to tick off that point some 25 years later. This book is based on my PhD, which I wrote at the School of Oriental and African Studies, under the guidance of Gilbert Achcar. Gilbert's supervision has simply been outstanding and this study would never have seen the light of day without him. Yair Wallach and David Feldman provided excellent further supervision on the PhD.

A big thank you to the Evangelisches Studienwerk Villigst, who funded most of my PhD studies.

Some further professional thank you notes: I profited immensely from discussions with my friend and colleague Jan Rybak about the research interests we share. I also thank Tom Segev, Moshe Zuckermann, Ofried Nassauer and many other interviewees wishing to stay anonymous for offering me their time, expertise and divergent views. Among the conferences I attended over the past years, the following were especially helpful in shaping the direction of this research: a workshop at the Leo-Baeck Institute in London with Moshe Zimmermann, a panel chaired by James Renton at the European University Institute in Florence, the 'Zionism and Antisemitism' conference organised by the Pears Centre for the Study of Antisemitism in London and the 'Jewish Friends' conference at the Free University of Berlin.

The archivists at the German foreign office in Berlin have been very helpful. This book would be much less interesting without them. The archivists at the Israel State Archives and the Ben-Gurion Archives have been more than kind, yet constraints of time and space led me to focus on German sources and German foreign policy.

Whilst the wisdom of doing a PhD is debatable, moving to London and studying at SOAS is not. I made amazing new friends. As I dislike making the private all too public, I won't list names, but you know. An equally big shout-out to everybody in Bremen and Berlin.

My family will always come first and last. It is thanks to your endless support that this was possible.

A disclaimer: whilst I could not have written any of the following on my own, all mistakes are mine.

FOREWORD TO THE PAPERBACK EDITION

This book first appeared in the spring of 2020, just as the world went into a pandemic shutdown. The question of Israel and Palestine—and the German question within that question—did not rank highly on the world's political agenda. This has since changed.

On 7 October 2023, Hamas overwhelmed the border between Israel and the Gaza Strip. Along with other Palestinian forces and individuals, Hamas fighters committed a massacre, largely against unarmed civilians, and took as many hostages as they could, including children and the elderly. About 1,200 people were killed, and about 250 taken hostage.

A few days after the attack, then German Chancellor Olaf Scholz said in the Bundestag, the country's parliament, that there could be 'only one place' for Germany. That place was 'by Israel's side'. Following this declaration of support, Scholz flew to Israel to underline his commitment. At the closing press conference, Israeli Prime Minister Benjamin Netanyahu declared that Hamas were 'the new Nazis'. The implication was clear. This time around, Germany could stand on the right side of history by supporting the Jewish state against its enemies of today.

From a German perspective, Netanyahu's equation of Hamas with Nazi Germany was both an offer of exoneration, and a veiled threat. If these militants were the new Nazis, the Germans were, by implication, no longer such—unless they proved lacking in their support for Israel's existential fight.

In Germany, or rather among Germany's political class and public sphere, Netanyahu's statement fell on receptive ears. German memory culture, as it has evolved over the past few decades, tends to reduce the complexity of Nazi barbarism to one of its ideological components—namely, antisemitism. Once this reduction is undertaken, it is not difficult for German public imagination to cast off the role of the antisemite and impose it on other groups; for example, Muslim immigrants, foreign intellectuals, left-wing students, or, for that matter, the civilian population of Gaza.

This blurring of Palestine with Nazi Germany leads easily to an equation of Gaza with Dresden. This comparison was made in Germany during the first months of the Israeli assault on Gaza especially: today's eliminatory antisemitism must be broken by merciless bombardment. Of course, leaving aside the many other differences in this problematic comparison, the bombing of Gaza since October 2023 exceeds what the populations of Dresden or Hamburg endured during World War II. The coastal strip has effectively been destroyed, its surviving population turned into permanent refugees living in their own ruins.

What also got lost in Germany's projection of its own past onto the Middle East was, among other things, the fact that Nazi Germany was a major imperialist power. Hamas, by contrast, is one of many radical and armed groups in the region. Its breeding ground is the suffering of its own population— ground partly fertilised, of course, by religious fundamentalism, authoritarianism, and antisemitism. There was, therefore, no need to mistake for legitimate resistance the events of 7 October; even without holding this view, it was evident early on that what Israel was doing in Gaza offered no political solution, only further despair and radicalisation. This, of course, was an opinion expressed in United Nations resolutions from the very first weeks of Israel's war.

Yet Germany chose to support the war, in military, moral and diplomatic ways. In previous years, around 30 per cent of Israeli arms imports had been of German origin. Almost 70 per cent came from the USA. Weapon deliveries to Israel surged after the Hamas attacks. Between 7 October 2023 and mid-May 2025, Germany exported weapons and military materiel to the value of almost half a billion euros, as the Bundestag disclosed following an inquiry by the left-wing party Die Linke. When South Africa accused Israel of the crime of genocide before the International Court of Justice in late 2023, the German government stepped in, disparaging such accusations as 'baseless'. Within Germany, expressions of pro-Palestinian sentiment have been repressed politically to an extraordinary degree. German support for the Israeli destruction of Gaza has thus proceeded without much internal dissent.

Whitewashing and statebuilding

Others have written about the relationship between Germany and Israel in tame or even jubilant terms, reflecting the official narrative more than critical scholarship. The goal behind this book, originally a doctoral dissertation completed at SOAS University of London in 2018, has been different. The idea was to shed light on the strangeness, the blind spots, and the manifold cruelties that characterise German–Israeli intertwinement. As per the book's title, I think the relationship is best characterised as an exchange of whitewashing for statebuilding.

The currently ruling discourse in Germany around the country's *Staatsräson*, translatable as 'reason of state', is the culmination of this exchange. Under Konrad Adenauer, the first chancellor of postwar West Germany, the rapprochement with

Israel served to demonstrate the Federal Republic's integration into the West, and to gloss over the failures of denazification. Today, or at least until recently, the German political class and leading media outlets have been engaged in a one-sided and self-congratulatory moralisation of the relationship. Thus, over time, Adenauer's calculation that solidarity with Israel would absolve Germany of its guilt became Germany's dominant motivation for the relationship. This, in turn, has developed into a form of state-orchestrated identity politics—or nationalism—organised around the idea that, the closer Germany's ties to Israel, the greater its distance from the Nazi past. Not only is the relationship primarily about moralising and absolution; it has few positive implications for the fight against antisemitism and fascist tendencies within Germany. It also has little to do with assuming a constructive role in the Israel–Palestine conflict.

If the symbolic and moral reconstruction of Germany is linked to the material reconstruction of Israel, so, too, is Germany's moral dismantling. Up until recently, Germany enjoyed a relatively positive reputation in the Middle East. Berlin's refusal to participate in the Iraq War in 2003, and opening of the country's doors to Syrian refugees in 2015, are particularly well-regarded in regional memory. Furthermore, Germany's memory culture has long been seen as exemplary beyond the country itself. Despite all the criticisms one may have against it, one would be hard-pressed to find another nation that has placed not its past glories, but its past sins at the centre of its culture of remembrance.

Germany has long been viewed by many as a country that had confronted its history. One such erstwhile admirer was the writer Pankaj Mishra, who, in the first months of Israel's offensive in the Gaza Strip, wrote in the *London Review of Books* that 'the German authorities risk failing in their responsibility to the rest of the world: never again to become complicit in murderous ethnonationalism.'

One day, even Germany will have been against this

In May 1965, the Federal Republic and Israel officially entered into diplomatic relations. In May 2025, mutual state visits took place to celebrate the sixtieth anniversary of mutual diplomatic recognition. Israeli President Isaac Herzog visited his counterpart, Frank-Walter Steinmeier, in Berlin. A German delegation made a return trip to Israel. Both sides lauded their 'friendship'. The Germans expressed gratitude for what they continue to view as a miraculous success story of reconciliation. Whilst in Israel, the newly appointed German foreign minister, Johann Wadephul, publicly expressed support for the use of humanitarian aid as a weapon of war.

Politicians of any country are professional experts in sustaining cognitive dissonance. It comes with the job. Yet German politicians seem to be capable of extraordinary moral flexibility. How is it feasible to celebrate a supposedly miraculous friendship after the German barbarism of the Holocaust, whilst a few kilometres away, a largely defenceless population is being bombed and starved? President Steinmeier was in fact with President Herzog and Prime Minister Netanyahu as the Israeli army bombed two hospitals in the Gazan city of Khan Younis. Now that Israel has few allies left, such open political support from a key European player has direct and deadly consequences. According to the latest figures from Gaza, at the time of writing the death count is reaching 60,000,[1] a majority of whom are women and children. Uncounted in this figure are those still missing under the rubble, as well as indirect deaths from lack of healthcare, water, and food.

Shortly after the state visit to Israel, however, the German political class seemed to be backtracking, in the same sort of uniform movement with which it had initially supported the Gaza war. Both Chancellor Friedrich Merz and Foreign Minister

Wadephul argued that, whilst Israel's security may be Germany's reason of state, friendship should not extend to tolerating breaches of international law. Yet the government had not only become aware of what was happening in Gaza in May 2025. What spurred this sudden change of heart? One reason was that the tone had changed in other Western capitals. On 19 May, Canada, the UK and France warned of 'concrete actions' if Israel were to continue its latest offensive and restrictions of humanitarian aid.

The week prior to this, the Spanish prime minister, Pedro Sánchez, had gone further and called Israel a 'genocidal state'.

Given that Merz, sworn into office on 6 May, had promised to be a European chancellor in a time of US decline, it would be difficult for Berlin to stand in the way of a European and wider Western change in policy toward Israel. That said, whilst the tone seems to be shifting somewhat even in Berlin, at the time of writing this hasn't yet amounted to any more profound policy shift—such as a ban on weapons exports, or the cessation of Israel's association agreement with the European Union.

On the book's publication in paperback

When I first wrote this book, I could not have foreseen the abyss that would one day open up beneath the German–Israeli relationship. Yet, re-reading the text as it was published in 2020, it brings me little pleasure to say that its explanatory framework has held up rather well; or, at the very least, much better than others. I have chosen, therefore, not to change the original text in light of the horrors that have since emerged.

The pages that follow can be read as a critical biography of Germany as it was reinvented after 1945. Given that Germany needs to reinvent itself once more, in an age of American decline, a hostile Russia, and renewed great power rivalry, such a biography may help to enlighten the future paths that the country could possibly take. As the German question is also a European one, understanding Germany is important not only to Germans. This book, then, may also be read as a modest contribution to the literature on the asymmetrical, but mutually existential, conflict between Israelis and Palestinians.

Lastly, and in more general terms, the following pages tell a story of international relations and politics after Nazi Germany's wars of annihilation, its downfall and the Holocaust. Of what does political morality consist, in a nihilistic age in which politicians from Vladimir Putin to Benjamin Netanyahu claim that they are fighting Nazis, while themselves perpetrating evil against hapless civilians?

For students of international relations, I hope this book demonstrates that one learns most about foreign policy if one takes a critical distance from it. This, of course, should be the goal of any critically thinking person, be it inside or outside of academia.

Daniel Marwecki
Berlin, June 2025

xvii

PREFACE

Visitors to the German capital rarely fail to visit the East Side Gallery, a row of murals painted on remnants of the Berlin Wall, running from the Ostbahnhof along the Spree river. Amongst the most well-known of these murals is that of the artist Günter Schäfer. Called *Fatherland*, it shows a combination of the German and Israeli flags, with the Star of David superimposed onto the black, red and gold of the Federal Republic of Germany (FRG). Next to this merging of national symbols, a universalist message of reconciliation is written; it speaks of 'peace and unity of all peoples' and describes the artwork as a 'memorial against any fascist tendency'. The dates of 9 November in 1938 and 1989 are also painted to the sides of the picture. According to the artist, these two dates symbolise a low and a high point in German history. The pogroms of November 1938 were a key event in the lead-up to the Shoah (Holocaust). In contrast, German national narratives tend to perceive the fall of the Berlin Wall in November 1989 as an 'end' to the 'punishment of separation' for the crimes of Nazism. While November 1938 represents the descent into barbarism, November 1989 stands for the culmination and reward for Germany's journey back to 'the West'.

Schäfer's work has often been vandalised. Next to swastikas and antisemitic slurs, the Israel-Palestine conflict is also re-enacted on the mural. While the artist differentiates between clear cases of antisemitism and 'Free Palestine' slogans, he personally cleans his mural of all types of graffiti and sloganeering (Schmidl 2015).

What Schäfer communicated in the mural was officially expressed by the German parliament in April 2018 when it celebrated the seventieth anniversary of Israel's founding: that the German 'fatherland', built on the ashes of Nazism, cannot be reimagined without a close relationship with Israel. In the Bundestag debate, speakers shared the view that the depth of the German commitment to Israel indicates the degree to which Germany has overcome its Nazi past. For the Social Democratic Party (SPD), Party Leader Martin Schulz said that 'by protecting Israel, we protect ourselves from the demons of the past of our own people' (Bundestag 2018). Green Party Speaker Katrin Göring-Eckardt echoed the sentiment: 'The existence of Israel is directly connected to the existence of our country as a free democracy [...] we must be the guarantor of Israel'. She condensed her message in a phrase that captured the gist of the whole debate: 'Israel's right to exist is our own' (Bundestag 2018).

Parliamentarians of the Christian Democratic Union (CDU), the Bavarian Christian Social Union (CSU) and the Free Democratic Party spoke in the same vein. Across parties, speakers echoed or explicitly referred to Chancellor Angela Merkel's famous statement to the Israeli Knesset in March 2008, when she declared that the German 'special historical responsibility for Israel's security' is part of the German *Staatsräson* – its very *raison d'état* (Merkel 2008).[1]

While a state's interests easily change according to outer circumstances, its *Staatsräson* does not. Because the commitment to Israel is a pillar of German statehood, the two parties on both ends of the parliamentary spectrum adhere to this commitment as well. In the Bundestag debate, the speaker for Die Linke ('The Left') framed Germany's 'special responsibility' for Israel with reference to philosopher Theodor Adorno as part of 'the moral duty to do everything so that Auschwitz may not repeat itself' (Bundestag 2018).

Today, many in the German political mainstream, including the just-quoted Martin Schulz, would argue that the 'demons of the past' had entered the German polity again. The 2017 federal elections were a shock to German democracy, being the first time since the FRG's founding in 1949 that a party to the right of the CDU/CSU entered the Bundestag as a significant force. With almost 13 per cent of the vote, the far-right Alternative for Germany (AfD) had become the third-largest party. Nevertheless, it also adopted the parliamentary perspective on German-Israeli relations, with Co-Leader Alexander Gauland declaring that Israel originated from the 'singular break of civilization' which 'will forever be connected with Germany's name: the Shoah' (Bundestag 2018). The guilt-evading formulation of the phrase 'connected with Germany's name' is noteworthy, as it is part of the AfD's attempt to belittle the place of Nazism in German history as much as possible. Two months after this debate, Gauland likened Nazism to a 'bird's poop' within the overall course of German history.[2]

What Germans (don't) talk about when they talk about Israel

The Bundestag debate shows that when German politicians talk about Israel, what they really tend to talk about is the Nazi past – and, in doing so, about present-day German identity.[3] A blunt statement such as this needs to be academically qualified, but it is revealing to read German governmental and public debates about Israel as socio-psychological projections, with Israel serving as a displacement object onto which different ideas of German national identity can be articulated.

Understanding German debates about Israel as debates about Germany helps in making sense of the following observation: speakers in the Bundestag did not talk about the actual *content* of German-Israeli relations, even though doing so would help explain what German politicians so often find inexplicable and miraculous. For example, in the same debate, Andrea Nahles of the SPD called the 'unique friendship' between Germany and Israel a 'miracle', and she expressed her 'awe' and 'gratitude' for the 'reconciliation' between the two countries (Bundestag 2018). Only one parliamentarian of the CDU/CSU spoke briefly about current military relations between Germany and Israel and their early origins in the postwar era, urging his colleagues to talk more openly about this undoubtedly crucial area of bilateral relations.

In fact, the history of German economic, financial, military and political support to Israel is highly underappreciated. A research report by the US Congressional Service found that 'Germany's commitment to Israel's sovereignty and security has historically been the strongest influence on its policy in the Middle East and a key factor in its cooperation with the United States in the region' (Belkin 2007: 1). According to the report, '[t]he extent and precise value of arms shipments to and from Germany through the mid-1990's remains unclear, yet analysts assert that German arms played a considerable role in Israeli military victories in 1967, 1973 and 1982' (Belkin 2007: 5). The report further asserted that:

> German leaders have consistently chosen to support Israel – whether militarily, financially or politically – despite periods of public, political or even international opposition. This support, however, has often been carried out secretively. In fact, historical accounts suggest that German success in maintaining relatively positive relations on both sides of the Arab-Israeli conflict has depended largely on its ability to avoid a high-profile leadership role in the region. (Belkin 2007: 15)

Scholarship on international relations and the Middle East typically focuses on the preponderant role of the United States in the region and their support to Israel. Yet this focus omits that the US–Israeli military alliance only truly developed after 1967, while the crucial role played by the FRG in Israel's consolidation prior to this remains largely unknown.

Also absent from the 2018 Bundestag debate was the issue of the Palestinians and their right to self-determination. As this debate shows, Palestinians hardly figure in the German narrative of reconciliation and friendship with Israel. Palestinian dispossession – the birthmark of Israel's founding in 1948 – is apparently too problematic and unwieldy a topic to enter the celebratory discourse of the German Bundestag. In fact, it was the far right which spoke most about Palestinians in the debate, framing them as aggressors, unwilling to compromise and fuelled by antisemitism. However, Palestinians are more than just a significant, if often invisible, 'Other' to German-Israeli relations. Germany has had a concrete impact on the Palestinian situation, both indirectly through its relations with Israel, and more directly through its role as a major supporter of the Oslo process (1993–2000) and subsequent funder of Palestinian 'statebuilding'. Nevertheless, it is an impact that is rarely pondered.

The Bundestag debate and the *Fatherland* mural both draw, albeit with different instruments, a picture of Germany's Israel policy which suggests national reconciliation and a German mastering of its barbaric past. It is much more a German picture than an Israeli one. The framing of German-Israeli relations as a form of reconciliation seeks to cleanse Germany of antisemitism, which time and again seems to creep back into view. Likewise, the Palestinian question does not disappear by ignoring it. The image of reconciliation that German political discourse draws is itself a function of Germany's Israel policy, a policy which remains unexplained if one only looks at how German governments talk about their relationship with Israel.

Astonishingly enough, however, the topic remains largely unexplained in academia as well. Given the importance of FRG-Israel relations to our understandings of the contemporary Middle East, and the central role of Israel in German foreign policy and domestic discourse, one would assume this to be a well-covered topic in the intersecting fields of international relations, Middle East studies, and studies of antisemitism and racism. Yet, this is simply not the case.

A few historians have done the indispensable work of carefully researching, describing and contextualising specific periods of German-Israeli relations (see especially Fink 2019; Jelinek 2004; Trimbur 2000). As is the nature of such studies, they cannot provide a historically encompassing analysis of their topic; providing the 'big picture' of German-Israeli relations is a task for political scientists. However, existing works from a political science perspective suffer from a remarkable tendency to uncritically adopt the discourses of the two states whose relations they claim to analyse. This unwillingness to significantly move away from a reproduction of political self-descriptions towards critical analysis results in an affirmative writing of diplomatic history. The effect of such affirmative writing is a 'moral bias', especially in the German literature on German-Israeli relations.[4] 'Moral bias' denotes the idea that postwar West Germany turned to Israel predominantly for moral reasons, and that morality has since remained central to the German-Israeli relationship. Conversely, Israeli academia does not share the German academic tendency of portraying bilateral relations as grounded in 'morality' (Hestermann 2016: 19ff.). The moral narrative is unconvincing simply because of the well-documented fact that under the first West German administration, led by Konrad Adenauer, the early process of denazification instigated by the

Allied powers was aborted and partially even reversed. The newly-found FRG was characterised by Nazi continuities on the level of state bureaucracy, functional elites and societal attitudes. The 'reintegration and amnesty' (Frei 2002; see also Taylor 2012) of former Nazi criminals was but one element in the moral wasteland of postwar West Germany, in which the different levels of involvement in National Socialism were repressed and German victimhood narcissistically upheld.

Whitewashing and statebuilding

It is one of the many ironies of the German-Israeli relationship that Germany was most important to Israel when it was least guided by moral considerations. Amongst other things, this book shows that prior to the decisive Arab–Israeli War of 1967, it was not the United States but West Germany which was the most important supporter of the newly-found Jewish state in the Middle East. Postwar German reparations, financial aid and military support helped in turning Israel from a risky enterprise of destitute refugees and committed settlers into a regional power.

Why would Israel, which claimed representation for both the victims and survivors of the German horror, seek such close relations with the successor state to Nazi Germany? 'Friendship' or the 'miracle of reconciliation' – catchphrases of today's German discourse – obfuscate rather than answer this question. The answer is simple: material need. David Ben-Gurion, Israel's primary founding figure, asserted his German policy against the emotional opposition of Israeli society because he knew that the new state needed all the help it could find to survive in a hostile environment. The overriding aim was to consolidate the new Jewish homeland against the overbearing odds. *Statebuilding*.

For the young FRG – a silent community of perpetrators and onlookers – supporting the Jewish state was firstly a brushstroke to facilitate western integration; a symbolic political act indicating an exorcised democracy where it could not have previously existed. *Whitewashing.*

It would of course be mechanistic and ahistorical to simply understand German-Israeli relations, from their postwar origins to today, as an exchange between whitewashing and statebuilding. The title of this book serves as a conceptual lens through which to assess and explain change in German-Israeli relations; an analytical tool helping us to make sense of the many questions raised by this strange relationship.

Sources, definitions, delimitations

The book is based on research from the archives of the German Foreign Office, the Auswärtiges Amt (AA), for the time period from the early 1950s until 1967.[5] The amount of material on the topic reflects its political significance; the fact that a lot of this material has so far remained ignored reflects a form of academic negligence, especially on behalf of German-language political scientists. This is a general examination of the most important aspects of Germany's Israel policy, which means that historical detail was neglected in favour of recently declassified files labelled 'confidential', 'secret' or 'top secret'. Other primary sources used include cabinet protocols, parliamentary debates and interviews with experts.

A political history bringing together Germany, Israel and the 'Palestinian question' needs to be clear about its underlying understandings of antisemitism. When this book talks about antisemitism, it is mostly in the context of 'secondary antisemitism', a specific guilt-related form of prejudice and hostility that developed in post-1945 West Germany. With racial antisemitism tabooed in the public sphere after the nation's defeat, expressions of antisemitism continued to take a coded form. Secondly, post-1945 antisemitism is mostly guilt-related, seeking to direct the burden of transgenerational guilt towards Jews. Victim-perpetrator inversions – such as likening the Israeli state or its actions to Nazi Germany – are a good example of such projection-based unburdening in a German context.

A good example for guilt-related antisemitism directly relating to the topic of this book is the not-too-distant popularity of Norman Finkelstein's 2000 polemic *The Holocaust Industry*. Finkelstein argued inter alia that Jewish organisations in the United States 'extort' Swiss and German banks for restitution payments. He essentially portrayed those banks as victims of what he assumes to be the (Jewish) 'Holocaust industry'. Concern for the 'exploitation of Jewish suffering' was, one may safely assume, not the main factor behind the book's bestseller status in Germany. While the book was applauded by the organised neo-Nazi fringe, its main theme speaks to a much wider problem in German society. For example, one well-regarded, large-scale study from 2014 found that 55 per cent of Germans feel angry at 'still being reminded of the German crimes against the Jews' (*Bericht des Unabhängigen Expertenkreises Antisemitismus* 2017: 55).

It is not possible within the scope of this book to compare the Israel policy of West Germany with that of the 'other' Germany to the East. However, it is easy to see how the 'antifascist', formulaic, state-sponsored anti-Zionism of East Germany could serve as a smokescreen behind which to hide antisemitic continuities (see Maeke 2017; Herf 2016; Timm 1997). The German Democratic Republic may have imagined itself as the political and economic antithesis to the FRG, but it was similar to it in its integration of former Nazis and the myth of a new beginning on old and unquestioned soil. In both cases, East and West, the aim of unloading guilt is linked to the desire for an unburdened, unhindered national identity. In the case of West

Germany, historian Wolfgang Benz aptly refers to secondary antisemitism as a 'patriotic project' (Benz 2004: 19).

Anti-Jewish ideology has been central to German national identity-making in the nineteenth and early twentieth century (Goldhagen 1997: 45). Looking at the history of postwar Germany's relations with the Jewish state, it is difficult to escape the impression that Israel, as it appears in the German mind, as well as a figurative 'Jewish Other' more generally, have been key to reimagining the 'fatherland'. What tends to get lost in the often narcissistic German debates about Israel is the 'actual' German role in the Arab-Israeli conflict. This is what this book is largely about.

Structure of the book

The chapters in Part I read the 1952 Reparations Agreement between the FRG and Israel as the original exchange between whitewashing and statebuilding. For West Germany, the rehabilitation the agreement provided eased western integration, while for Israel, it was dramatically important to the industrialisation of its economy.

Part II is about the most important period in German-Israeli relations: the years between the aftermath of the 1956 Suez War and the 1967 Arab-Israeli War. The FRG was the only western state at the time to support Israel militarily, financially and economically. In doing so, West Germany played a pivotal role in the making of Israel's status as the strongest regional military power, and although rehabilitation continued to be a German motivating factor, it was to a lesser degree.

Generally, Germany's Israel policy must be contextualised within wider Cold War dynamics. In 1964–65, for instance, the FRG fulfilled a proxy role for the United States in its military support of Israel, with the US gradually taking over the role of

Israel's principal backer. After 1967, German-Israeli relations lost a lot of their initial drama and importance, with the relationship maturing in the shadow of the US-Israeli alliance. Hence, the period after 1967 is treated with broader sweep.

From the mid-1960s onwards, the catchword of Bonn's Israel policy became 'normalisation'. Part III analyses the 1965–67 transition period of Germany's Israel policy in more detail, before tracing German efforts at 'normalising' relations with the Jewish state, evaluating the German engagement with the Palestinians in this context.

Part IV assesses the intensification of Germany's Israel policy after unification in terms of strategic interest and German national identity. Examining German support of the Oslo process (1993–2000) and of Palestinian 'statebuilding' afterwards, it also asks why this support has not helped in bringing about the two-state solution Germany desires. The conclusion concludes.

PART I

The 1952 Reparations Agreement

Relations between Israel and the Federal Republic of Germany (FRG) begin with the 1952 Reparations Agreement, otherwise known as the 'Luxembourg Agreement'. For the FRG, these reparations turned out to provoke a moderate strain on its budget, if at all. For Israel, however, the agreement was crucial, offering a clear material purpose: building the state. To Germany, the principal purpose was symbolic: distancing the FRG from its immediate Nazi past in order to facilitate western integration. This structural convergence of corresponding interests which those two states were so compelled to fulfil for one another explains what seems incomprehensible on a different, individual level: that the State of Israel – which integrated so many survivors and relatives of Nazi victims – and the German state – which incorporated so many Nazi criminals and countless enablers in its institutions – could forge such important relations at such an early point.

A discussion of the Reparations Agreement should begin with the contrasting names given to it by the two sides involved. These names are not incidental, but express differing political rationales, expectations and framings. Moshe Sharett, the Israeli foreign minister, coined the term *Shilumim*. Based on Jewish legal tradition, *Shilumim* denotes a punitive payment. It signifies an attempt to repair, the handing back of stolen property; it is debt paid, not guilt forgiven (Segev 1993: 196). This framing was important to the Israeli government in order to de-escalate dramatic domestic protests against the prospects of accepting 'blood money', as it sought to avoid the impression of absolving Germany. However, this was exactly the German expectation, as conveyed in the cruel and purposefully naïve term they gave to the agreement (and which is still used in official parlance today): *Wiedergutmachungsabkommen*. Literally, this translates as 'to make good again'.

The closeness between reparation and absolution is also illustrated by the fact that in German, the words 'guilt' and 'debts' share the same root, which is why German historian Constantin Goschler fittingly titled his study of German postwar reparations *Schuld und Schulden* ('Guilt and Debts'). The contrasting name pairs of *Schuld* and *Schulden*, or *Wiedergutmachung* and *Shilumim*, reflect the conceptual framing of this book: whereas Germany intended to absolve its guilt and rehabilitate itself, Israel sought a contribution to its consolidation in the form of a partial debt repayment. Conceiving the origins of German-Israeli relations as an exchange between rehabilitation and consolidation, or whitewashing and statebuilding, allows for an analysis deeper than the normative philosophical considerations and official representations inherent in the above name pairs. This makes it possible to assess with more distance and clarity the stakes and profits involved in the exchange which this agreement represented.

1

THE COSTS OF WHITEWASHING

In 1966, two years into retirement from office, the FRG's first chancellor, Konrad Adenauer, was asked on German television about his policy of reparations towards Jews and the State of Israel. Adenauer, whose name is identified like no other with the 'rebirth' of Germany after 1945, replied as such:

> We had done to the Jews so much injustice, committed such crimes against them that somehow these had to be expiated or repaired, if we were at all to regain our international standing [...]. Furthermore, the power of the Jews even today, especially in America, should not be underestimated. (Adenauer 1965)[1]

Adenauer firstly states his aim to pay reparations in order 'to regain [Germany's] international standing'. This goal of rehabilitation is then closely intertwined with a central idea of modern antisemitism: that of Jewish power. Adenauer was at no point in his life a Nazi. The stereotyped content of the above statement is also, of course, far removed from a genocidal nature. What may surprise the reader though is that Adenauer so openly admitted to his motivations in addressing the German public. The aim of rehabilitation, coupled with an overblown idea of

Jewish power, seemed self-evident, a natural thing to say on German television, even in 1966.

It is indeed difficult to separate constructions of assumed Jewish might from the goal of rehabilitation, which stands at the historical core of the German turn towards Israel. According to Israeli historian Tom Segev, Nahum Goldmann, chief negotiator for Israel and the Jewish Claims Conference, was aware of Adenauer's weakness in this regard and used it to his advantage in the negotiations, pointing to ominous 'consequences' if there was a failure to reach an agreement.[2]

The literature on German-Israeli relations rarely reflects upon the undoubtedly quite interesting finding that fear of 'Jewish power' played a role in the founding moment of Germany's Israel policy. Usually, Adenauer's evocations to this effect are conveniently ignored or, in rarer cases, actually cited in order to be downplayed (Hansen 2002: 242).

That ideas about 'Jewish power' apparently played a role in the early German turn towards Israel makes for a good story, but the importance of this narrative should not be overstretched. Pivotally, the West German decision to pay reparations to Israel needs to be seen within the context of Adenauer's overarching goal of *Westbindung*, which implies regaining the sovereignty, autonomy and power of West Germany by firmly embedding it in the West.

There does not seem to be much disagreement in historical scholarship that rehabilitation and integration into the western alliance were Germany's main motivating factors for the 1952 agreement. For example, even the introduction to the West German cabinet protocols for the year 1952, a publication of the German Federal Archives, downplays the role of moral considerations, and concludes that 'a decisive motive' for concluding the agreement was 'not to endanger [...] the Federal Republic's integration into the Western world' (German

Federal Archives 1952a). The question of why Germany sought an agreement with Israel relates to the question of American influence. Goschler concludes that without the United States, the FRG would have felt much less compelled to pay reparations (Goschler 2008: 928; see also Trimbur 2003: 265; von Jena 1986).[3]

It is in the context of rehabilitation and western integration that the question of lingering antisemitic attitudes, or their temporary transformation into philosemitic ones, needs to be addressed, as has indeed already been convincingly attempted by critical observers at the time. Eleonore Sterling escaped the Nazis at the age of thirteen. Her parents perished in a concentration camp in France. She returned from the United States to Germany and became the first female professor of political sciences there. Today, Sterling and her works on antisemitism, as well as her role as a Jewish woman in postwar German academia and the public, are largely marginalised and forgotten. In 1965, she wrote an article for the weekly *Die Zeit* in which she argued that the western powers, on whom the early FRG depended politically, militarily and economically, mistrusted its supposedly novel democratic character. In order to decrease this mistrust, the FRG began to use symbols and substitute acts to demonstrate its postwar humanity and democratic credentials. Sterling argued that a functional philosemitic attitude has served as a substitute to a true act of understanding, repentance and future vigilance (Sterling 1965: 2f.; see also Stern 1992). German self-understandings and the perception of Germany abroad have become inextricably linked with how the country discursively deals with its Nazi past. Echoing the historian Dan Diner's notion of a 'negative symbiosis' (Diner 2018) between Germans and Jews since Auschwitz, Anson Rabinbach observed that 'every stage in the emergence of West German sovereignty has been linked to the question of responsibility for the German past' (Rabinbach 1988: 160). As Adenauer himself has put it, the

1952 Reparations Agreement is the foundational moment in the history of the postwar relationship between German sovereignty and the German attitude towards Jews.

The agreement in the context of West Germany's postwar goals

In Europe and the United States, there continues to exist an overly positive academic and public picture about the German 'reckoning' with its past. What seems to be the case is that present-day German memory culture (itself not without its problems) is projected back to the beginnings of the Federal Republic. According to a recent comparative study on postwar reparations in Europe, German restitution is generally perceived in the academic literature as an historical benchmark, an interpretation which 'mainly dwells on the most spectacular event of German reparations, the Luxemburg Agreement of 1952', a treaty which 'commonly serves as the model of redress, the one seminal example that 'changed forever the concept of reparations." (Ludi 2012: 76).

The Reparations Agreement between Germany and Israel of 10 September 1952 was the first major treaty regulating German reparations for the genocide of the Jews. While it laid the groundwork for future individual compensation, this treaty was about reparations to the State of Israel. In it, the FRG committed to paying $823 million (3.45 billion Deutsche Mark [DM]) to Israel, approximately $7.8 billion in today's terms). Two-thirds of this sum were paid in the form of goods and services, predominantly investment goods. Only one-third was paid in foreign currency. A London bank received DM1.05 billion in pound sterling, with which Israel was able to buy crude oil from British companies (Ebeling 1966: 25). The second protocol to the agreement committed Germany to paying DM450 million to the Conference on Jewish Material Claims against Germany (otherwise known as the 'Claims Conference'), an umbrella group of Jewish-American organisations created for the purpose of the agreement.

In the first two years of the agreement, reparations paid to Israel amounted to no more than 0.2 per cent of German gross national product (GNP). In the course of rapid economic growth, the percentage share of reparations to GNP fell to 0.06 per cent by 1965 (Könke 1988: 533; see also Gardner-Feldman 1984: 90). These numbers underline Goschler's finding that reparations were 'seen by the Allies and by the Germans as a more peripheral aspect of Germany's regaining of sovereignty, while they played a central role on the Jewish side' (Goschler 2008: 175). In terms of direct costs, German rehabilitation was indeed modestly priced. A look at the German federal budget at the time gives some further perspective. Historian Adam Tooze demonstrates the underlying economic dimension to those histories which stress the amnesty and reintegration of Nazi criminals (Frei 2002), and the politics of selective memory and of balancing German suffering against that of the German victims (for example, see Moeller 2001). In 1953, German expenditures for the integration of German expellees from the East was thirteen times higher than payments to Israel for that year (Tooze 2011: 55). The numbers Tooze advances clearly show that among the overall postwar demands of internal stabilisation, pacification, Cold War military contribution and paying reparations to the victims of Nazism, the latter was the least important (Tooze 2011: 47).

On the history of German reparations

Looking at the overall history of German reparations, government numbers indicate that by the year 2013, the FRG had paid a total of €71 billion in the form of reparations and individual compensation for victims of World War II. The majority of this sum – about

€47 billion – was paid as individual compensation under the Federal Indemnification Law, or *Bundesentschädigungsgesetz* (BEG) (Goschler 2015). Recipients of individual restitution payments were, in practice, predominantly Jewish survivors. To be eligible for restitution, victims had to be connected to the territory of the German Reich of 1937, 'a crucial limitation, of course, because the overwhelming majority of the victims of the Holocaust were neither German nor Austrian, nor did they suffer their fate on the territory of Germany' (Tooze 2011: 56).

The Iron Curtain also acted as a border for individual restitution, something which the Claims Conference unsuccessfully lobbied against. According to Tooze, more astonishing than the delimitation of indemnification to Jews of German origin was the slashing of the FRG's pre- and postwar debts following the London Debt Conference, ratified on 27 February 1953, which took place in parallel to the reparation negotiations. The treaty foresaw a German debt reduction of more than 50 per cent, from DM30 billion to DM14 billion. However, the FRG only agreed to these terms under the condition that further Allied postwar reparation claims would have to be deferred until a final peace treaty between the Allied powers and a reunified Germany was in place (Tooze 2011: 56).

A comparative glance at the history of East German reparations and restitution shows the determinant role of the Cold War in this question: the German Democratic Republic (GDR) paid substantial reparations en bloc to the Soviet Union and Poland. Individual compensation went to Nazi victims living on GDR territory and was focused on communist victims, while Jews on GDR territory were compensated not as Jews, but as 'antifascists'. Although the GDR's and the FRG's reparation policies mirrored their positions in the Cold War, they held one thing in common: individual indemnification only benefited Germans (Goschler 2015).

The reparations and restitution paid to compensate for the limitless violence unleashed by Nazi Germany are but one of the ways in which the Nazi past was dealt with in both West and East Germany. Yet in being by definition the most costly, material expression of confronting past criminality, they are instructive of how both the FRG and GDR have, as states, dealt with a past that defies coming to terms with on an individual level. The majority of Germany's victims have, of course, not seen any forms of compensation, including the Roma and Sinti, homosexuals, victims of medical experiments or the politically persecuted. Incidentally, the omission of the politically persecuted has meant that those few in Germany who actually resisted the Nazis politically, namely communists and socialists, never became part of German public memory. Instead, those whom philosopher Hannah Arendt had considered an abyss away from the rest of humanity – the officers who plotted to kill Hitler in 1944 for his military ineptitude – are those whose memory is upheld. Similarly, it was possible in the postwar FRG to re-channel some of the previous antisemitic sentiment against the 'Red Scare'.

'Forced labourers' – a euphemism for the millions of mostly Eastern European slaves utilised in the German war industry – received only limited compensation in 2000, when few were still alive to claim them. Meanwhile, the list of uncompensated victims includes the million Polish and Soviet victims of the *Vernichtungskrieg* ('war of annihilation'), as well as victims of the war elsewhere.

When retrospectively thinking about the gap between the limitless nature of Nazi violence and the limited reparations and compensations which were eventually paid, one needs to also bear in mind that war reparations and individual indemnification somehow proportional to Nazi violence would have meant foregoing German postwar recovery, just as a thorough denazification of Germany would have meant giving up on the

West German state. Among the Allied powers, the United States had initially pursued an extensive denazification policy, yet the continuity of the German *Volksgemeinschaft* ('ethnic community') and its drive to forget, reintegrate and 'look ahead' frustrated these efforts. As the Cold War took shape in the immediate aftermath of World War II, the US administration became gradually less interested in the persecution of Nazi war criminals, placing a priority on West Germany's rehabilitation and integration into the US-led alliance (Breitman and Goda 2010). By 1949, Washington's interest in a stable West German frontline state in the Cold War had trumped political efforts at denazification. Limited reparation and compensation was thus just another of the prices exacted by the Cold War. Ultimately, the fact that German reparations for World War II appear as highly significant in the history of reparations in the twentieth century also needs to be related to the paucity of acknowledgement, reparation and restitution for other European genocides, such as the Turkish genocide of the Armenians in 1915, as well as for the other major crimes of European modernity: imperialism, colonialism, slavery. In this context, one should also bear in mind that the German government refuses to pay reparations for the genocide of the Herero and Nama in Namibia, a refusal which relates to German societal amnesia about the crimes of German colonialism.

The Nazi past in the post-war present

The practice of paying reparations and restitution, then, is also a practice of writing history; of determining who is remembered and who is forgotten. Quite certainly, it is also the decomplexification of Nazi criminality as it appears in reparation praxis which has made it possible for the German Federal Ministry of Finance to proclaim in the mid-1980s that Germans should be 'proud' of postwar reparation policies (Musial 2015: 65).

Conversely, in focusing its reparation and restitution policies on Jewish victims, the FRG has restored a difference that was at the heart of the Nazi project of extermination. Not only were Jews the largest victim group of Nazi genocidal policy, but the specificity of the attempt at their destruction was that the means and ends were the same: Jews were exterminated for no other purpose than their extermination, an extermination which continued even after defeat had become inevitable. As Hannah Arendt said on German television in October 1964, Auschwitz was 'truly as if the abyss had opened. One imagines that everything else could have, somehow, be repaired, just like everything in politics can be repaired. Not this. This has never been allowed to happen' (Arendt 1964).

It is questionable, however, whether the postwar West German move of focusing on Jewish victims was motivated by considerations of the specificity of the Jewish genocide. A hierarchical view of criminality wherein the Shoah is the most evil of Nazi crimes was not prevalent in German postwar society at the time. According to survey data, in December 1951, only 5 per cent of Germans admitted to feeling guilt towards Jews. The majority was equally divided between those who thought that only people 'who really committed something' should pay and those who found that Jews were 'partly responsible' for their fate (Judt 2010: 271f.). Viewed in this light, reparation and restitution elicited discourse on a topic that was generally not talked about in the Federal Republic, namely the German crimes against the Jews. What, then, is it that led to selective reparation policy in the postwar period?

One could think of an answer in terms of power, in an ironical double sense. With Israel, there existed a Jewish *state* that was able to claim reparations and present itself as the legitimate representative of the survivors, which was not the case for any other victim group of Nazi genocidal policies.

Secondly, German decision-makers continued to be influenced by ideas of 'Jewish power', ideas not held, for example, about the Sinti and Roma people. An explanation along these lines, however, fails to fully convince.

International affairs scholar Elazar Barkan, in what one reviewer called an 'ill-informed history' rather than an analysis of reparations (Chesterman 2000), argued that Adenauer's willingness to push for reparations despite popular sentiments to the contrary was testament to his moral commitment (Barkan 2000: 12). Prior to this, Lily Gardner-Feldman, a political scientist at Johns Hopkins University, argued that '[t]he overall experience of West German-Israel relations since 1952 bears witness to the impressive role of morality in international affairs' (Gardner-Feldman 1984: 274). She drew an explicit connection between a supposed societal reckoning with the past and the turn to Israel: 'What is important to understand [...] is that the perception of morality, which was shared by Adenauer, his Christian Democratic supporters and his Social-Democratic opponents, was essential in the launching of the special relationship. This moral view is tied, explicitly, to the psychological response, the feelings and emotions, *embedded in the German people*' (Gardner-Feldman 1984: 41, emphasis added; see also Gardner-Feldman 2012: 18). This is a crude misrepresentation of German postwar society. Gardner-Feldman reproduces Konrad Adenauer's naturalisation of a German people, the same *Volk* which had been hitherto cast as the Aryan master race, imbuing it with a rather undefined morality.

It is clear that this simplistic moral explanation cannot account for the fact of Nazism's afterlife in the Federal Republic. Hannah Arendt once publicly said this about postwar Germany: 'The Germans may call their terrible past mastered once they have condemned the murderers that still live among them and once they have removed those who are guilty from public offices' (cited in Geisel 2015: 439). This has never happened, as can be seen with the '131er' law, for instance, which reintegrated the 'victims' of Allied denazification policies. Witnessing West German efforts at amnesty and reintegration of former Nazi perpetrators and enablers turned Arendt into a sharp critic of the Adenauer government, as attested to in several passages in her famous coverage of the Eichmann trial. Historian Norbert Frei, in his landmark study on the subject, agrees that the postwar German state needed to be built partly on previous elements, for the fact was that the depth of Nazism in the German state and society made a clean slate impossible (Frei 2002). What Frei sees as the most troubling outcome of his study, however, is the degree of voluntariness with which West Germany pursued its policies of amnesty and reintegration of former Nazi criminals (Frei 2002: 11; see also Taylor 2012). Adorno stated in 1959 that he considered 'the continued existence of National Socialism *within* democracy potentially more threatening than the continued existence of fascist tendencies *against* democracy' (Adorno 1986: 115, original emphasis).

It is precisely this afterlife of National Socialism within postwar German democracy – specifically, the reintegration of former criminals and the societal amnesia about the Nazi past – which makes the morality explanation to German-Israeli relations so very spurious. In an article aptly titled 'The Jewish Question in the German Question', Anson Rabinbach argued cogently how the reparations question and the afterlife of Nazism were connected in the postwar FRG. The first was used, not least, to allow for the continued existence of the latter. Rabinbach spelt out the implications of this so well that it is worth quoting him in full:

The discovery of the Jewish question as a way of distancing the present German government from the past created a peculiar situation which necessitated that German leaders be more philosemitic than their constituents, legislate political morality and prohibit antisemitism by strict sanctions, perpetuating a deep disjuncture between public professions of responsibility and popular attitudes. If the famous paragraph 131 permitted the reintegration of former Nazis into the civil service, the reparations declaration sanctioned the substitution of the Jewish Question for the Nazi question. The implicit power accorded to the Jewish Question [...] also produced what Saul Friedländer described as a negative form of Jewish power in contemporary Germany: the power of absolution. That this power would eventually become the source of resentment was not hard to predict. (Rabinbach 1988: 167)

Bartering over guilt: Adenauer's 1951 Bundestag declaration

The idea of demanding indemnification for Nazi crimes had been debated by some Jewish organisations in the United States as early as 1941 (for this pre-history of the agreement, see Deutschkron 1970: 42ff). Adenauer had already suggested an offer of about $2 million before the official Israeli request in 1951. This rather ludicrous sum may give some indication as to how Adenauer would have preferred to handle the matter. The starting point for the negotiations that would lead to the 1952 agreement were two notes sent by Israel to the four Allied powers in January and March 1951, demanding $1.5 billion from West and East Germany ($1 billion from the FRG; $500 million from the GDR – a demand the FRG was able to reduce in the subsequent negotiations). The Soviet Union did not reply, and the western powers referred Israel to direct negotiations with Germany. In April 1951, a clandestine meeting between two Israeli government representatives and the German chancellor himself paved the way. In this meeting, the Israelis made clear that what they needed from the chancellor was a public declaration of guilt, as Israel could not negotiate with an unrepentant Germany.

Adenauer's resulting speech in the Bundestag on 27 September 1951 was the first German declaration about responsibility for Nazi crimes. As such, it may be read as one of the FRG's founding documents. The decisive, short passage of the speech had been drafted in a back-and-forth between the German and Israeli governments, as well as the World Jewish Congress (Segev 1993: 203-5). Adenauer accepted a number of Israeli amendments to the speech, yet he remained firm on his positions regarding the fundamental questions of German guilt and responsibility. Ben-Gurion wanted the chancellor to admit to the guilt and responsibility of the German nation as a whole. This was rejected by Adenauer. Here is the relevant paragraph of Adenauer's speech:

> The government of the Federal Republic and with it the great majority of the German people are aware of the immeasurable suffering that was brought upon the Jews in Germany and the occupied territories during the time of National Socialism. The overwhelming majority of the German people abominated the crimes committed against the Jews and did not participate in them. During the National Socialist time, there were many among the German people who showed their readiness to help their Jewish fellow citizens at their own peril – for religious reasons, from distress of conscience, out of shame at the disgrace of the German name. But unspeakable crimes have been committed in the name of the German people, calling for moral and material indemnity, both with regard to the individual harm done to the Jews and with regard to the Jewish property for which no legitimate individual claimants still exist. In this field, the first steps have been taken. Very much remains to be done. The Federal Republic will see to it that reparation legislation is soon enacted and justly carried out. Part of the identifiable Jewish property has been restored; further restitution will follow. (cited in Segev 1993: 202)

This statement has been extensively and critically commented upon (see Herf 1997: 282f.). If 'the overwhelming majority of the German people' supposedly opposed the genocide, one may wonder who had actually committed the crime. In an ingenious construction of guilt evasion, Adenauer spoke of crimes not committed by Germans, but 'in the name of the German people'. The picture that emerges from Adenauer's statement is that of a German people in its majority opposed to Nazism, of which it was itself a victim, since its name had been abused for Nazi crimes. Nevertheless, seemingly out of generosity, the 'German people' would be willing to pay reparations for a crime for which it felt it was not responsible.

The Israeli 'response' to Adenauer's speech, drafted a day before the speech was made, reflected the prior tug of war over the speech's contents. In direct contradiction to what Adenauer said, Israel's official statement read that 'the entire German people bears responsibility for the mass murder of European Jewry' (Lustick 2006: 59). The asymmetry between Adenauer's attempt to absolve the German nation and the Israeli government's depiction of all its individual members as equally accountable brings to mind Hannah Arendt's observation that 'there is no such thing as collective guilt or, for that matter, collective innocence, and that if there were, no one person could ever be guilty or innocent' (Arendt 1994: 297f.).

For practical purposes, Israel then acknowledged Adenauer's declaration as 'an attempt on the part of the Federal Government to solve the problem' (cited in Lustick 2006: 59). Political scientist Ian Lustick called this whole episode 'a carefully choreographed performance of minimal substance and maximum form.' As part of this performance, he gives a detailed account of subsequent journalistic and scholarly reporting, which 'hailed Adenauer's speech in terms considerably more dramatic than was warranted by the text itself' (Lustick 2006: 60). *The New York Times* saw the speech as a 'moral regeneration', while the *Washington Post* described it as 'the best thing that has come from Germany since before 1933' (cited in Lustick 2006: 61).

For the United States, the Reparations Agreement smoothed German integration into the Western Bloc and consolidated the Israeli state, which, by the time of the 1967 Arab-Israeli War, would become its key ally in the Middle East. When pointing to the United States' and Israel's role in the early rehabilitation of Germany, it must be borne in mind that the FRG's record on reparations would have been a much less significant one without the pressure of these two states. The history of the 1952 Luxembourg Agreement illustrates the two main roles of Israel in the perception of the FRG. On the one hand, Israel is a powerful reminder to Germany of its Nazi past. On the other, as the carefully staged episode of Adenauer's speech and the Israeli acceptance of it shows, Israel has been utilised, but also contributed to, the early whitewashing of the FRG. At the end of the day, this was the price Israel paid for German support. In 1965, Ben-Gurion stated in retrospect that Adenauer had 'recognized the moral responsibility of the entire German people for the crimes of the Nazis' (cited in Lustick 2006: 61). While Adenauer's commitment to Israel cannot be doubted, this had certainly not been the case.

Defining the German interest: Moral demands, financial constraints and the need for rehabilitation

It is worthwhile to describe the opposing German positions on the agreement, and to hone in on the negotiations between Germany and Israel in order to show which perception of the German national interest eventually won out and why. Studying the amply documented negotiations, one can point to three different lines of argument: the morality-driven argument; the financial argument; and the argument of longer-term political rehabilitation, which eventually prevailed.

German-Israeli negotiations over the actual content of the agreement took place on neutral Dutch ground from March to June 1952. The FRG simultaneously conducted the above-mentioned negotiations in London over the settlement of its pre- and postwar commercial debts. Contrary to prior promises, the FRG made negotiations with Israel and the Claims Conference dependent on the outcomes of the London negotiations.

Law professor Franz Böhm and lawyer Otto Küster, who led the German negotiating team, represented a morality-driven approach towards the question of reparations for Nazism's Jewish victims.[4] Böhm and Küster were opposed by Hermann Josef Abs and Minister of Finance Fritz Schäffer. Abs, executive board member of the Deutsche Bank under the Nazis, who oversaw 'Aryanisation' measures of Jewish property, became a close adviser of Adenauer on financial questions after the war. In line with their institutional positions, the argument of Abs and Schäffer was that the FRG was unable to agree to a substantial payment of reparations to Israel, when it was simultaneously working to reduce the repayments of German interwar debts. Schäffer was especially adamant in his opposition. It was also not beyond him to chafe at what he saw as the 'overblown expectations of the *Weltjudentum*' (Bundestag 26 February 1952). While the term *Weltjudentum* literally translates as 'world Jewry', it is part of the German antisemitic vocabulary and alludes to the idea of a Jewish global conspiracy.

According to Goschler, Adenauer found himself riven between the positions of Böhm and Küster and those of Abs and Schäffer (Goschler 2008: 311). Indeed, the chancellor's zigzagging on the reparations question seems to support this claim. For example, while he agreed on the Israeli note of March 1951 in a meeting with Goldmann in December of that year, he sent off the German delegation to the negotiations with orders 'to go and find out what these gentlemen really want' (cited in German Federal Archives 1952b). This certainly came as a surprise to Böhm, since Adenauer knew well what 'these gentlemen' wanted, having personally discussed it with them. However, as Tooze demonstrates throughout his above-cited analysis, Adenauer's manoeuvring on the issue was less a form of aberrant personal behaviour than part of an overall strategy aimed at a positive outcome in all the negotiations in which the FRG engaged itself at the time, as well as a reflection of the differing structural constraints under which the chancellor found himself.

Thus, Böhm and Küster were forced to employ a wait-and-see tactic at the negotiations table. In April, crisis ensued as Abs and Schäffer intervened in the negotiations, seeking to exploit Israel's dire economic and financial situation by making an offer much below the initially agreed-upon terms. Böhm and Küster, after harsh confrontations with Schäffer, resigned from their posts in protest. Adenauer now faced a public opinion disaster in the eyes of western publics.

It is in this context that Minister of Economic Affairs Ludwig Erhard, commonly referred to in Germany as the 'father of the economic miracle', intervened in the discussion. Contrary to the moral advocates and the financial opponents of the agreement, he argued that the political and the economic dimensions were in fact inseparable. In a letter to Adenauer, he expressed his support for the Reparations Agreement with Israel in the following terms:

> If we do not bank on further economic expansion, we abandon ourselves [...]. From a more dynamic assessment of the situation and particularly from the political aspect it may very well serve the German interest better to acknowledge a greater amount of debt, if we thereby strengthen Germany's credit and in the end even reconcile the Jews of the world to the German past. The difficulty is that the possibilities cannot be weighed or measured and therefore also do not impress the German public [...]. But either we have a future, in which case we may wager something, or we are lost, and then all agreements are without significance. (cited in Tooze 2011: 68)[5]

Following Tooze, this statement signifies the transitional moment of the West German state at the time, in which the future did not appear as fixed (Tooze 2011: 68). Under direct pressure from the US administration and the SPD, Adenauer intervened decisively to prevent an irreversible breakdown of negotiations. Following the advice of Böhm, who reassumed his position in the German negotiating team, Adenauer offered the Israeli side an outcome based on the initial agreements. This is the background to Adenauer's final imploration to his cabinet to come to an agreement on the reparations question. The protocol of the meeting, on 17 June 1952, states:

> The chancellor underlines the paramount importance of the matter in relation to the entire western world and especially to the USA. Breaking off negotiations with Israel without a result would summon the gravest political and economic dangers for the FRG. Therefore, even considerable financial sacrifices must be made in order to come to an agreement with Israel. (Bundestag 17 June 1952)

Here, as in almost all other internal statements, Adenauer does not make moral arguments for paying reparations. Secondly, the audience for Adenauer is not primarily the Israeli state, nor, for educational purposes, German society. The audience lies in the West and, specifically, the United States. Adenauer warns of great political and economic dangers. It is for this reason that a certain financial sacrifice has to be made, in order to ensure the political and economic well-being of the FRG in the long run. In summary, in line with the statement of Ludwig Erhard quoted above, Adenauer proposed paying substantial reparations to Israel in order to ensure Germany's political rehabilitation in the West, which would in turn make possible German economic expansion as well.

The last hurdle to take was ratification by the German parliament, which occurred on 18 March 1953, with 239 delegates in favour, thirty-five against and eighty-six abstentions.[6] With

126 delegates present, the SPD voted unanimously in favour. Adenauer's governing Christian Democratic Union (CDU) and Christian Social Union (CSU) coalition voted with eighty-four in favour, five against and forty-five abstentions. The only party to unanimously vote against the agreement was the Communist Party (KPD), with thirteen votes. Delegates of the parties to the right of the CDU/CSU mostly abstained, with yes and no votes rather evenly scattered. The Free Democratic Party (FDP), which then contained strongly revisionist and hard-right nationalist elements, voted seventeen in favour, five against and twenty abstentions.

Reading the speeches by representatives of the major parties shows a number of important points. Firstly, all those speaking in favour of the agreement argued in terms of the positive impact on the German global reputation and the clearing of its name. This argument became more pronounced, or seemed to become the core argument, on the right-wing spectrum. Walther Hasemann spoke for the FDP, referring to the agreement as 'an act which wants to be seen as a moral one, its aim being to clear the German name and reputation' (Bundestag 18 March 1953). Hasemann, who voted in favour, was already a member of the Nazi Party prior to Hitler's accession to power and a party loyalist until 1945. Other parliamentarians who in the Nazi years profited from 'Aryanisation' measures, such as Hans-Christoph Seebohm or Hans-Joachim von Merkatz, a regime supporter, voted in favour. Both of these figures later changed from the Deutsche Partei (DP) to the CDU.

One obviously finds many former Nazis among the abstainers and no-voters in the right-wing parliamentary spectrum. An interesting case is that of Franz Josef Strauss. An ex-officer of the Wehrmacht, he was to soon become one of the figureheads of German postwar conservatism. He also abstained. Yet within a few years, he would become the central figure on the German side for establishing close military ties with Israel.

The potentially most interesting division ran between the KPD and the SPD, the two left-wing parties in the parliament who voted en bloc against and in favour, respectively. Kurt Müller of the KPD had suffered severe injuries inflicted by the Nazis in a German jail, before being sent to the Sachsenhausen concentration camp, where he survived until its liberation by Soviet troops in 1945. Müller started his speech by stating that 'the death and murder of six million Jews is an accusation against a terrible, odious system of barbarism [...]. But we oppose the fact that there are speakers today, who, when the demand of the hour was to oppose these crimes, either stood aside or supported them' (Bundestag 18 March 1953). He continued by criticising the fact that, at the time, individual restitution was not yet underway. Citing from the agreement, he argued that it would be Israeli, German and American industrialists who would profit from the agreement, not individual Jewish victims of National Socialism. He then argued that the agreement ultimately served an American purpose to build up Israel as a military spearhead in the Middle East. The fact that former Nazis now sitting in the Bundestag were in its favour added insult to injury regarding the memory of Nazi victims and the fate of survivors.

The Social Democrat Carlo Schmid, while not a follower of Nazi ideology, was a former member of the National Socialist Association of Legal Professionals and Wehrmacht mayor. He spoke about the barbarism of the Nazi regime, pointing out that Jews were singled out by Nazi terror. Schmid recognised the collective claim of Israel for Jewish representation, yet argued that this should not prevent the payment of individual compensation to all victims of Nazism without consideration of origin, residence, race or faith. While thus presenting both general and specific cases for reparations and restitutions, Schmid was also aware that German reparations were helpful in restoring the German reputation.

Eugen Gerstenmaier, who had not been a Nazi due to his Christian convictions, spoke in favour of the agreement on behalf of the CDU. His speech closely resembled the positions and framings of Adenauer on the issue. Gerstenmaier began his speech with a statement on the 'outbreak of lunacy' that was Nazi barbarism; he also claimed that the 'counter-strike of history' was to 'transform the whole of Germany into a large ghetto. Even more insurmountable than an oriental ghetto were, to us Germans, the walls of hate, contempt and rejection, which were drawn around us already before the war and which held us imprisoned after the war' (Bundestag 18 March 1953). He then framed the Reparations Agreement as a central means to display a novel attitude and to overcome these 'ghetto walls'.

2

BUILDING ISRAEL

The Israeli motive for seeking German reparations was clear: to attempt to build the fledgling state. By 1952, the Israeli economy was in crisis and the survival of the state was not guaranteed. The Reparations Agreement was a crucial contribution to Israel's consolidation. This material need contrasted with an emotional one: to exorcise everything German (Diner 2015: 9).[1] Understandably, Israeli society identified the Germany of Adenauer with that of Hitler. Boycotting Germany was 'what personal loss, revenge, and national honour required' (Segev 1993: 190). Israel at first 'did indeed seem likely to forbid all contacts with Germany and to boycott it for generations [...]. This reaction was largely instinctive: It expressed what most Israelis believed was the right thing to do' (Segev 1993: 191). The Israeli path to Germany, which Segev so artfully reconstructs, principally consisted in the victory of the demands of the state over 'instinctive' individual reaction. This struggle between individual adversity and the demands of statebuilding was acted out not least in biblical terms, which also shows the difficulty of finding a political language for a case which, in so many ways, knew no precedent. This was the situation at a time of silence over the Holocaust, not yet named as such, when the rules of memory still needed to be established (see also Slyomovics 2014 for a personal and wide-ranging reflection on the question of accepting German reparations).

In the world of international politics, boycotting the FRG was neither possible nor practical. Ben-Gurion wanted to firmly embed Israel in the western camp. For Jerusalem, the road to Washington went via Bonn; for Bonn, the road to Washington went via Jerusalem. Ben-Gurion's drive for ties with Germany led the Israeli state and society into a political crisis. Yet in retrospect, from a state-making perspective, this policy was successful, maybe even without a plausible alternative (Segev 1993: 191f.). While Israel was driven towards Germany out of material interest, the fact of accepting German reparations was the first step towards the 'normalisation' of mutual relations, as expected and desired by the German government (Goschler 2008: 173).

The prospect of negotiating with the FRG provoked a massive contestation in the Israeli public sphere, which peaked with the attempted storming of the Knesset on 7 January 1952, following a mass rally organised by the Herut and led by future Prime Minister Menachem Begin. Herut was the successor party to Vladimir Jabotinsky's Revisionist movement and the predecessor to Likud, Israel's current governing party. Direct negotiations with Germany were opposed from the right and left of the political centre. Herut organised the right; communist Maki and socialist Mapam led the struggle from the left (Tovy 2017). Independent media and survivor organisations were important to the opposition outside of parliament, with former ghetto fighters and partisans tending to lend their authoritative voices to Mapam (Segev 1993: 211). Israeli left-wing opposition, meanwhile, argued along similar lines to those of West German communists. At this stage, both Maki and Mapam were oriented towards

Moscow. Their opposition to the agreement was 'schizophrenic' (Segev 1993: 217), as both deemed relations with West Germany an abomination, whereas relations with East Germany were considered legitimate (Segev 1993: 217; see also Tovy 2017: 493). It must be noted that throughout the Cold War and especially in the postwar years, denouncing the reintegration of Nazis into the FRG's administration was a favourite propaganda tool of the Soviet Union and the GDR, propaganda which contained, of course, much more than a kernel of truth. In pointing out the rehabilitating functions of the agreement for the FRG, the Israeli left may be said to have opposed the agreement for plausible reasons, yet it has done so in defence of a totalitarian state ideology which did not recognise a specifically Jewish claim to restitution and which was no stranger to antisemitism, as demonstrated by the 1952 Slánský trials (which led to Mapam's split and distancing from Moscow).

Herut's campaign under Begin was one of emotion and national honour. To Begin and his many followers, the whole affair appeared as a despicable trade of the memory of the victims for bloodstained German money. Begin argued for upholding the anti-German boycott, insisting that negotiating with Germany would mean '[n]egotiations with a pro-Nazi regime', and Herut, along with the other opposing parties, asserted that 'Adenauer's government was helping to revive Nazi ideology in West Germany' (Tovy 2017: 490). Those opposing the negotiations also argued that direct negotiations were not worth the moral degradation, as the FRG would pay very little and thus not provide serious economic help to the state (Tovy 2017: 491). According to Tovy, those favouring negotiations, namely the Labor Party under Ben-Gurion, which was firmly in command of the state, made three principal arguments. Firstly, reparations would strengthen Israel; a strong Jewish state 'would be the Jewish people's greatest victory over Nazi ideology, which had attempted to wipe out all vestiges of Jewish existence, and the best possible guarantee against the perpetration of another Holocaust.' Proponents also argued that reparations from Germany would constitute the first time in history that those who persecute Jews would be made to pay for their crimes, and that those who stole and murdered should not be allowed to also benefit from their crimes (Tovy 2017: 491f.).

Three specific arguments were levelled against those of the opposition. Firstly, in terms of upholding the boycott, supporters of negotiations argued that Israelis and Jews outside of Israel were already engaged with Germany over restitution questions. Secondly, the rehabilitation of the FRG would proceed with or without Israel, as the FRG was already practically aligned with the Western Bloc. Thirdly, reparations were to be a singular instance, and not a 'prelude to the establishment of economic and diplomatic relations between the two countries.' Israel would remain committed to the boycott and 'there would be neither reconciliation nor forgiveness for the horrifying events of the Holocaust' (Tovy 2017: 492).

How is one to retrospectively evaluate the above arguments favouring and opposing reparation negotiations? As will be shown shortly, the main argument in favour – namely that reparations would lead to a fortification of the Israeli state – was proven entirely correct, and the opposition's fear to the contrary turned out to be unfounded. It is also plainly evident that the fact of accepting reparations had not simply been a singular instance of accepting partial compensation for Nazi crimes. Instead, the agreement opened the door towards economic normalisation and a military relationship between the two countries, as well as diplomatic relations (topics dealt with further below). As such, proponents and opponents were both proven right: the agreement led to the consolidation of the Jewish state, but it also opened the door towards the 'normalisation' of bilateral relations, as well as playing a role in the rehabilitation of Germany.

The argument that the FRG's integration into the West would have proceeded with or without Israeli help does not detract from the fact that for the West German administration, the agreement was perceived as an important factor in regaining the FRG's 'international standing', as stated in the quote from Adenauer at the beginning of the first chapter. Again, it needs underlining in this context that the exchange between whitewashing and statebuilding was differently priced, reflecting both countries' economic and political status at the time. For the FRG, the rehabilitation that the agreement provided turned out to be cheap. For Israel, its effects were crucial.

The Israeli government prioritised state reparations over individual restitution for statebuilding purposes. David Horowitz, director general of the Israeli Ministry of Finance, argued 'for en bloc reparations as the centrepiece of Israel's demands on Germany. Indemnification of individual Jews was vital [...] but only reparations to Israel would make the difference between economic survival or collapse' (Sachar 1999: 35). Nahum Goldmann called the agreement 'a downright salvation' for Israel (cited in Vogel 1969: 99).

The relevance of the Reparations Agreement to the early consolidation of the Israeli state is often noted, but rarely systematically assessed (for an exception, see Könke 1988). This may seem peculiar in light of the importance of German-Israeli relations to Germany's self-image, especially since after unification. One would assume that the German contribution to Israel's build-up could even be turned into source of national pride, linked to the German 'mastering' of its past. As for German policymakers at the time, a key reason for downplaying the significance of the agreement to the consolidation of Israel was to not further endanger relations with Arab states, a topic dealt with below.

In fact, the story of this consolidation (via reparations) can be told quite quickly. The pre-state Jewish economy in Palestine, the Yishuv, necessarily depended on foreign capital inflows and financial assistance. The structural characteristic of economic dependency on outsiders has marked Israel since its founding, with economic self-sufficiency only achieved relatively recently (cf. Nitzan and Bichler 2002: 27ff.). Israel imported much more than it exported, a trade deficit which could not be evened out by the state budget, and foreign currency reserves were chronically low. Reparation payments to the Israeli state helped bridge the trade deficit, giving the Israeli administration capital to undertake a program of state-led import-substituting industrialisation (Könke 1988).

German reparations came at a crucial time in Israel's development, helping the economy out of a bottleneck. After the ceasefire agreements of 1949, the Jewish population of Israel doubled: 340,000 immigrants had arrived from Europe's displaced persons camps by the end of that year; a further 345,000 arrived over the course of 1951, mostly Jews from Arab countries (Halevi 2008). The government needed to impose a strict austerity and rationing program on the population to meet basic housing and welfare needs. Compared with West Germany, the population of Israel was poor and lacked basic amenities (Lustick 2006: 55). Population growth overburdened the economy to such a degree that immigration was halted in early 1952, shortly before reparation negotiations with the FRG began. This, of course, was directly contrary to the key Zionist objective (Arlosoroff 2018).

From 1950 to 1965, GNP increased by 11 per cent annually (Halevi 2008). This 'expansion was driven by two main forces: population growth and foreign aid' (Nitzan and Bichler 2002: 122). The significance of German reparation capital as part of foreign aid is indicated by breaking down the growth rate in the 1950s. While GNP rose by 1.8 per cent between 1952 and 1953, its growth rate increased almost ten-fold, to 17 per cent, in the years 1954–55, which is when the deliveries under the agreement started (Rivlin 2010: 37). The capital inflow provided by the Reparations Agreement was in fact three times higher than grants in aid provided by the US government at the time. According to Gardner-Feldman, Israel received $757.3 million worth of reparations capital from the FRG between 1953 and 1965. In comparison, US grants stood at only $214.7 million for that period. Following Fanny Ginor, who assessed the impact of German reparations for the Bank of Israel, German reparations and individual restitution taken together made up more than a quarter of overall capital imports in a nineteen-year period (see Gardner-Feldman 1984: 97).

In summary, Israel's doubled population was put to work in a program of industrialisation, enabled by capital from abroad, much of it from Germany; Arab-Jewish immigrants, the Mizrahi, provided the cheap labour necessary for this task (Hanieh 2003: 7). Incidentally, reparations would thus help perpetuate Israel's ethno-class structure. This happened in two ways, as individual restitutions paid to German Jews would also contribute to the wealth gap between European and Mizrahi Jews. By 1978, 40 per cent of individual restitution payments had been granted to Israeli citizens (Gardner-Feldman 1984: 94), which relieved the state of welfare payments and helped to stock up Israel's chronically low foreign currency reserves. Thus, state-to-state reparations can be seen to have tackled the structural economic problem of the Israeli trade deficit, whereas individual restitutions pumped money into the Israeli economy.

As this is a book about German-Israeli state relations, the following discussion ignores the topic of individual restitution, focusing on the qualitative impact of capital deliveries under the 1952 treaty. A dissection of these deliveries shows that the agreement is best understood as a targeted statebuilding program.

Contrary to Ben-Gurion's initial fears, the German government took care to smoothly implement the agreement, which contrasts with the hesitancies and tactical manoeuvres characterising the negotiations. It is helpful to first understand how the 1952 agreement actually worked in practice. The way in which it was carried out forcibly contributed to the creation and gradual intensification of bilateral relations.

The Israel Mission, created under the terms of the agreement and located in Bonn, was responsible for Israeli purchases in Germany. The federal government paid the agreed yearly instalments into the Mission's account with the Bank deutscher Länder (later Bundesbank). The Israel Mission was subordinated to the Israeli Ministry of Finance, where the Israeli purchasing lists were first drawn up (Könke 1988: 516). According to the agreement, the Israel Mission was 'entitled to engage in all activities which may be required in the Federal Republic of Germany in connection with the expeditious and effective implementation of the present agreement' (Article 12). Moreover, in the eyes of German law, the Israel Mission was a juridical person, and its rights and duties resembled those usually accorded to consulates and embassies. Extraterritoriality applied, the mission was exempted from taxes and its staff was accorded diplomatic immunity. Accordingly, in the files of the Auswärtiges Amt (AA), Felix Shinnar, the head of the mission, was referred to as the 'Israeli ambassador' in Germany long before the establishment of formal diplomatic relations in 1965. The scope of his activities soon expanded beyond those demanded by the Israel Mission, serving as both the Israeli mouthpiece in Germany and, in lieu of official diplomatic relations, as a channel of communication for the German government towards Israel.

To deal with questions emanating directly from the agreement's implementation, the Mixed Commission was formed, consisting equally of German and Israeli government officials, with the Israeli members drawn from the Israel Mission. The central task of the Mixed Commission was to agree upon the delivery lists for each year of the agreement. The Bundesstelle für Warenverkehr (Federal Office for Trade Transactions), an exclusively German body, was tasked with oversight of the agreement and helped the Israel Mission to find adequate German companies for its orders. Via the Bundesstelle, the German government saw to it that areas of special economic need such as West Berlin, as well as companies employing German refugees, were 'adequately considered' in the placement of Israeli orders (Ebeling 1966: 17f.).

Felix Shinnar, who had already been one of Israel's chief negotiators over reparations from Germany, stated the importance of the agreement in an interview with German journalist and chronicler of German-Israeli relations, Rolf Vogel:

> For Israel, the necessity of receiving goods was important because thus she had the opportunity, putting aside the urgent needs for daily consumption, to obtain substantially only those goods that served the peaceful, industrial, or agricultural upbuilding of Israel. Some 80 per cent of the agreement was accepted in shipments of capital goods of all kinds, and accordingly the shipments under the agreement (and I believe that this does justice to the meaning, the inner meaning of the agreement) were a visible, lasting constituent of the building-up of Israel in those first years, so decisive for the economic consolidation of Israel. (cited in Vogel 1969: 88)

As the German economic historian Günter Könke demonstrated, the significance of reparation payments was that they constituted a 'substantial contribution to the economic modernization of Israel in the 1950s and 1960s, which enabled the accession of Israel to the group of industrialized countries and which, over the longer-run, helped secure the political and economic existence of the Israeli state' (Könke 1988: 534). The New Economic Policy (NEP) devised in 1952 sought to reduce Israel's import dependency and to achieve industrialisation via the strong steering hand of the state within the economy (Könke 1988). The very name of this policy shows Israel's orientation towards state planning at the time. The German 'economic miracle', built on a free market shock therapy prompted by Marshall Fund capital, thus aided the 'economic miracle' of Israel, built upon a state-planned industrialisation, and afforded to a high degree by German reparations capital.

As one-third of the agreement was earmarked for procuring oil from British companies, the agreement simultaneously helped Israel to build its industry and to cover the energy requirements for its modernisation. Article VI of the agreement divided German deliveries into five groups: ferrous and non-ferrous metals; products of the steel manufacturing industry; products of the chemical industry and other industries; agricultural products; and services.

Situating the deliveries under the agreement within the context of Israel's NEP reveals its modernising functions. The official report issued by the Mixed Commission on the agreement's implementation in 1966 gives an overview of the deliveries of goods under the agreement between 1953 and 1965 (Ebeling 1966; see also Vogel 1969). The report disaggregates the deliveries into the five main categories agreed upon in Article VI of the treaty, and also offers a survey of the specific types of deliveries within each group.

Groups 4 (Agriculture) and 5 (Services) are rather insignificant: agricultural products made up only 3.8 per cent of overall deliveries; and while services amounted to over 10 per cent of the overall sum, they mostly covered corollary costs to the deliveries, such as freight, insurance and the financing of the Israel Mission. As such, only the first three groups are important, which account for over 85 per cent of the sum invested in deliveries to Israel.

Raw materials went into the construction of factories and plants. As the German report of the Mixed Commission explains, those materials 'involved chiefly the procurement of structural steel for the large facilities that were later to house

FIG. 1: Deliveries under the Reparations Agreement

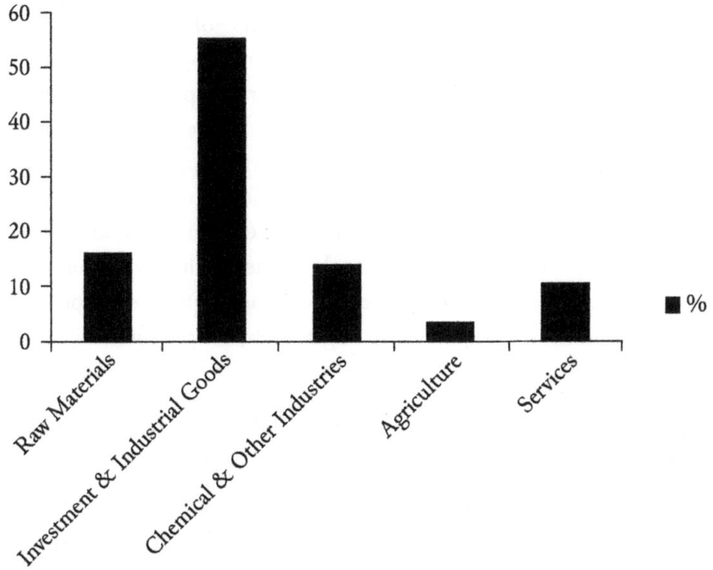

Data source: Ebeling 1966: 26

the manufacturing plants of varied industries [...]. Shipments of structural steel covered chiefly the first nine years of the total period, declining sharply in the last four years, since the major projects were concluded by 1962' (cited in Vogel 1969: 89). The investment goods delivered under Group 2 (Investment & Industrial Goods) were the core of the statebuilding program, amounting to 55.3 per cent of the overall share. These deliveries comprised capital-intensive investment goods, especially of the engineering sectors. The report of the Mixed Commission explains why this was the case:

From the first drafting of the agreement the parties both felt that the need for investment goods should be given primary consideration in order to set up an efficient economy in Israel [...]. The supplying of capital goods was also of special importance to the economy of the Federal Republic and the various suppliers, since these were products whose manufacture [...] is particularly labour- or wage-intensive. The products of the mechanical engineering industry in all their variety were supplied chiefly from 1957 onwards, that is from the point when the projected factories in Israel were sufficiently far along so that they could be equipped with machinery. Machinery of all kinds was supplied, and all the branches of the industry shared in the orders – textile machinery, machinery for the chemical industry, metal- and woodworking machinery, motors, machine tools, construction and highway equipment, cranes, locomotives, transport equipment, pumps, farm machinery, equipment for sugar mills, office machinery, and various others. (cited in Vogel 1969: 90)

Könke found that deliveries under Group 2 played 'a key role for the build-up of the Israeli economy', as the investment goods of this group equipped the newly built factories and enterprises that would serve as the backbone for the transformation of the Israeli economy (Könke 1988: 518). Further disaggregation of deliveries under Group 2 shows that machinery made up 13.2 per cent of the overall share in deliveries. The electrical industry (which also fell under Group 2) made up a significant 9.3 per cent share of the overall amount. Between 1955 and 1960, the FRG delivered five electrical power plants to Israel. Electricity demand rose not only with population growth and expansion of agriculture, but most notably in relation to the pace of industrialisation (see Könke 1988: 518).

The largest single item was shipbuilding, also delivered under Group 2; this made up 24.4 per cent of the overall share of deliveries. The report of the Mixed Commission explains why:

More than DM 585 million of funds under the agreement were invested in ships. This large sum is the easier to understand when we reflect that Israel has only one open frontier, that to the Mediterranean and the Red Sea, and must carry on her entire goods traffic by sea. In addition, at the beginning of the agreement, in 1953, Israel had only an insignificant merchant fleet with a few, over-aged ships. A total of 60 vessels with a total tonnage of about 450 thousand was supplied, with 13 West German yards participating in the construction. (cited in Vogel 1969: 90f.)

The report adds that 'Israel would hardly have been able to expand her industry at such a pace and to supply it with raw materials and transport its products abroad, if she had not had her merchant fleet' (cited in Vogel 1969: 97). However, the emphasis on shipbuilding also served German industrial interests. As the report explains, a large number of German companies not directly related to the shipbuilding sector profited as subcontractors, which is why the Mixed Commission was able to agree to place an emphasis on this sector (Ebeling 1966: 30). Furthermore, due to the demilitarisation measures of the 1945 Potsdam Agreement, shipbuilding was prohibited in the FRG until 1951. After the lifting of restrictions, this sector saw a massive rise in production, with the FRG holding a world market share of 17 per cent in this sector by 1956. Certainly the construction of the Israeli merchant fleet played its part in this rise in production, helping to solve a problem of unemployment in these sectors.

It is not only the above-mentioned tough German stance in the reparation negotiations, but also these hard economic facts which clearly refute a widely held misperception of the German-Israeli relationship as a one-sided affair in which Germany pays and Israel receives (as one would expect for such a moral act of contrition). The misperception of unequal relations originates with the Reparations Agreement, which however involved little German selflessness. The way the Reparations Agreement was carried out and the available economic data actually indicate that the agreement was beneficial to Germany not only for the already explained purposes of rehabilitation and whitewashing, but also in plain economic terms alone. This was, of course, not coincidental. Importantly, Israel would have preferred for reparations to be paid in hard currency, not goods. Nevertheless, paying in terms of goods was a German condition set prior to the start of negotiations, and already contained in the letter signed between Adenauer and Nahum Goldmann, president of the World Jewish Congress, in December 1951. In exchange for this concession, Israel demanded that the rest of the overall sum would be spent on oil deliveries. Thus, with Israeli orders from German companies paid for by the federal budget, these effectively served as a stimulus to production, helping to revive those sectors of the German economy mainly geared towards export, such as the shipbuilding and machine-building industry, as well as the ferrous steel, petrochemical and electronic engineering sectors.

The Reparations Agreement also enabled Germany to gain a foothold in the Israeli market, which helps to explain the strong economic relations between the two countries to this day (at the time of writing, Germany is the fourth-largest trading partner of Israel and its most important trading partner within the European Union). Indeed, just ten years after the signing of the Luxembourg Agreement, regular German exports were already larger than exports of commodities under the terms of the agreement, mostly because of follow-up orders and because Germany was able to establish itself ahead of others in a number of key economic sectors (Ebeling 1966: 40). Contrary to boycott threats and protests, German exports to Arab countries were generally not afflicted by the Reparations Agreement. And while it is true that individual German companies, industrialists and businessmen argued against reparations for fear of losing Arab markets, German industry overall was greatly interested in the agreement, competing strongly for Israeli orders (Könke 1988: 531f.). In summary, reparations paid to the Israeli state in the form of goods turned out to be a profitable, long-term investment for the FRG. 'Normalisation' between the two countries thus proceeded, first of all, in the economic sphere.

50

3

THE AGREEMENT AND THE ARAB STATES

While the Reparations Agreement is generally portrayed as a German-Jewish affair, it unavoidably meant the FRG's assumption of a political role in the Arab-Israeli conflict. It was especially in the period between the signing and the ratification of the Reparations Agreement that Arab League states lodged complaints against it. Heinrich von Brentano, at the time chairman of the CDU/CSU faction in the Bundestag, and who would succeed Adenauer as foreign minister in 1955, wrote to his predecessor about these complaints. Von Brentano cautioned against swift ratification of the Reparations Agreement:

> It is apparently not the case that solely egoistic or even antisemitic tendencies are behind the protests. These [Arab League] states partly also feel seriously threatened in their existence if because of an uncontrolled fulfilment of the agreement Israel receives commodities which could facilitate new warfare in this tense situation [...]. I would like to suggest once more to eventually alert the American government of this specific situation and to ask for a friendly intervention on our behalf. (*Politisches Archiv des Auswärtigen Amtes* [PA AA], B130, Bd. 6428, 11 December 1952).

Adenauer's reply summarises the official German weighing of priorities on this matter:

> I do not see how we can exceed our current offer to the Arabs without defaulting from our agreement with Israel and the Jews. This would cause incomparably more damage to our standing in the world than a passing tension in German-Arab relations. The American government naturally is constantly informed by me and my staff about the state of German-Arab relations. (PA AA, B130, Bd. 6428, 23 December 1952)

On 4 March 1953, Adenauer presented the Luxembourg Agreement to the German parliament, prior to its vote on ratification (Bundestag 4 March 1953). In this speech, he also addressed the Arab protests, summarising them in the form of two key arguments. The first was that Israel's claim for reparations on the basis of its integration of Jewish refugees was illegitimate as long as Israel did not meet its obligations regarding the Arab *Palästina-Flüchtlinge* ('Palestine refugees'). Adenauer stated in response to this argument that the question of German reparations to Israel and the question of the refugees from Palestine were separate issues which each needed to be addressed on their own terms. The issue of compensation for Jewish refugees who escaped Nazi persecution was to be solved between the German state and the Jewish people. Germany neither possessed the right nor the capacity to position itself towards the problem of refugees from Palestine. However, Adenauer added, Germany wished for a swift and satisfactory solution to this problem, as it knew too well from its own experience of the needs and sorrows of refugees.

Following Adenauer, the second complaint against the agreement was that it supported a state which was at war with its Arab neighbours. In reply, Adenauer claimed that the agreement 'in no way constituted a breach of neutrality', emphasising its stated prohibition of 'the delivery of weapons, ammunition and other military material to Israel' (Bundestag 4 March 1953). The chancellor spoke of the 'traditionally friendly German relations towards the Arab world', and stated that he was willing to further these relations. He offered closer economic ties to all Arab countries willing to negotiate with the FRG, warning that such negotiations 'could only be successful if led in a spirit of friendship and not weighed down by prior threats' (Bundestag 4 March 1953).

There is an abundance of files in the archives of the AA on 'Arab reactions to the Luxembourg Agreement', scrupulously collected by the AA's chief 'Arabist', Hermann Voigt. A systematic assessment of this topic is not possible here and would stray too far from this book's purview. But we can look at two complaints which cover a great deal of the diverse Arab governmental and non-official reactions to the agreement. The first complaint is a letter by the Arab Higher Committee for Palestine, led by the infamous Mufti Amin al-Husseini (PA AA, B130, Bd. 6426, 7 June 1952). The second is an official protest note ushered by the Arab League (PA AA, B130, Bd. 6426, 21 July 1952).

The Mufti's ideological sympathies for the Nazi regime have been amply documented and hardly require further evidence. His letter is a chilling document of Jew-hatred written directly after the genocide, of which the Mufti had full knowledge. In his letter to the chancellor, the Mufti addressed the 'Jewish' (never 'Zionist') aggression against Palestinians as well as against 'the German citizens' in Palestine. The letter frames Jews as an aggressive, merciless collective, a danger for both Germans and Arabs alike. The Mufti asserted that 'after the termination of the Second World War [...] there hardly exist Jews who suffer persecution and homelessness. Those Jews who claim compensations for the losses and sufferings of German Jewry, have themselves committed against the Arabs of Palestine a most brutal aggression and inhumane persecution [...] the Arabs are the party who deserves to be compensated and redressed' (PA AA, B130, Bd. 6426, 7 June 1952). Al-Husseini closed by stating that paying German reparations not to 'the Jews', but to the 'Palestine Arab refugees' would 'open a new epoch for the cementation of the traditional German-Arab friendship' (PA AA, B130, Bd. 6426, 7 June 1952). It is clear on which fundaments this friendship was supposed to rest.

The Mufti's letter was studied in the AA and a note was prepared for the chancellor, clearly stressing the letter's 'anti-Jewish' content. It suggested that the letter should remain unanswered, because 'the Arab Higher Committee cannot claim to be the representative body for the Arab population of Palestine, as it does not even have influence on those parts of Palestine that are not in Jewish possession' (PA AA, B130, Bd. 6426, 23 July 1952). This, incidentally, gives further support to the majoritarian historical view that the Mufti's influence on the Palestinians after World War II was relatively small.

In contrast, Bonn could not ignore the note of the Arab League. While the Mufti falsely claimed to represent what was a dispersed and powerless Palestinian population, the Arab League note represented the view of the Arab governments:

> The Arabs differentiate between the paying of an indemnity to an unjustly treated person, whether Jew or not, and between the paying to Israel in her quality of alleged representative of all the Jews in the world, of funds which will permit Israel to carry on her aggression and maintain her threat to the security of the Arab States. (PA AA, B130, Bd. 6426, 21 July 1952)

Furthermore, the letter stated:

> Without wishing to discuss the state of the Jews in Germany, during and before the last war, or the well-foundedness or not of their allegations, the Arabs firmly believe that Germany is by no means under any obligation to a state created after the war, hostile to the Arabs, and on the latter's soil. The Arabs categorically deny

that this state represents the Jews of the world. (PA AA, B130, Bd. 6426, 21 July 1952)

The Arab League note acknowledged the validity of individual reparations, yet opposed any being paid to the Israeli state. The note is certainly historically insensitive regarding the fate of the Jews under the Germans. Problematically enough, it speaks of a German–Arab friendship 'both before and since the war' (PA AA, B130, Bd. 6426, 21 July 1952). However, historical judgement should maintain equal standards. The FRG, the state in which most of the perpetrators continued to live, had itself not been especially sensitive about the Holocaust at that time.

In their overview of public Arab reactions to the Reparations Agreement, Litvak and Webman summarise that 'mainstream discourse' in the Arab world did not deny 'Germany's right to compensate Jews on a personal basis [...] but Israel's right to represent and receive reparations in the name of those Jews':

> A large part of the discussion about the agreement evolved around its political aspects and implications for the balance of power between Israel and the Arab states. The assertion that the Arab refugees were more entitled to compensation, which implied an equation between the suffering of the Palestinians and the suffering of the Jews under Nazi persecutions, also seemed to stem from political considerations rather than from an intention to minimize the Holocaust. (Litvak and Webman 2011: 78)

Before Bonn's ratification of the Reparations Agreement, Moshe Sharett suggested transferring some of the German reparation payments to the 1948 refugees, 'in order to rectify what has been called the small injustice (the Palestinian tragedy), caused by the more terrible one (the Holocaust)' (cited in Lustick 2006: 53f.). However, linking German reparations with the issue of the 1948 Palestinian dispossession would have meant linking the two single-most explosive political topics in Israel at the time and was thus deemed unfeasible (Fischbach 2003: 191).

The AA concluded that the FRG should avoid engaging with the Arab League's arguments. A note sent to all German embassies in September 1952 instructed ambassadors to frame the agreement as being borne 'solely out of a feeling of moral responsibility for the Jewish victims of national-socialist persecution', and that it was 'based on humanitarian and not on any political motives' (*Aktenedition zur Auswärtigen Politik der Bundesrepublik* 1952/209). The note, signed by Adenauer's confidant Herbert Blankenhorn, stated unequivocally that the FRG did not see itself in any way responsible for the 1948 refugees. The idea of depicting the FRG's support of Israel in moral-humanitarian and not political terms was, of course, itself the outcome of a political debate, as explained previously. That Bonn sought to avoid getting mired in arguments about an 'indirect' German responsibility towards Palestinians is thus not surprising: the decision to consolidate the Israeli state was in itself not a moral, but a political one, aimed at the rehabilitation of the West German state during the Cold War.

The decision to pay reparations to the Israeli state followed a logic of its own that was wholly unrelated to the Palestinian issue, which was seen as marginal and in primarily humanitarian terms until after 1967. Palestinians did not appear within German state discourse in terms of national identity, but were rather referred to in the archival files of the AA as 'Arab refugees' or as 'Arab Palestine-refugees'. Palestinians emerged as political interlocutors to the FRG only after the Arab-Israeli War of 1967, a topic covered in the following chapters. However, awareness of the Palestinian refugee question did exist within the West German state administration (Schölch 1985).

The earliest hints of an engagement with the Palestinian refugee question which this research unearthed date back to January 1957. AA official Voigt argued in an internal communiqué that the FRG should augment its payments to the United Nations

(UN) organisation responsible for the humanitarian care of the 1948 refugees, the United Nations Relief and Works Agency (UNRWA). He argued what he found to be an obvious point, namely that German contributions were too low:

> [...] the hitherto paid amount of 70.000 DM must without doubt be seen as minimal. States of comparable size [to the FRG] have [...] paid a multiple of our amount [...]. The political reasons for a contribution of the Federal Republic [...] are evident in regard to our relations to the UN as well as the Arab countries [...] it does not require further justification that for optical reasons, our contributions cannot be lower than those of Scandinavian countries and Belgium. (PA AA, B130, Bd. 3739, 24 January 1957)

What one can see here is a form of instrumental humanitarianism. Payments to UNRWA are argued for largely in relation to German relations with Arab countries and the UN.

As for the second complaint – that the Reparations Agreement served to build the Israeli state which was in a state of war with its Arab neighbours – it cannot be doubted that the agreement strengthened Israel's position in the conflict. Moreover, this did not just happen indirectly by freeing up resources for military purposes. Military relations between the FRG and Israel actually harken back to the earliest days of bilateral relations. According to Israeli historian Yeshayahu Jelinek:

> Neither the Jewish community of the British Mandate in Palestine, nor the Israelis ever hesitated to buy German-produced weapons or to procure weapons with German help. Many entries in Ben-Gurion's diary testify to this. In 1947, before the end of the British Mandate and only two years after the downfall of the Third Reich, the Jewish underground army, the Haganah, used German weapons and led negotiations with Germans. (Jelinek 2004: 402)

During the 1948 Arab-Israeli War, Israel bought German-produced Messerschmidt planes and light weapons from Czechoslovakia. According to Jelinek, the Israeli Ministry of

Defence (IMoD) went on a purchasing mission to West Germany no later than 1951. The IMoD was interested in surplus weapons from the stockpiles of the North Atlantic Treaty Organisation. It was evident to the Israelis, and most certainly known to the German government, that goods delivered under the Reparations Agreement were also to be used for the construction of Israeli military industries. In February 1952, shortly before the start of official negotiations over the Reparations Agreement, the IMoD sent an expert to Germany to explore procurement possibilities in this regard. The Israeli army (Israeli Defence Forces [IDF]) and IMoD were involved in the allocation of the funds disposable under the agreement (Jelinek 2004: 402). The Israeli historian Roni Stauber concurs, on the basis of IDF and IMoD files, that '[c]ontrary to the Israeli-German agreement and the repeated claim that the reparations money was intended solely for peaceful purposes, it served the IDF and the armaments industry for the purchase not only of raw materials but of military equipment and armaments in Germany' (Stauber 2013: 238).[1]

Israeli officer Avigdor Tal became part of the Israeli Mission in Cologne in 1955. Jelinek describes his role as procuring armaments and military goods, as well as forging ties with the West German army, the Bundeswehr, and German politicians in charge of military questions: 'Tals' presence was surely known to the German military and civil authorities. West German military aid to Israel started in 1956' (Jelinek 2004: 403). Indeed, German-Israeli military relations became crucial only after the 1956 Suez War. The next part of this book examines the period between 1956 and 1967, the most dramatic and important phase in the history of German-Israeli relations.

PART II

The Military Alliance
A German *Sonderweg* in the Middle East?
(1956–67)

THE PERIOD BETWEEN the Reparations Agreement and the Arab-Israeli War of 1967 is both the most complex and important one in German-Israeli relations. It is the most complex because German foreign policy in the Middle East at the time was influenced by a number of countervailing factors: changing US geostrategy, West German-East German competition, and growing Soviet influence in the Middle East, in tune with the radicalisation of anti-western, anti-colonial Arab nationalism. At the same time, it is the most important because, from 1956 until 1965, the Federal Republic of Germany (FRG) was the only western power to extend to Israel all three forms of conventional geopolitical support: economic, financial and military. The FRG thus played an overall role in Israel's early consolidation that was more important than that of the United States, France or Britain.

Part I told the story of economic support, of industrialisation via reparations. Deliveries under the Reparations Agreement

59

began to be phased out in 1965. Meanwhile, another vital form of German aid at the time was in the form of a financial loan, dubbed *Aktion Geschäftsfreund* ('Operation Business Friend'), which was, like the weapons, also given in secrecy. After the establishment of diplomatic relations in 1965, the loan was transformed into official development aid. According to an official governmental reply to a parliamentary request, from 1961 to 1965, Germany transferred 644,8 million Deutsche Mark (DM) in a low-interest, long-term loan to Israel (Bundestag 2012).

Up to 1967, France and the FRG were the two most important sources of weapons for Israel, although French military supplies to Israel outweighed those of their German neighbours. One key difference, however, was that Germany did not sell its weapons, but delivered them free of charge. Prior to the Arab-Israeli War, Germany was a far more important source of arms for Israel than the United States. Regarding the pre-1967 period, Shimon Peres, then Israeli deputy minister of defence and the main architect of the military relationships with both France and the FRG, stated '[...] the USA helped us with money, but not with weapons. France helped us with weapons, but not with money. Germany could build a bridge over the past by delivering arms, without demanding money or anything else' (Peres 1970: 71).

The Israeli newspaper *Ma'ariv* quoted Ben-Gurion in 1964 as saying '[t]he contribution of the German government for our military security *exceeds* what any other government does for us' (cited in Gardner-Feldman 1984: 127, original emphasis).

From 1957 to 1962, Germany delivered light weapons (mostly Allied surplus material not needed by the German army) and motor patrol boats, as well as providing military training. But in 1962, Adenauer agreed to a major arms deal with Israel. Deliveries included heavy artillery, planes, helicopters, boats and submarines: 114 anti-aircraft guns, twenty-four Sikorsky helicopters, twelve Nord Noratlas transport planes, 250 Cobra anti-tank missiles with 1000 rounds of ammunition, six Jaguar speedboats, four Do28 planes and two 350-ton submarines. The overall value of these deliveries stood at DM240 million (*Aktenedition zur Auswärtigen Politik der Bundesrepublik* [AAPD] 1964/289).

In 1964, the US administration pressured Bonn to add 150 M48 'Patton' tanks to the delivery list, the most important part of German arms supplies. As a key component of the Israeli tank corps, they were crucial to Israel's victorious Sinai ground battle in the Arab-Israeli War of 1967.

Looking at the overall history of German support to Israel until 1965, it seems clear that the military force displayed by Israel in the decisive war of 1967 could not have been developed to this level without the FRG's prior support. The period from 1945 until 1965-67 is thus a key one for comprehending the overall German-Israeli relationship. The United States fully took over its role as Israel's pivotal external backer only after 1967, when Israel's status as a regional hegemonic power had already been demonstrated, due to German help.

The FRG supported Israel out of its best interests as it conceived them. To understand the determining factors of Germany's Israel policy after the Reparations Agreement, one needs to first take a closer look at the years 1955-56. In 1955, the FRG joined North Atlantic Treaty Organisation (NATO) and developed the Hallstein Doctrine, while the Soviet Union entered the Middle East with the Egyptian-Czech arms deal; in October 1956, Great Britain, France and Israel attacked Egypt. How do these events relate to one another and how have they influenced German Middle East policy?

West German integration into the Cold War alliance was achieved and formalised with the FRG's accession to NATO, which can be seen as the logical continuation of the Marshall Plan (Hobsbawm 1990: 304f.). This meant that the rehabilitation factor became less determinant for West Germany's Israel policy. However, it retained importance, not least because Bonn feared that Jerusalem could use Nazi continuities within the West German state and society to bring the FRG into international disrepute. Furthermore, after the Reparations Agreement, 'West Germany needed Israel as proof of its unswerving commitment to the democratic camp, the Jewish state needed West Germany to escape from its isolation in the Middle East and link itself to a partner with growing impact in Western Europe' (Trimbur 2003: 275).

The Hallstein Doctrine testified to Bonn's increased independence on the international scene. This doctrine was a diplomatic tool for enforcing the West German claim to sole representation for the whole of Germany (*Alleinvertretungsanspruch*). It postulated that diplomatic recognition of the German Democratic Republic (GDR) by third-party states would be regarded as an unfriendly act by the FRG. A possible response by Bonn would be to break off diplomatic relations between the FRG and any state recognising the GDR. Developed in the context of the Cold War in Eastern Europe, the Hallstein Doctrine tied German hands in the Middle East, handing Arab states a formidable diplomatic tool. From this point, Arab states could now threaten to diplomatically recognise the GDR in order to counter German support of Israel. The Hallstein Doctrine thus instilled a new level of risk into German Middle East politics. For Arab nationalism bent on carving out political autonomy in the Cold War confrontation, diplomatic manoeuvres towards East Germany became an important playing card until 1965. German-Israeli relations in this period therefore need to be understood not least in the context of the principal dilemma the FRG created for itself with the Hallstein Doctrine: between supporting Israel and upholding the claim to *Alleinvertretung*. This dilemma was dissolved when Israel and Germany finally forged diplomatic ties in 1965, which also marked the end of the Hallstein Doctrine for German Middle East policy.

Importantly, the FRG increased its support of Israel because it was seen, as Adenauer told Ben-Gurion in March 1960, as a 'fortress of the West' (cited in Blasius and Jelinek 1997: 337). Israel stood against the forces of Arab nationalism, epitomised by Egyptian President Gamal Abdel Nasser. The Adenauer administration, often misjudging the autonomy-seeking, non- or anti-communist orientation of 'Arab socialism', feared that Egypt would drift decisively into the Soviet camp, for which the 1955 Egyptian-Czech arms deal indeed gave cause to worry.

The key moment for the formation of military ties between Germany and Israel was the aftermath of the 1956 Suez attack by Great Britain, France and Israel. The attack was opposed by the United States, which consequently distanced itself from Israel, as well as from its European allies. The intervention also marked the end of French and British colonial influence in the Middle East. It is against this backdrop that the FRG emerged as a key supporter of Israel from 1957 until 1965.

As for the Israeli leadership around Ben-Gurion, the reliable fulfilment of the Reparations Agreement demonstrated the FRG's commitment to the Zionist project. After the Luxembourg Agreement, the Israeli government continued to deepen ties with the FRG in order to integrate Israel as much as possible into western Cold War structures.

Both Germany and Israel attached great importance to the secrecy of military ties and financial support. This means that the full extent of German-Israeli military cooperation cannot be accounted for with certainty, as much information remains classified in the relevant military archives of both countries. Furthermore, military cooperation was often based on informal, often solely oral agreements. The Auswärtiges Amt (AA), at least until 1965, was never directly involved in military questions negotiated between the two countries (see also Jelinek 2004: 401). Even in the German Federal Ministry of Defence (Bundesministerium der Verteidigung [BMVg]) itself, only a handful of people were informed. For the military historian interested in reconstructing military cooperation between the two countries in detail, these factors make for a frustrating undertaking. The available material suffices, however, for the broader analytical ambitions pursued here. On the one hand, one can follow investigations made by officials of the AA in the BMVg about the question of military cooperation. As German military support of Israel became public and a point of contention with Arab states, the AA was able to gather more concrete information on the extent of the deliveries, in order to be able to adequately deal with the ensuing political-diplomatic problems.

The data the following chapters present largely stems from research in the archives of the AA. The published archival editions of the AA also provide ample material in support of the arguments presented here. Regarding the secondary literature, the exemplary research in Jelinek's underrated study of the period from the immediate postwar period until 1965 needs to be highlighted (Jelinek 2004). Given that sufficient data is thus easily available for a substantive examination of German-Israeli military cooperation before 1967 and, moreover, considering the importance of this period to German foreign policy specifically and Cold War history in the Middle East generally, it is astonishing that the question of German support to Israel in this period has received so little focused scholarly attention.

4

AFTER SUEZ
THE ALLIANCE BEGINS

As shown in Part I, the Israeli military orientation towards Germany predated the Reparations Agreement. It was mutually understood that this agreement would also help in building Israel's domestic military industry, with relations starting in earnest in 1956-57. Shlomo Shpiro, military analyst and security expert at the Bar Ilan University in Tel Aviv, who stresses the early importance of bilateral military cooperation, found that the first substantial German military delivery to Israel consisted of two motor patrol boats in 1956 and 1957. He explained this deal in pragmatic military terms. At the time, the Israeli navy was only 'equipped with a motley collection of ancient vessels [...] totally unfit for defending Israel's long Mediterranean coastline against the vastly superior Egyptian navy. Germany, with its long expertise in building military ships, its shipyards eager for new orders, was the ideal place for purchasing new boats for Israel' (Shpiro 2002: 31). Most accounts date the beginning of military relations to the meeting between Shimon Peres, the Israeli deputy minister of defence, and Franz Josef Strauss, the German minister of defence, to December 1957. Although the two had met before and would meet several times afterwards, this meeting can be said to have instituted the official, yet highly secretive military relationship between the two countries that characterised German-Israeli relations until the advent of diplomatic relations in 1965 (see also Jelinek 2004: 407). The emergence of Germany as a principal military backer of Israel needs to be explained in the context of the 1956 surprise attack by Britain, France and Israel against Egypt following Nasser's nationalisation of the Suez Canal. Following Stauber's article on the understudied connection between the Suez aftermath and FRG-Israeli relations (Stauber 2013: 236), the German reaction to the events of 1956 demonstrated to the Ben-Gurion administration 'Adenauer's commitment to the existence, security and prosperity of the State of Israel' (Stauber 2013: 235). It is also after Suez that the FRG 'began to see Israel as a strategic asset in the Cold War' (Stauber 2013: 235).

Britain, France and Israel were aware that the United States opposed an attack on Egypt, but calculated that, once underway, the United States would back its western allies. This proved to be a mistake. The United States and the Soviet Union cooperated at the United Nations to reinstate the status quo ante. The FRG, officially neutral, was as surprised by the attack as it was by the decisiveness with which the United States opposed it. The German embassy in Washington explained that the United States viewed its reputation among Arab states as an 'indispensable requirement' for its relations towards the Middle East (*Politisches Archiv des Auswärtigen Amtes* [PA AA], B130, Bd. 6436, 11 March 1957). In another report about the changes in US Middle Eastern strategy in 1957, the embassy found that Washington was compelled, 'surely against its will', to position itself against its European allies. With a hint of irony, the report suggested that the United States had so far played the role of an 'anti-colonial' non-partial observer in the Middle East (PA AA,

B130, Bd. 6438, 8 January 1958). The United States could not allow itself to alienate Arab public opinion, especially at a time of decolonisation, where any project of imposing hegemony in the Middle East had to dissociate itself from formal types of colonialism (Achar 2004). Across the Arab world, and indeed the entire, decolonising global south, the 1956 attack was widely perceived as a colonial undertaking, and dealt a deadly blow to French and British independent imperial ambitions.

The US State Department contemplated the idea of enlisting German support in pressuring Israel towards withdrawal from the Sinai Peninsula and the Gaza Strip. The FRG was especially suited to play such a role due to Israeli economic dependence on the reparations deliveries (PA AA, B130, Bd. 6436, 11 February 1957). In February 1957, the US Secretary of State John Foster Dulles 'suggested' to the German ambassador in the United States 'to nudge the Israeli government towards a withdrawal from occupied Egyptian territory [...]. The FRG would be especially capable of doing so, since Israel economically depended on it' (PA AA, B130, Bd. 6436, 19 February 1957). Washington actually considered using the 'reparations weapon' immediately after the Israeli campaign in the Sinai Peninsula started at the end of October 1956 (Stauber 2013: 237). However, whenever the question of utilising Israel's economic dependence on the FRG to force the country into compliance arose, Adenauer remained firm that deliveries under the Reparations Agreement would not be halted, since, he claimed, as reparations, they stood outside of politically utilisable development aid (PA AA, B130, Bd. 6436, 11 February 1957). According to Wolffsohn, '[t]his decision on Adenauer's part represents the true turning-point in German-Israeli relations. From that point on, Ben-Gurion pressed not just for restitution, but above all for cooperation, for diplomatic relations – which he had sought to avoid before – and not least of all for military cooperation' (Wolffsohn 1993: 127).

This raises the historiographical question about the extent of US pressure on Germany to halt implementation of reparations deliveries, as well as about German views of the Suez War. Stauber cautions not to exaggerate the firmness of the German stance, since there never existed anything akin to an explicit US order to halt deliveries (Stauber 2013: 245; cf. Trimbur 2003: 281). The research for this book undergirds this finding. The files of the AA speak of 'suggesting' and 'contemplating', not of firm orders. Of course, this raises the counterfactual question of how the German government would have reacted to a more formal order. According to Stauber, 'Jewish and Israeli personages who were familiar with the complex relationship of Israel, Germany and the U.S. tended to doubt that the FRG would refuse a decisive American demand on this subject' (Stauber 2013: 246). One such personage was Nahum Goldmann, who had the most extensive personal rapport with Adenauer over the reparations negotiations. Goldmann was of the opinion that 'if the U.S. takes measures against us, Germany will stop the reparations' (Stauber 2013: 246). This belief concurs with the view that the German commitment to Israel worked within the overall constraints of US geostrategic priorities, even though it sometimes came close to putting those constraints to the test.

There was also an obvious economic German interest in not interrupting the reparations deliveries. German industry and the banking sector were relieved when learning that implementation of the Reparations Agreement would not be suspended, a decision they had lobbied for (Stauber 2013: 237). Furthermore, Ralph Dietl's argument about the 'Europeanist' agenda behind the Suez War (Dietl 2008) allows us to see the German pro-Israel stance in light of the overall German view on the attack. While officially declaring neutrality, the FRG made clear during internal discussions with its European allies that it supported the offensive. The German historian and Adenauer biographer

Hans-Peter Schwarz, certainly not critically disposed towards the subject of his study, described the chancellor as a 'late-nineteenth-century colonialist' who 'unconditionally approved of the Suez intervention' (Schwarz 1997: 191 and 242). The FRG was taken aback by the decisiveness with which the United States acted to enforce a return to the status quo ante, thus rebuffing and embarrassing Germany's European allies. It is important to recognise, however, that no principal rift existed between NATO states on the question of opposition to Arab nationalism as led by Egypt and personified by Nasser. In personal conversations with Adenauer, Dulles was not beyond likening Nasser to Hitler, describing the former's manifesto, *Philosophy of the Revolution* (1956), as the "Mein Kampf' of Arab nationalism' (PA AA, B130, Bd. 6439, 26 July 1958). In fact, the Suez War provides a major and early example of 'nazifying' Arabs in order to help legitimise interventionist wars. The Nasser/Hitler or Suez/Munich analogy was used throughout the crisis, especially by Britain and France (Kyle 2003). The actually divisive question among NATO states was how to respond to Arab nationalism. In the above-cited conversation with Dulles, Adenauer expressed his 'great fear' that the United States 'did not take Arab nationalism seriously enough' (PA AA, B130, Bd. 6439, 26 July 1958). To the Europeans, the US-Soviet handling of the crisis drove home the lesson that the two superpowers would, if need be, cooperate over their heads in order to maintain the bipolar world order. Trimbur consequently interprets the German decision to continue reparations deliveries not least as a 'warning' to the United States, 'a gesture that could be viewed as assistance to a country at war' (Trimbur 2003: 287).

After Suez, Israel found itself in a situation where it had impressed upon the Middle East and the outside world its military capacities, yet also incurred a setback in its overall effort to ally itself militarily with the United States. Acquiring American weapons had now become a rather more distant prospect; meanwhile, the Middle Eastern influence of its war allies, Britain and France, was severely curtailed. Furthermore, its alliance with the French was to a large degree predicated on the Algerian War of Independence (1954–62). The French supplied Israel mainly because of the threat it posed to Nasser's Egypt, which was arming the Algerian National Liberation Front. Accordingly, French support of Israel waned after De Gaulle extracted the French forces from Algeria in 1962.

It is in this post-Suez context that the FRG emerged as a potential informal military ally. Stauber argues that, for Israel, deepening relations with Germany was important in order to shield the Reparations Agreement against eventual future jeopardization from the outside, as well as because of the rising political importance of the FRG in the Western Bloc.

It is within this same context that Ben-Gurion's policy of the 'New Germany' emerged (Stauber 2013: 250). The name of this policy reveals its purpose: to demarcate Adenauer's Germany from that of Hitler. It was directed to a critical Israeli audience in order to legitimise ties with the FRG, and it was also the symbolic resource Israel was able to offer to the FRG. Extending this resource rested on the continued German commitment to the consolidation of the Israeli state, and represented a symbolic concession to acquire material support. Stauber perceptively follows through on the ways in which this concept affected the Israeli view of the Arab-Israeli conflict: 'according to the founding father of the Jewish State, the German state which was founded on the ruins of Nazi Germany and where millions of its former citizens still lived – officers, soldiers, and murderers – would help the Jewish People against those who arose to destroy their state' (Stauber 2013: 252).

The effects of German reparations and military support on the build-up of the Israeli state in political, military and economic terms were decisive to the Israeli government's acceptance of the West German turn. Building Israel was conceptualised as 'the ultimate answer to activities against the Jewish people' (Stauber 2003: 112). To achieve this end, even cooperation with West Germany could be justified (Weitz 2000). As Ben-Gurion himself put it to the Knesset in 1959 on the question of military relations with the FRG:

> [T]he injunction bequeathed by the martyrs of the Holocaust is rebuilding, strengthening, advancing and ensuring the security of Israel. For that purpose we need friends who are able and willing to equip the Israel Defence Forces in order to guarantee our survival [...], but if we regard Germany or any other country as Satan we shall not receive arms. (cited in Stauber 2003: 115)

The German defence establishment was impressed by the show of Israel's military proficiency during the Suez War. Stauber refers to a conversation involving Franz Josef Strauss and Hans Speidel in December 1956. Speidel was a founder of the Bundeswehr and later chief-of-staff of NATO's Central European ground forces. He had also been a Wehrmacht senior commander on the Eastern Front, where Strauss had served as a junior officer. Strauss was also formerly a member of the *Nationalsozialistischer Kraftfahrerkorps*, a *Sturmabteilung* suborganisation. Strauss and Speidel were dissatisfied with the French and British military handling of the Suez crisis. In light of the military capabilities shown by the Israel Defence Forces, one of the two (it is unclear from the file who) claimed that 'perhaps it would have been better to have let the Jews defeat the Egyptians' (cited in Stauber 2013: 242). It is interesting, as Stauber rightly notes, that Speidel and Strauss were impressed by the military capacity of 'the Jews'. In fact, what the last chapter of this part will explain as the re-imagination of Israeli Jews as German soldiers is closely intertwined with changes in West German geostrategic and military thinking about the Middle East. After Suez, the FRG began to perceive Israel as a defender of western interests in the Middle East, pitted against Arab nationalism.

Guns instead of embassies: The Hallstein Doctrine in the Middle East

The question of German-Israeli military relations is related to the question of diplomatic relations between the two countries. Both issues, in turn, need to be looked at within the overall context of Germany's contradicting interests in, on the one hand, a useful relationship with Israel and, on the other, the territorial and political claim over East Germany. Germany and Israel established diplomatic relations in 1965, which means that bilateral relations were at their most important when there was no official form to them. For the FRG, the optimal timing for diplomatic relations would have been upon the conclusion of the 1952 Reparations Agreement, as signalled by Adenauer in the Bundestag at the time and by what German diplomats have told the Israelis since. In 1952, diplomatic relations with Germany were impossible for Israel for purely domestic reasons. By 1956, however, diplomatic relations had become defendable to the public, not least due to Germany's reliability in fulfilling the Reparations Agreement (PA AA, B130, Bd. 8448, 15 August 1963). It is again indicative of the weakness of the moral explanation of Germany's Israel policy that the FRG was virtually the only major western nation not diplomatically represented in Tel Aviv until 1965, *despite* the Israelis requesting it. As one German political scientist noted, German politics towards Israel are less an illustration of morality than a confirmation of Marx's quip that morals regularly embarrass themselves in front of interests (Scheffler 1988: 77).

The overriding West German interest was to preserve its claim over the GDR. The Hallstein Doctrine, as explained at the beginning of this book section, now began to shape Germany's Israel policy. The countless internal discussions and debates with the Israelis about the diplomatic question (which can be found in the AA's archives) always end on the same argument: offering diplomatic relations to Israel would run the risk of Arab states recognising East Germany in return. This would then lead into a dilemma made of the FRG's own volition, for if Arab states were to diplomatically recognise the GDR, Bonn could either break off diplomatic relations with Arab states, thus significantly decreasing its clout in the Middle East, or it could abdicate from the doctrine, thus abandoning its claim over the GDR (see also PA AA, B130, Bd. 8448, 15 August 1963).

For Israel, diplomatic recognition by the FRG would have meant a further bridge towards NATO states and further integration into the Western Bloc. The US State Department was of the opinion that Israel also sought diplomatic relations with the FRG to open up indirect communication channels with Arab states (PA AA, B130, Bd. 2876, 17 April 1957). This makes sense insofar as the FRG enjoyed a much better reputation in the Middle East than ex-colonial powers of Britain and France. Both the United States and Israel believed German fears of Arab states recognising the GDR to be exaggerated, as, they argued, Arab countries would not risk losing German economic aid and trade relations. As explained further on, this argument turned out to be well-founded.

Accepting the German refusal of diplomatic relations was a concession Israel had no reason to make gratuitously. The Ben-Gurion administration pursued its policy of the 'New Germany' in tune with the flow of weapons. For Israel, military aid was at this stage more important than diplomatic recognition (Jelinek 2004: 401). 'The substance of German-Israeli relations', the Israeli ambassador to the United States told the German Minister of Foreign Affairs Heinrich von Brentano in 1958, 'is more important than its form' (PA AA, B130, Bd. 3767, 7 June 1958). While Adenauer observed that the substance of German-Israeli relations remained satisfactory to both sides, towards the end of his term in office he invested personal energies towards the diplomatic formalisation of bilateral relations, much to the shock of his foreign minister. Adenauer was certainly not least motivated by a desire to embellish his personal legacy, crowning his work *Wiedergutmachung*. He remained committed to his idea of the term, telling Felix Shinnar, the head of the Israel Mission in Bonn, that diplomatic relations with Israel needed to be achieved in order to nix any renewed legal efforts in the FRG to bring former Nazi criminals to trial, since such endeavours would threaten the global reputation of the FRG (AAPD 1965/182). Despite this, diplomatic relations would be established only under Adenauer's successor in office, Ludwig Erhard. This happened, as we will see, primarily as a result of changed US geostrategy in the Middle East.

Military ties with Israel were a highly contested issue within the German state administration, with the AA arguing against weapons deliveries to Israel on the grounds of *Alleinvertretung*. Proponents of military cooperation with Israel defended their policy by pointing to its secrecy, given that it was to be executed under the radar of Arab states' suspicion. Franz Josef Strauss was, on the German side, the driving force behind military ties with Israel. Strauss was one of the most controversial German postwar politicians, his name invariably connected to the revisionist tendencies in the early Federal Republic. Pushing for early German rearmament, as well as nuclear armament, he was opposed to any moves towards legal and political confrontation with the Nazi past.

Strauss was not initially favourable towards Israel. As mentioned previously, he abstained in the Bundestag vote on the ratification of the Reparations Agreement, arguing that the agreement posed a threat to German relations with Arab states. However, he changed his mind once he became minister of defence. His interests in relations with Israel reflected closely his interests in Germany regaining its military power, the growth of German arms industries, as well as his views on Cold War confrontation, in which he foresaw a role for Israel as a western bastion against Arab nationalism and Soviet influence in the Middle East. It is interesting to see how Strauss framed military ties with Israel in terms of Germany's positioning towards its past. The following is taken from an interview with the already mentioned German publicist Rolf Vogel, one of Adenauer's confidants and a chronicler of German-Israeli relations.[1] In this interview, Strauss framed his politics towards Israel in the form he wanted them to be presented to the public:

> I was of the opinion that effective co-operation between the Federal Republic of Germany and Israel would be a significant contribution towards the task of leaving the past behind us. I meant this in the sense, not only of the reacceptance of Germany in the world, but acceptance of the Federal Republic of Germany as a state with equal rights in the field of present-day world politics. (cited in Vogel 1969: 124)

And further:

> [W]here lives were concerned aid to Israel was more than a matter of obligatory reparations; it was of especial moral and political consequence to us all. I came to this conclusion with the fact in mind that millions of Jews were murdered as a result of criminal German policy and with German weapons. It is not for us to criticize the setting up of the State of Israel [...]. It is an established fact that some of the Jews of the world have found a new home and accomplished a marvellous task of reconstruction. Many threats have been uttered against this country and its people; threats from a hostile world that it will be conquered and its people wiped out. If therefore the Federal Republic of Germany can make a modest contribution to keeping the peace in the Middle East – a critical factor for us too – then this goes some way towards reparation in the very sphere in which Germany committed some of her worst crimes. (cited in Vogel 1969: 124)

There is a contradiction in Strauss' argument. In the first quote above, he makes clear that relations with Israel constituted a means 'of leaving the past behind us'; yet in the second quote, he speaks of the 'moral and political consequences' of aid to Israel. One would assume that a moral approach towards the past would mean confronting it. However, Strauss meant the exact opposite: to leave the past behind. It is also worth noting the abstraction and de-personification of the German persecution of Jews: Jews have been murdered 'as a result of criminal German policy' and 'with German weapons', not by actual human beings. Having been a Wehrmacht officer on the Eastern Front, Strauss was witness to German mass executions of Jews. The hostile, at times eliminatory, rhetoric of some Arab states' leaders towards Israel served Strauss as an invitation for exculpation: the 'German weapons' that previously killed Jews could now be delivered to the Jewish state, as it was faced with extinction.

Shimon Peres thought the Bavarian to be primarily motivated by a fear of Soviet influence in the Middle East and by respect for Israel's military capacity (Jelinek 2004: 408). One immediate effect of post-Suez cooperation was that the Israelis handed over to the FRG Soviet weapons captured in the war for inspection. After the 1967 war, Israel would again offer captured Soviet weapons to Germany. Shpiro, in his contributions on the topic, attaches great importance to this fact, viewing it as highly beneficial to German development of arms technology in the Cold War arms race.

German-Israeli military cooperation as it developed after Suez consisted firstly of Israeli arms sales to Germany, then of German arms deliveries to Israel. In 1958 and 1959, Germany ordered grenades, mortar shells and, most significantly, 50,000 'Uzi' submachine guns from Israeli companies in the form of long-term orders. Later, smoke mortars were added to the delivery list. A summary note from the AA in July 1965 reviews German purchasing orders until that point. This summary, for which information had been gathered in the BMVg, years after the heat surrounding these deliveries had abated, stated that the overall value of ongoing military deliveries from Israel to Germany stood at about DM250 million (roughly equivalent to one of the fourteen instalments paid under the Reparations Agreement) (PA AA, B130, Bd. 2582, 16 July 1965).

Israeli weapons deliveries had a further afterlife, as Jelinek recounts. Of the 50,000 Uzis Germany ordered, only 40,000 were needed by the Bundeswehr. The BMVg thus sold 10,000 Uzis to Portugal, which was at the time engaged in a counter-insurgency against anticolonial Angolans striving for independence. In the words of Jelinek, '[t]he Angola-affair was the worst possible combination: Germans give Israeli weapons to Portuguese colonialists to fight down the African struggle for independence' (Jelinek 2004: 409).

As Jelinek explains, the decision to introduce the Uzi as the standard submachine gun of the Bundeswehr was justified by referring to its superiority and competitive price. However, the transaction was also intended as an indirect form of economic aid to Israel, supporting its growing military industry (see also Gardner-Feldman 1984: 126). Moreover, equipping the Bundeswehr with Israeli weapons needs to be considered as a tactical move to pre-empt criticism of German rearmament (Jelinek 1997: 75). Journalist Rolf Vogel had a hand in the Uzi deal, creating links between relevant officials in both countries. Vogel summarised the German rationale as such: 'The Uzi in the hand of the German soldier is better than any brochure against antisemitism' (cited in Hansen 2002: 134). The statement conveys the idea that German rearmament in the 1950s with Israeli weapons was a tool for overcoming antisemitism in Germany. This statement can be read as an aphorism which succinctly sums up the whole rationale of German politics towards Israel from the postwar era to the 1960s. Yigal Allon, a Knesset member of the left-leaning Ahdut HaAvodah and later minister of defence, understood the German motivation for buying Israeli weapons well: 'The Germans have purchased these weapons not because the weapons are good, but because they are Jewish. The Germans desperately need rehabilitation' (cited in Segev 1993: 316).

The above quotes of Vogel and Strauss present the fact of early German-Israeli military ties in terms of overcoming the past. One of many possible ways of criticising such a perception is to point to the symbolic violence inherent in this relationship. In his collection, Vogel relates how the Israeli sales to Germany included textile products, subsequently used for the new German army's uniforms. Israeli workers tasked with the production of these textiles 'stage[d] strikes that were easily broken by internal exchange schemes' (Vogel 1969: 125). The cold language in which Vogel glosses over this telling episode is rather striking. Apparently, survivors who refused to participate in the re-militarisation of the successor state to Nazi Germany stood in the way of 'reconciliation'.

Israel lobbied for increased NATO protection in the West European capitals by working on the tensions between Europe and the United States that had resulted from the Suez War. In mid-December 1957, Giora Joseftal, Mapai leader and Histadrut functionary, visited Konrad Adenauer in Bonn. Having headed the Israeli delegation during the negotiations over the Reparations Agreement, Joseftal was no stranger to German politics. Accompanied by Felix Shinnar, Joseftal 'delivered a personal message from Ben-Gurion. He described to the chancellor the precarious situation which had developed following the Soviet intrusion into the Middle East, precarious to Israel, and, thus, to the whole Western world' (PA AA, B130, Bd. 3767, 13 December 1957). He then explained Ben-Gurion's wish for a NATO security guarantee for the Israeli state.

As Germany had no formal representation in Israel, it was difficult for the AA to gather information about Israel's political intentions. A contact from the British embassy in Bonn would occasionally relate news items he received from his colleagues in Tel Aviv. According to the British diplomat, 'Mr Joseftal returned to Israel exceedingly satisfied from his visit to the chancellor. He gained the impression that the chancellor was very open to the Israeli wishes, which is why he recommended to Ben-Gurion to deploy a high-ranking personality to Bonn' (PA AA, B130, Bd. 3767, 8 January 1957). This personality was to be Moshe Dayan, Israeli commander in chief of the Sinai campaign. However, the secret leaked and the first Israeli cabinet crisis over military relations with Germany ensued. Ben-Gurion refrained from dispatching Dayan and decommissioned the whole cabinet on 31 December 1957, to present the same cabinet to the Knesset a week later and thus renew its parliamentary support.

Thus, in late December 1957, 'three Israelis found themselves stuck in their car in the snow somewhere on the way to Bavaria. One of the three would later be appointed Israel's first ambassador to Germany, the second would be army chief of staff, and the third, minister of defence and prime minister' (Segev 1993: 302). The director general of the Israel Ministry of Defence (IMoD) Asher Ben-Natan, who would later become the first Israeli ambassador to Germany, military officer Haim Laskov and Shimon Peres were travelling to meet Franz Josef Strauss, the German minister of defence, in his private residence in Rott am Inn. This was not the first meeting between Strauss and Peres, which, according to Jelinek, went ahead on 4 July 1957, but it was the most important (Jelinek 1997: 407). According to Strauss, in the December talks with Peres, as well as in a discussion he had with him earlier that year, Peres expressed the wish not only to salvage two sunken submarines, but also to order new ones. Peres also asked if Israeli officers could be trained in West Germany. Strauss and Peres further discussed Israeli options regarding the joining of the Organisation for European Economic Co-operation (OEEC), the predecessor of today's Organisation for Economic Co-operation and Development (OECD), and the European Payments Union (EPU) (PA AA, B130, Bd. 6398, 13 January 1958). According to Shimon Peres:

> Within only a few months of our first meeting, very valuable equipment began to reach the Israel army. It consisted of German army surplus and equipment manufactured in Germany [...]. We obtained ammunition, training devices, helicopters, spare parts and many other items. The quality was excellent and the quantities were considerable – compared with what we had been used to, though they were still far short of what the Egyptians were receiving. For the first time the impoverished Israel army, which had had to skimp and scape and stretch its thin resources to the utmost, felt almost pampered. (Peres 1970: 72)

The AA was against the military contacts established by the BMVg. In January 1958, Heinrich von Brentano, the West German minister of foreign affairs, wrote to Franz Josef Strauss regarding Peres' visit:

> I am seriously worried that news of this sort may become public, either via inconsiderate comments by the German parties involved or by foreign sources, especially certain political circles in Israel. The consequences for the position and the reputation of the Federal Republic in the Middle East would be unforeseeable. The Foreign Office's explicit denial of any alleged weapon deliveries and military aid to Israel would lose all of its value. The public reactions in the Arab world may lead some of these states to establish diplomatic relations with the GDR. (PA AA, B130, Bd. 8410, 5 January 1958)

This was to become the refrain of the AA until 1965: avoid a situation in which the German commitment to the Hallstein Doctrine would be put to the test. However, another reason may well be Nazi continuities in the German foreign policy establishment (see Conze et al. 2010), which shed a troubling light on the somewhat undefined notion of the 'traditional German-Arab friendship'. A further reason for not endangering relations with Arab states was their economic importance in terms of markets for German exports, as well as sources of petroleum. The 'oil factor', however, would drastically rise in importance by the late 1960s, a topic discussed further below.

Kept in the dark, German diplomats attempted to learn about the content and details of military cooperation from their counterparts in the BMVg. However, the majority of those who were theoretically responsible for matters of military imports and exports to non-NATO areas were also uninformed (PA AA, B130, Bd. 3767, 24 August 1958). At this early stage, military ties with Israel seemed to be known only to Strauss himself and an 'Officer Becker' (PA AA, B130, Bd. 3767, 25 September 1958). The arguments brought forth either in favour or against military ties with Israel to some degree reflected institutional positions held in the German administration. Erhard, the economics minister, argued against military ties for economic reasons. The Reparations Agreement, he argued, had undoubtedly secured the FRG a place in the Israeli market, but trade with Arab states was three times as large as trade with Israel. Furthermore, Israel was insignificant as a source of raw materials, whereas Arab states were very important in this regard. Since military ties with Israel constituted a threat to trade relations with Arab states, he felt they should not be pursued (PA AA, B130, Bd. 6398, 5 September 1958).

The main proponents of military ties with Israel on the German side were Strauss and Adenauer. They forged these ties out of an interest in rehabilitation and in strengthening Israel as a western Cold War bastion in the Middle East. Military ties in the 1950s were significant, but their importance rose dramatically in the first half of the 1960s. In March 1960, the German chancellor and the Israeli prime minister held their first (and last) official meeting. A closer analysis of this first meeting is helpful for understanding the rationale, dynamics and context of the consequent deepening of military ties.

5

SHIFTING IMAGES
'NEW GERMANS' AND 'ARAB NAZIS'

The State Against Fritz Bauer, a 2015 multiple-award-winning German movie by director Lars Kraume, shows the efforts of state attorney Fritz Bauer in bringing former Nazi criminals to trial in West Germany. The movie revolves around Bauer's role in the capture of Adolf Eichmann. A short scene brilliantly captures the meaning of Germany's policies towards Israel in this context. Bauer, himself of Jewish descent, talks to his confidant, the minister of the federal country of Hessen. The lawyer is desperate. He knows of Eichmann's whereabouts, but does not dare relay this information to the West German government, rightly afraid that Eichmann's former comrades in the judiciary would warn him. It is March 1960, and in the background of the room, a television screen shows the global news: David Ben-Gurion and Konrad Adenauer sit amiably together during their meeting at New York's Waldorf Astoria hotel, shaking hands. Bauer, aggravated, turns to the screen, points to Adenauer and exclaims: 'I cannot listen to his damned talk of reconciliation anymore!'

Adenauer's policy of *Wiedergutmachung* towards Israel and the simultaneous abortion, in part even reversal, of Allied denazification policy within the German state apparatus were not contradictory, but two sides of the same coin. Two images convey the rapid changes of the German-Israeli relationship in the postwar era. The first – the photograph of the March 1960 meeting between David Ben-Gurion and Konrad Adenauer in the Waldorf Astoria – shows them sitting next to each other in a relaxed, friendly attitude of mutual understanding. By contrast, the photograph of the 1952 signing of the Reparations Agreement in Luxembourg displays a frosty, speechless atmosphere of impossible communication (see also Diner 2015). Both images are carefully crafted political compositions. Their different character indicates a deepening of relations. With the *Shilumim* making a great contribution to Israel's build-up over the 1950s, cooperation between the two states intensified further, with the individual statebuilding interests of both sides served in an ever more stable exchange. The Waldorf Astoria meeting exemplifies the continuity of the exchange between symbolic rehabilitation and material consolidation. To Germany, the meeting was relevant for the image and rhetoric it produced for a global (and specifically American) public. Israel obtained the promise of significant flows of financial and military aid and thus the continuity of German material support.

Upon their declassification in 1997, the English-Israeli and the German transcripts of the meeting were published (Shalom 1997; Jelinek and Blasius 1997). At the time, even though bits of information were revealed to the press, the transcripts of the discussions were kept secret, as they conveyed politically sensitive information about German military and financial support to Israel. The Waldorf Astoria meeting thus gave rise to much speculation, but what it showed to the world was first of all an image. German historian Rainer A. Blasius writes in his introduction to the German publication of the two meeting transcripts: 'A picture went global and was memorized – a representative of the people of the victims and a representative of the people of the perpetrators, sitting together at a small table like old friends, smiling amiably, exchanging friendly gestures and shaking hands' (Jelinek and Blasius 1997: 309).

This image, taken after the two-hour discussion in Adenauer's hotel room, was followed by pronouncements to the international press. Adenauer declared to be 'deeply moved' by the meeting, and that cooperation between Israel and Germany was to remain fruitful. In response, Ben-Gurion evoked his prior Knesset pronouncement, repeating that 'the Germany of today is not the Germany of yesterday' and that '[a]fter today's meeting with the Chancellor, I am convinced that my judgement then was correct' (Jelinek and Blasius 1997: 310). The impression the image sought to convey should not be confused with the political intentions behind it. Claims for representation are political and thus inherently disputable. It was certainly in the German interest to convey the idea of a public handshake between Jews and Germans, to produce a public display of forgiveness. As such, this image of absolution and the rhetoric surrounding the Waldorf Astoria meeting were the symbolic capital Israel was able to provide to Germany.

To assign to Adenauer the role of a 'representative' of the 'people of the perpetrators', as Blasius does, did not make sense from the official German perspective at the time. This description did not correspond to either Adenauer's self-image or to the self-descriptions of the West German state. While the FRG was the legal successor to the Nazi regime and accepted paying reparations to Jewish victims, Adenauer repeatedly used the formula of a 'crime committed in the name of the German people', while maintaining the claim that the majority of Germans opposed Hitler's regime (see also Stern 1992: 306-10). It was in consequence to this guilt-evasive strategy of attributing the crimes of Nazism to a small circle of perpetrators that Adenauer could perceive of obligations towards the past only as something that was demanded by 'honour' (*Ehrenpflicht des deutschen Volkes*) (Stauber 2003: 116). The handshake extended by Ben-Gurion became a key moment in the restoration of that 'honour' inasmuch as it symbolised absolution, albeit only from an uncritical perspective oblivious to political intentions.

The Waldorf Astoria meeting was a well-timed public display. From the end of 1959 until February 1960, a wave of anti-Jewish incidents swept the FRG. Jewish cemeteries were vandalised and antisemitic graffiti smeared in public places. The FRG denounced these events firstly because of their negative impact on Germany's international standing, and the government produced a white paper documenting the incidents. Along with the AA, which sent instructions to all its delegations, the white paper concluded that the incidents, which went into the hundreds, were severely harming the FRG's international reputation (Stauber 2003). The international criticism levelled against the presence of former Nazis in Adenauer's administration was utilised by the GDR to paint the FRG's Nazi continuities in the strongest colours possible. For its part, the FRG put the entire blame for the 'swastika epidemic' on alleged GDR agents, a reaction that was perceived negatively as an effort to deflect guilt without actually confronting the truths contained in the accusations (Stauber 2003: 104). Jewish organisations in the United States were much alerted by the wave of antisemitic incidents sweeping Germany, publicising the events and sending high-profile delegations to investigate them (Stauber 2003: 105).[1]

Gerhard Schröder (no relation to the later chancellor), German interior minister and a former member of the Nazi Party as early as 1933, presented the following interpretation of the incidents. Niels Hansen approvingly quotes Schröder's message to the German public, broadcasted on the evening news in late December 1959: 'What is horrible [...] is that here, there was a violation of the public will to *finally overcome* the most despicable and inexcusable chapter of [National Socialist] history by compensation, reconciliation and tolerance' (cited in Hansen 2002: 539, emphasis added). What is lost in the English translation is the historical-religious gravitas behind the original terms *Wiedergutmachung* and *Versöhnung*, translated here as 'compensation' and 'reconciliation'. The paradoxical idea of 'finally overcoming' an 'inexcusable past' falls neatly into Theodor Adorno's criticism of Germany's *Aufarbeitung der Vergangenheit* ('coming to terms with the past'), incidentally published in the year the 'swastika epidemic' started (1959). Adorno criticised a conception by which the Nazi past was talked about with the aim of forgetting about it:

> The question 'What does working through the past mean?' must be elucidated. It is based on a phrase that has recently become highly suspect as a slogan. 'Coming to terms with the past' does not imply a serious working through of the past, the breaking of its spell through an act of clear consciousness. It suggests, rather, wishing to turn the page and, if possible, wiping it from memory. The attitude that it would be proper for everything to be forgiven and forgotten by those who were wronged is expressed by the party that committed the injustice. (Adorno 1986: 115)[2]

What Adorno argues is that the official slogan of 'coming to terms with the past' denotes the opposite of what it presents itself as. Here, the intention is to forget the past, not a conscious attempt to confront the unspeakable: 'the tendency toward the unconscious and not so unconscious defensiveness against guilt is [...] absurdly associated with the thought of working through the past' (Adorno 1986: 115). It is this 'absurd connection' which captures so clearly the paradox in the former Nazi Gerhard Schröder's statement.

The meeting between Adenauer and Ben-Gurion, while planned before the wave of antisemitic incidents, was now scheduled for March 1960, in order for both to meet during respective visits to the United States. The place of the meeting was also telling because, from the 1960s onwards, the German-Israeli alliance was to unfold even stronger under the United States' Cold War umbrella, as Israel's military importance to the United States was to increase dramatically, in tune with the rise of anti-western Arab nationalism.

A look into the actual contents of the discussion shows that the Waldorf Astoria meeting is indeed best understood as an exchange of public absolution for the secret promise to continue to help build the Israeli state. Ben-Gurion spoke English, Adenauer spoke German; both protocols are remarkably congruent (Jelinek and Blasius 1997: 326f.). While the Israeli translator recorded the discussion in the form of dialogue, the German translator used indirect speech. The following quotes are taken from the Israeli-English record as found in the 1997 publication by Jelinek and Blasius. The German version, from the same publication, is used only to highlight nuances or eventual differences in translation.

Ben-Gurion and Adenauer begin by expressions of mutual admiration. Adenauer lauds Ben-Gurion's statebuilding efforts, while Ben-Gurion compliments Adenauer on his politics of reconciliation, notably towards the Jews (Jelinek and Blasius 1997: 330). Ben-Gurion continues with an emblematic interpretation of the relationship between the Shoah and the Israeli state, culminating in the phrase that 'historically, Hitler almost murdered the Jewish state' (Jelinek and Blasius 1997: 334), as the genocide had destroyed European Jewry, the supposed force behind the Zionist program (Jelinek and Blasius 1997: 330). This exposition is only punctually interrupted by Adenauer, and ends with the requests for financial and military aid, which Adenauer agrees to. The rest of the talk is devoted to US politics, the Cold War and the question of African countries, about which the generally much more talkative Ben-Gurion is relatively more sensitive than the strongly paternalist and Eurocentric Adenauer.

Both speak of morality when describing and justifying the German-Israeli relationship. Ben-Gurion tells his counterpart that 'what you have done, you did out of your conscience. This fact, why and how it was done, we appreciate even more than what was done. I consider the moral aspect more important than the material' (Jelinek and Blasius 1997: 330). Adenauer invokes morality to give reasons for his promise of material support: 'We will help you, out of moral reasons and out of reasons of practical politics. Israel is the fortress of the West, Israel has to develop in the interests of the whole world. I can already now tell you that we will help you, we will not leave you alone' (Jelinek and Blasius 1997: 337).

There is no methodological reason to assume that Ben-Gurion or Adenauer were insincere when they gave moral meanings to the German-Israeli relationship. Instead of trying to uncover a plain material interest behind their formulations, it is empirically more revealing to ask what Adenauer and Ben-Gurion meant when they evoked terms of morality, and why they did so. Shortly before agreeing to Ben-Gurion's requests, Adenauer makes an elucidating comment in this regard. As Ben-Gurion outlined that the Nazi regime destroyed European Jewry, Adenauer interrupts him, stating: 'The fate of the Jews is somewhat similar to ours. We also suffered the loss of a whole layer in German society. We also are missing the personalities that were lost with that layer' (Jelinek and Blasius 1997: 332).[3]

This deflection of guilt was not a stand-alone lapse in historical judgement, but exemplary for the spirit of the Adenauer era. Interestingly, statements such as these, even though they can readily be found, are widely ignored, excused and not properly explained in the academic writing on German-Israeli relations. For instance, Blasius does not allude to this comment in his introduction to the Waldorf Astoria meeting. Career diplomat Niels Hansen, in his deeply hagiographic, apologetic work on German-Israeli relations in the Adenauer era, pursues a different strategy. He quotes Adenauer's equalisation of German and Jewish suffering in full and then attempts to explain it. This attempt reads as a surreal excuse and affirmation of Adenauer's initial statement, and is exemplary for the political drive of Hansen's whole work. Without denying the validity of Adenauer's comment, Hansen claims that Adenauer meant to 'affirm' Ben-Gurion's prior statement about the impact of the Holocaust on the Israeli state. He continues by enumerating German victims during World War II. He mentions 5.3 million German soldiers killed in battle, adding 2.5 million victims of 'flight, persecution and displacement'. Having thus listed these, he proceeds to claim, without proof, that it was not Adenauer's intention to 'balance the losses' (*aufrechnen*). Yet, by uncritically reproducing Adenauer's initial statement, Hansen himself draws parallels between soldiers of the Wehrmacht killed in battle and Jewish victims of the Holocaust (Hansen 2002: 546f.).

If to a contemporary reader Adenauer's equation between German and Jewish suffering may sound absurd or disconcerting, it is a discursive strategy explicable in its historical context, a context that historians and political scientists should elucidate and explain, not reproduce and excuse.

Jelinek and Blasius claim that the main motivation of both Ben-Gurion and Adenauer was to meet publicly in order to make a political statement regarding 'the future of both peoples' (Jelinek and Blasius 1997: 329). This is hardly a tenable proposition. Ben-Gurion's conciliatory politics towards West Germany, especially in its early stages, was risky to his political position, provoking strong resistance in the state administration, the Knesset and Israeli society. Even though protest against the Waldorf Astoria meeting was not comparable to the massive mobilisation against the Reparations Agreement (Weitz 2000: 275), it is hard to believe that Ben-Gurion would continue to risk his political position for moral overtures to the successor state of the Nazi regime. As Ben-Gurion told reporters of the Israeli newspaper *Ma'ariv* in September 1960, he went to meet Adenauer because he 'hoped that from this discussion, something great would emerge for Israel, and I have good reason to believe that this hope will not be disappointed' (cited in Jelinek 1997: 533). He also justified his meeting with the West German chancellor in religious-moral terms. Again, however, the evocation of morality is best understood as the way in which a structural interest of the state is communicated in the language of politics. This interest was the consolidation of the state. Ben-Gurion's willingness to make public gestures of reconciliation was predicated on a specific interpretation of the Jewish catastrophe in Europe. In the first paragraphs of the Waldorf Astoria discussion, he develops an argument revolving around the detrimental effect of the genocide for the building of the Zionist state: 'The real historical damage [...] was something that never happened in history [...]. The Jewish people received a deadly blow from the Nazi regime. Those of our people who had vision, knowledge, ability, idealism, readiness for self-sacrifice, and material means, that was European Jewry, they were destroyed' (Jelinek and Blasius 1997: 330). This exposé logically culminates in a request for a German contribution to Israel's statebuilding efforts:

> Hitler not only murdered six million Jews [...] historically, Hitler almost murdered the Jewish State: Our hope and heritage for 3000 years. We are not going to submit to such a fate. We will overcome it. If you do not agree, that is your right. For the life of six million people, there is no such thing as reparation. But something can be done to lessen the terrible damage that was done to the idea of the Jewish home. We want you to participate in developing our country. (Jelinek and Blasius 1997: 334)

Ben-Gurion came equipped with two specific wishes for how West Germany could help in the development of the Israeli state. The first was a loan: 'You cannot undo what Hitler did, but you can help giving us the means to rebuild Israel. Either you participate or you lend us every year for ten years forty to fifty million dollars' (Jelinek and Blasius 1997: 336). The German transcript quotes Ben-Gurion as asking for a loan of 'forty to fifty million dollars over a time span of ten to twenty years'; however, Ben-Gurion's formula of $40-50 million over ten years would become the reference point for future political haggling about the exact criteria of the German loan (Jelinek and Blasius 1997: 311ff.). After Adenauer's agreement to the loan in principle, later codenamed 'Operation Business Friend' by the German side, Ben-Gurion moves on to the topic of weapons, asking for submarines and missiles. In so doing, he evokes the military relationship Israel had had with France, and in this light expresses his satisfaction with the postwar cooperation between Germany and France (Jelinek and Blasius 1997: 336). For both streams of support – financial and military – Ben-Gurion refers to discussions that had previously taken place between Israeli representatives and Hermann Josef Abs, as well as Franz Josef Strauss (Jelinek and Blasius 1997: 336). These streams of financial and military aid agreed upon at the Waldorf Astoria meeting were to become intertwined with the trial of Adolf Eichmann in Jerusalem.

The Eichmann trial in German-Israeli relations

Adolf Eichmann, the 'logistician' of the Shoah, was captured in Argentina by Mossad agents in May 1960. He was on trial in Israel from April to December 1961, and executed on 31 May 1962. The trial drew global attention and placed the Holocaust into public debate in Germany and Israel, as well as the wider western world. Prior to this, the Holocaust had been foremost a private affair of its survivors.

Years after the trial, the Israeli philosopher Yeshayahu Leibowitz wrote that it was 'a conspiracy by Adenauer and Ben-Gurion to clear the name of the German people. In exchange they paid us billions' (Segev 1993: 365). What the trial illustrates is the exchange structure specific to German-Israeli relations, namely that of whitewashing for statebuilding, or, specifically, of dissociating West Germany from the Third Reich in exchange for financial and military support. Contrary to what one may expect, the Eichmann trial had led to a deepening of German-Israeli state relations. Even on the societal level, it 'moderated anti-German sentiment in Israel' (Segev 1993: 366).

Tom Segev has shown how Ben-Gurion personally ensured that the trial differentiated between a (Nazi) Germany of the past and a Germany of the present (Segev 1993: 346), thereby disconnecting the FRG from its past. As Holocaust scholar Hanna Yablonka (2004) has shown, and as historian Idith Zertal (2005) has criticised, the trial was also used to connect Israel's Arab enemies to Nazism. The one element this book adds is to enter into the equation the issue of German support to Israel, as promised by Adenauer to Ben-Gurion in New York shortly before Eichmann's capture. There is ample evidence, in the files of the AA alone, to suggest that a threat hung over the trial: if Israel had not differentiated the FRG from Nazi Germany in the Eichmann proceedings, convicting the criminal pars pro toto for a Nazi Germany of the past (thus severing the links between the deeds of Eichmann and the FRG), the Adenauer administration would have withheld its promised financial and military support. Thus, Germany was 'denazified' by Israel in exchange for weapons and money. On the other hand, Arab states were 'nazified' in a move that sought to legitimise the Israeli position in the Arab-Israeli conflict.

The 'Nazification' of Arabs is a long-standing trope in the Arab-Israeli conflict, ranging from the 'Hitler on the Nile'

(Nasser) to the 'Hitler in Beirut' (Arafat), and to the framing of Palestinian opposition to Zionism as guided principally by antisemitism (for a concise summary of this question, see Achcar 2012: 77-81). This is not to make the converse claim that antisemitism does not play any role in Palestinian and Arab enmity to Israel. It is clear that Nazis had 'travelled' to Arab states not only in a social-psychological sense, but also in a rather literal sense (see also Rose 2017: 39-62). This is an equally complex and politically charged topic that cannot possibly be addressed here. The relevant fact to underscore in the context of this topic is simply that most Nazis and their host of enablers continued to live where they came from, which is Germany. The question of the roles of antisemitism in the context of the Arab-Israeli conflict should be disentangled from Nazi antisemitism and its afterlife in the FRG.

The FRG centrally perceived the Eichmann trial as a threat to its reputation, as it was worried that the trial would identify the postwar country with its Nazi past. The following statement of German President Heinrich Lübke, who formerly worked as an engineer under Hitler ally Albert Speer, sums up well the dominant thinking of the West German political elite at the time:

> A few days ago in Jerusalem there began a trial the name of which has become at once symbol and stigma of the terrible crimes committed by Hitler and his supporters in the name of Germany. Even today we Germans, including former resistance-workers and those who opposed Hitler, are still filled with deep shame that some of our fellow-countrymen were accessories to such crimes. In spite of this we must establish, for the sake of that same justice that has brought Eichmann to trial today, that it is fundamentally incorrect to equate the term 'National Socialist' with 'German'. (cited in Vogel 1969: 129)

While one finds here the same guilt-deferring formulas as analysed previously, Lübke claims that by the token of the 'same justice', the Eichmann trial should not be used to equate the FRG with the National Socialist state. In March 1961, Adenauer held a press conference at which numerous foreign journalists were present. He expressed his 'sorrows' about the 'repercussions' of what will be debated in the trial on the 'overall judgement passed on us Germans' (cited in Deligdisch 1974: 66). He proceeded to explain his views on National Socialism and the question of German responsibility, formulated in the same spirit as Lübke: 'One should not forget', the chancellor said, that 'National Socialist Germans had perpetrated against Germans exactly the same crimes as Eichmann had perpetrated against Jews' (cited in Deligdisch 1974: 66). Furthermore, the chancellor claimed that the percentage of committed National Socialists had been relatively low and that most people 'joyfully helped fellow Jewish citizens whenever they could' (cited in Deligdisch 1974: 66).

In August 1961, Ben-Gurion gave an interview to Rolf Vogel for a German newspaper. Vogel was at the time part of the German observer delegation to the Eichmann trial, employed by the German secret service and with a direct line of communication to the chancellery (Wiegrefe 2011). In the interview, Ben-Gurion said that his 'opinion of present-day Germany remains unchanged. Nazi Germany no longer exists [...]. The development of our relations with Germany today depends on the intentions and the policy of the German Government. For our part, we are ready to take up normal and close relations and to co-operate to the fullest extent' (cited in Vogel 1969: 132). German Minister of Defence Franz Josef Strauss, in his interview with Vogel, suggested that since 'Germany had defended Israel's safety', the FRG should not be held 'collectively guilty for the crimes of a previous generation' in the Eichmann trial (cited in Vogel 1969: 124). Of course, Strauss himself was part of this 'previous generation' of Germans active in World War II. Nevertheless, he found that his Israeli counterparts were receptive to these worries.

While Bonn had a general interest in seeing the trial demarcate the 'Third Reich' from the Federal Republic, it had a specific interest in avoiding the implication of Hans Globke, state secretary in the chancellery and Adenauer's closest adviser. Globke, a jurist, had written an influential legal interpretation of the Nuremberg Laws which helped pave the way towards the juridical persecution of Jews, and there was a danger that Eichmann would connect his name to Jewish persecution in Greece.

The material available in the archives of the AA suggests that Germany made the delivery of the loan and weapons promised in the 1960 Waldorf Astoria meeting dependent on the Israeli handling of the trial (see also Winkler 2012: 303). Shortly before the opening of proceedings in 1961, Ben-Gurion met Strauss in Berlin, where he reminded him about the loan. Ben-Gurion stated that the first rate had been due on 28 March 1961, but Israel had not received this payment, and thus had to acquire the loan elsewhere. Strauss then asked the chancellor about the loan, who said that 'under no circumstances could anything be done before the beginning of the Eichmann trial' (AAPD 1965/2). In October 1961, Minister of Foreign Affairs von Brentano wrote to Adenauer about the Eichmann trial and the financial loan promised in 1960. He referred to Shinnar, Israel's representative in the FRG, who had stated that 'reservations concerning the Eichmann trial' had been dispelled, so the payment of the loan could now go ahead (PA AA, B130, Bd. 8414, 9 October 1961). When in February 1962, Strauss tried to convince Carl Carstens, state secretary in the AA, of weapons deliveries to Israel, he argued that 'the Israelis prevented extreme agitation against us' at the Eichmann trial, mentioning especially Globke (AAPD 1962/2).

Israel received the first tranche of the 'Operation Business Friend' loan in December 1961, after the verdict on Eichmann was given. A major delivery of arms was then agreed upon in August 1962, two months after Eichmann's execution (AAPD 1964/289).

Jelinek confirms that '[t]he Israeli government undertook great efforts to prevent a public debate about Globke' (Jelinek 2004: 83). His explanation for this finding is that it was the purpose of the Eichmann trial to 'elucidate the global public about the Nazi crimes against the Jewish people. The case of Globke was seen as a side issue, which would have distracted from this effort' (Jelinek 2004: 83). While it is of course true that Globke was not central to the trial, the problem with Jelinek's argument is that other 'side issues' played quite an important role. Although Israel downplayed the connections between the FRG and Nazi Germany, it stressed the connections between Arab states and Nazi Germany. This was done, as Idith Zertal explains:

> [...] in two distinctive ways: first, by massive references to the presence of Nazi scientists and advisers in Egypt and other Arab countries, to the on-going connections between Arab and Nazi leaders, and to the Nazi-like intentions and plans of the Arabs to annihilate Israel. The second means was systematic references – in the press, on the radio, and in political speeches – to the former Mufti of Jerusalem, Haj Amin El-Husseini, his connections with the Nazi regime in general and with Eichmann and his office in particular. In those references he was depicted as a prominent designer of the Final Solution and a major Nazi criminal. The deeds of Eichmann – and other Nazi criminals – were rarely mentioned without addition of the Arab-Nazi dimension. (Zertal 2005: 100)

In other words, the trial minimised the role of Globke and inflated the role of the Mufti in the history of the German persecution of the Jews. In her famous coverage of the trial, Hannah Arendt noted the obvious, namely that 'the former Ministerialrat of the Interior and present Staatssekretär in Adenauer's Chancellery doubtlessly had more right than the ex-Mufti of Jerusalem to figure in the history of what the Jews had actually suffered from the Nazis' (Arendt 1994: 19).

Ben-Gurion personally made three changes to the opening speech of chief prosecutor Gideon Hausner, 'all aimed at protecting West Germany's image and diminishing the guilt of the German people' (Segev 1993: 346). Ben-Gurion told Hausner that crimes should not be attributed to 'the Germans' but to 'Nazi Germany'. Secondly, he suggested to omit the thesis that Nazism was inevitable, in order to prevent discussion of a specific developmental path in German history. Thirdly, Ben-Gurion sought to emphasise the guilt of Hitler, apparently so as to reduce possible discussion of the collective guilt hypothesis.

The Germans perceived these efforts positively. The report of the German observer delegation to the trial noted the 'efforts of the prosecutor to never ascribe the crimes against Jews to the Germans as such. Whenever the context permitted, he spoke of Nazi-Germany, Nazi-criminals etc., in order to show the difference to present-day Germany. This was not a coincidence. We later found that the chief prosecutor consciously drew a clear distinction between the criminal German state elite and the German people as a whole' (PA AA, B1, Bd. 81, 13 September 1961).

The Eichmann trial shows the intersections, as well as the causal relationships, between a number of complex historical processes and ideological-discursive re-framings: the process of German postwar whitewashing and rehabilitation; the consolidation of the Israeli state in the Middle East; the framing of 'Arabs as Nazis'. In political language games, historical fact suffers. The following closing remarks of the above-quoted report of the German observer delegation to the Eichmann trial closes the circle of projections:

> One of the strongest impressions left on the European visitor is the novel and very advantageous type of the Israeli youth. This youth exhibits almost none of the features which one was used to view as Jewish. Of great height, often blond and blue-eyed, free and self-determined in their movements with well-defined faces, the

offspring of the German Jewish immigrants represent a new type of the Jew that was unknown until now. (PA AA, B1, Bd. 81, 13 September 1961)

Here, Jews seem to have finally become German. This perhaps rather astonishing type of openly racist German over-identification with Israeli Jews starkly illustrates how continuities of German antisemitism can express themselves in a pro-Israeli attitude. In this case, Israel is represented in terms of German self-descriptions of a distinctly pre-1945 era, whereby Israel becomes Aryan. The German identification with Israeli military capacity in terms such as these is a corollary to the fact that in their formative phase under consideration in this chapter, German politics towards Israel served not to confront the past but to whitewash its continuities, a rationale accepted by Israel in return for the means to build the state.

Business friends: Did the FRG finance Israel's nuclear project?

In 2015, Hans Rühle, an expert on nuclear proliferation who had held high positions in the BMVg and NATO, published an article in the conservative newspaper *Die Welt*, known for its staunch support of Israel. The article claimed that the FRG had financed Israel's nuclear project with the 'Operation Business Friend' loan in the 1960s, promised to Ben-Gurion at the Waldorf Astoria and paid out after the Eichmann trial. Rühle argues that while the French technical help for the construction of the nuclear power plant at Dimona is well-known, the question of who paid for the project had remained a riddle, as the costs far exceeded Israel's budget at the time. Contrary to normal development loans, 'Operation Business Friend' was never explicitly tied to any specific projects; in fact, the Kreditanstalt für Wiederaufbau, the state-owned German development bank in charge of the loan, has not disclosed its files on the topic to this day. For

Rühle, the strongest indication that 'Operation Business Friend' financed Dimona is that both Israeli and German officials involved in the matter used the same codewords in their communications. As Rühle relates, Adenauer and Ben-Gurion spoke about 'development projects in the Negev' during the New York meeting, and subsequent documents on both sides refer to 'nuclear-powered desalination plants' or a 'textile factory'. Of course, no water was desalinated in the desert and the 'textile factory' is a well-known codename for the Dimona plant. Rühle also refers to a discussion of Ben-Gurion with the editors of major Israeli newspapers in March 1963, where he spoke about the need to avoid confrontation with the Adenauer government, in order not to disturb 'the construction of a deterrent weapon whose significance for the security of Israel and the prevention of future wars cannot be valued highly enough' (Rühle 2015).

It is improbable that decision-makers in Bonn were not informed of French support for Israel's nuclear project. After all, France and Germany were Israel's most important military supporters at the time. The archival research undertaken for this study suggests the plausibility of Rühle's argument, but does not verify it. To give one of multiple indications supporting Rühle's argument, the first German ambassador to Israel, Rolf Pauls, wrote about the 'nuclear desalination plant' in fairly dramatic terms, indicating to his superiors in Bonn that this project had 'epochal' meaning, and that a German contribution to it would be a 'positive memorial' of Germany to Jews everywhere. These are surely big words for a desalination plant that never existed. Pauls wrote that the FRG could expect from such a contribution a more forthcoming Israeli view on German unification and a softer position on the finality of Germany's Eastern border – which at the time was disputed by Bonn (PA AA, B130, Bd. 8824, 21 September 1965). Nevertheless, that Bonn financed an Israeli nuclear bomb remains, until now, only a plausible story for which definite proof does not exist.

6

CHANGING THE GUARDS
AMERICAN STRATEGY AND THE DECISION FOR DIPLOMATIC RELATIONS

From 1962 to 1965, German arms became key to Israel's attainment of military strength in the Middle East. As the introductory pages of this part detailed, the deliveries agreed upon in August 1962 included heavy artillery, aircraft and submarines. In 1964, 150 M48 'Patton' tanks were added to the list upon American instigation, meaning it is necessary to analyse German arms deliveries to Israel between 1962 and 1965 in the context of overall American geostrategy in the Middle East. The West German 1964–65 'Middle East Crisis' provides excellent study material for such a purpose.

Before moving towards the analysis of this diplomatic crisis, however, the question of German rocket scientists in Egypt must be addressed. From 1962–65, a number of German scientists were employed in Egyptian rocket engineering programs, many of whom were former Nazis. Following this, Israeli Minister of Foreign Affairs Golda Meir and Herut opposition leader Menachem Begin agitated against Ben-Gurion's 'New Germany' policy in the Israeli Knesset and public, arguing that the employment of these scientists showed Germans were again plotting the destruction of the Jews. In contrast to other aspects of German-Israeli relations, the rocket episode is well researched (see relevant chapters in Jelinek 2004; Sachar 1999; Segev 1993) and thus requires only a brief summary here. Jelinek describes the episode as one guided by emotions. The rockets the Germans helped in building were, in fact, never able to leave the ground. Israel unsuccessfully pressed for legal German measures against participation in the Egyptian rocket program. However, the main reason German rocket scientists gradually left Egypt in early 1965 was that Egypt could no longer afford the costly and largely ineffective program, although targeted Mossad attacks and the global publicity surrounding the program also contributed (Jelinek 2004: 419-29). The rocket crisis contributed to Ben-Gurion's downfall in 1963, demonstrating once more that Ben-Gurion's 'New Germany' policy was highly contested within the Israeli government and society.

In 1963, Franz Josef Strauss visited Israel, now as the former defence minister. A *New York Herald Tribune* article about the visit quoted Shimon Peres as saying that 'Germany's importance to Israel's vital interests is no less than that of France.' The article continued by stating that '[i]t is known that France is a major supplier of weapons to Israel.' Peres praised Strauss for having provided 'the most substantial aid' to Israel's security. Not detailing what this 'substantial aid' had consisted of, Peres said that 'a day will come when the truth will be known' (PA AA, B130, Bd. 2314, 24 February 1964).

The 1962 arms deal, to which Strauss and Peres in all likelihood referred, emerged from their personal consultations, which had started in 1957. So what was the American role in the 1962 agreement? When Adenauer informed the chairs of the party factions in the Bundestag about it, he explicitly referred to American wishes. However, German Minister of Foreign Affairs

Gerhard Schröder and the American ambassador to Germany, George McGhee, both concluded in February 1965 that the 1962 deal came to pass without American involvement (AAPD 1965/89). Thus, Adenauer's invocation of American wishes could also be read as a pretext – if the United States wished for the delivery of arms to Israel, what could the chancellor do? Nevertheless, it is highly improbable that Germany would deliver a major arms package without US knowledge, especially given that the United States principally supported the arming of Israel, only refraining from doing so itself for fear of further radicalising Arab nationalism as led by Nasser.

The Israeli government asked Washington for tanks as early as 1962, but this request was denied. In 1964, Israeli Prime Minister Levi Eshkol visited Washington. The United States again refused to deliver tanks directly to Israel, but Erhard, visiting the country shortly after Eshkol, was informed that the FRG was to deliver the tanks, with the United States paying the bill. Erhard argued against the American wishes by pointing to the Hallstein Doctrine; however, he was told that the West German–East German dispute was irrelevant compared to the US position in the Middle East (Jelinek 2004: 414). The events of 1964-65 are important, then, as they demonstrate how the United States began to take over the role as Israel's principal backer.

In autumn 1964, German tank deliveries to Israel were discussed in the global press, a watershed moment in German-Arab relations, specifically those between Germany and Egypt. The 'Middle East Crisis', as it was dubbed in the corridors of the AA, was not a crisis of the Middle East, but a German crisis in the Middle East. From late 1964 to spring 1965, the FRG was forced to confront the key dilemma that hung over its Middle East politics since the inception of the Hallstein Doctrine: it could either trigger the doctrine, breaking off diplomatic relations with Egypt in order to be able to continue to arm Israel, or it could cease the arming of Israel in order to stabilise its relations with Arab states. This was a choice between Israel and Egypt, and thus, between rehabilitation and *Alleinvertretung*.

By definition, a problem can be solved whereas a dilemma cannot. For a dilemma to disappear, the basis of its construction has to disappear. In other words, ending the crisis depended entirely on the United States. As it was the US that pressured the FRG into the tank deliveries, it was not possible to discontinue the deliveries without US consent. On the other hand, the United States also made clear that it did not wish to see the Germans apply the Hallstein Doctrine. The German position in the Middle East needed to be held for the cause of overall western interest, as defined by Washington. In other words, *Alleinvertretung* was a game Bonn was allowed to play only when it did not endanger American Cold War strategy. The German dilemma was finally solved by a changing of the guards: in early 1965, the United States agreed to take over outstanding tank deliveries, with the FRG now paying for them. This decision reflects a fundamental shift in US Middle East strategy at the time. In tune with radicalising Arab nationalism, Washington now decided to openly arm the Israeli state. The beginnings of the US–Israeli military alliance, so decisive to the Middle East, especially after 1967, lie here. In consequence, Germany was able to offer Israel diplomatic relations on 7 March 1965.

This is the German crisis in the Middle East explained in a nutshell. In fact, the crisis is a highly illustrative episode for the study of German-Israeli relations, especially for the question of the role of the United States in them. The 1964–65 episode in the Middle East was perceived by the German government as the gravest diplomatic crisis it faced since 1945 (AAPD 1965/125), as attested to by the enormous volume of files dedicated to it in the AA archives. In the published archival editions of the AA, files dedicated to the crisis crowd out almost all other events in that period. However, a close descriptive reconstruction would be somewhat tiresome, as what the German handling of the crisis throws into stark relief is primarily the dogged attachment in Bonn to the Hallstein Doctrine and the claim over the GDR.

In November 1964, Chancellor Erhard bluntly informed his Israeli counterpart Eshkol in a letter that Germany prioritised its claim to *Alleinvertretung* over its relations with Israel:

> I may remind you that the policies of the German government are determined by our conscious responsibility for the fate and future of the whole of the German people. We cannot look at the German-Israeli relationship, which undoubtedly plays a role in this regard as well, as an isolated factor, but are forced to regard it in relation to the fateful question of the German nation, the reunification of all Germans in peace and freedom. (PA AA, B130, Bd. 2361, 4 November 1964)

Such statements clearly demonstrate that the FRG defined its policy towards Israel in terms of its own interests as it saw them. This fact needs to be underlined in response to those voices in Germany that frame German-Israeli relations as one-sided transactions undertaken out of guilt. This has never been the case.

The FRG has acted towards Israel as any sovereign state would, and, contrary to widely held views, never assumed the role of the penitent. In the following, we shall focus on the key issues of Germany's 'Middle East Crisis', comparing the perspectives and positions of the relevant actors in the crisis: Egypt, Israel, the FRG and the United States.

In the section of his book devoted to the 'Middle East Crisis', Hansen wrote disparagingly about Nasser, yet obscures the fact that it was the FRG which most clearly played a double-game in the Middle East: its military support of Israel contradicted its proclaimed policy of not delivering weapons into 'areas of tension'. The AA was clearly aware of this hypocrisy (PA AA B 130, Bd.

6402, 9 November 1964). It thus saw its criticism of military ties with Israel vindicated. A major reason for its Arab-leaning views, however, lay not in the Middle East but in Germany, as it feared for the West German claim over the GDR. It needs to be pointed out that Nasser had until this point in fact supported the FRG's claim to *Alleinvertretung*. At the conference of the Non-Aligned Movement in Cairo in August–September 1964, shortly before German tank deliveries to Israel became public, Egypt, according to the German embassy in Cairo, 'not only refrained from doing anything to harm our German policy, but [...] acted positively in our favour' (PA AA, B130, Bd. 2198, 15 October 1964; see also Blasius 1998). The reports of German embassies throughout the Middle East at the time underline that the revelations of German support to Israel fomented anti-German feeling. The reports speak explicitly of changing perceptions of Germany from a 'traditional friend' towards a 'colonial' power in the Middle East (see reports in PA AA, B130, Bd. 6402).

Thorough analysis of the crisis (and relevant GDR files) makes clear that Nasser had no intention of diplomatically recognising the GDR at any point (Blasius 1998). This was the case even when, on 24 January, he invited Walter Ulbricht, the first secretary of the GDR's ruling Socialist Unity Party (*Sozialistische Einheitspartei*), to visit Egypt at the end of February. Bonn knew of Nasser's intention to not diplomatically recognise the GDR even prior to the provocative visit (AAPD 1965/89). However, Bonn still toyed with the idea of utilising the Hallstein Doctrine at the beginning of March: in a meeting on 5 March between Chancellor Erhard and the American, British and French ambassadors to Germany, the chancellor was told by the American diplomat that it was not in the United States' interest for Bonn to break off diplomatic relations with Cairo. The brusque language used by McGhee reveals American exasperation at a German fixation on the claim to *Alleinvertretung*, which the United States clearly saw as subordinate to the overall western position in the Middle East: 'Germany has a good name in the Middle East. The Americans have little influence. The West needs this German influence.' The French ambassador, meanwhile, was of the opinion that 'no Russian could have ordered Ulbricht around more clearly as McGhee did with Erhard' (AAPD 1965/112).

A solution to Germany's diplomatic crisis had by then already been in the making. On 18 February, US Secretary of State Dean Rusk informed the German ambassador to the United States, Karl Heinrich Knappstein, that '[w]e will not let you in the foxhole' and that 'we will draw away a considerable amount of heat from you' (AAPD 1965/85). Previously, the FRG had asked Israel to accept a cessation of weapons deliveries, and instead offered financial compensation. This offer was flatly rejected. With the knowledge that the United States would take over outstanding weapons deliveries to Israel, the FRG was now able to offer diplomatic relations to Israel, which Erhard did on 7 March 1965. As Erhard stated, offering diplomatic relations to Israel constituted a means for Bonn to act autonomously and in a forward manner that was also in accordance with the interests of the United States (PA AA, B130, Bd. 8824, 2 February 1965). The FRG thus freed itself of the voluntary constrictions of the Hallstein Doctrine in the Middle East, throwing the ball into the court of Arab States.[1]

When Germany and Israel formally agreed upon diplomatic relations on 12 May 1965, ten Arab states, including Egypt, broke off diplomatic ties with Bonn. The AA files indicate that this move needs to be understood primarily as a face-saving gesture, necessary for domestic reasons alone, as by then the extent of German military aid to Israel had become public. Arab states subsequently communicated to the FRG their intention to not endanger trade relations and economic aid. The fact that no Arab state had diplomatically recognised the GDR created an opening for the eventual re-establishment of diplomatic relations. Quite fittingly, diplomatic relations with all Arab states were resumed between 1971 and 1975, the years following the 1967 Arab-Israeli War, which had pushed Arab nationalism towards its decline.

The year 1965 saw the end of the German *Sonderweg* in the Middle East. The beginning of diplomatic relations and the cessation of its role as a prime economic, financial and military supporter of Israel marks a caesura in the history of German politics towards Israel. If, however, we view German-Israeli relations from a broader perspective of the history of the modern Middle East, the turning point in German-Israeli relations is the 1967 Arab-Israeli War, as the German consolidation and arming of Israel until that point played an important role in the Israeli success that fundamentally altered the political landscape of the region.

7

TANKS AND FANTASIES
GERMANY AND THE 1967 ARAB-ISRAELI WAR

The FRG was implicated in the 1967 Arab-Israeli War because of its prior support of the Israeli state, most notably through its military assistance from the late 1950s onwards. The first Israeli ambassador to Germany, Asher Ben-Natan, told Chancellor Erhard in their first conversation that an eventual war in the Middle East 'would only last a few days. Israel thus had to always be prepared. German aid was a great contribution to the development of the country and military aid also played a very large role for the security of Israel' (PA AA, B130, Bd. 8825, 30 September 1965). On 8 June 1967, the day Egypt accepted a ceasefire, the German ambassador to the United States wrote to Bonn about the 'satisfaction in the U.S. Congress over the military victory of the Israelis and thus the victory of the West, which was not expected to be of such magnitude and of such swiftness' (PA AA, B130, Bd. 2604, 8 June 1967). Israel's sweeping victory was a success for the Western Bloc insofar as it sounded the death knell of Arab nationalism, thus severely weakening the Soviet position in the Middle East. The war demonstrated Israel's value as a 'fortress of the West' (to again quote the former German Chancellor Adenauer). While the interests of the United States, Israel and the FRG converged on the blow dealt to Arab nationalism, Israel also pursued a project of its own in the war with the subsequent occupation of the Sinai Peninsula, the Golan Heights, the West Bank, Gaza and East Jerusalem (Achcar 2004: 20).

On 12 June 1967, two days after the Arab-Israeli War ended, the German ambassador to Israel, Rolf Pauls, sent a short but telling telegram to Willy Brandt, who was then the FRG's foreign minister. Pauls informed Brandt that 'an officer of the general staff [highest army echelon] told me that the modernized, more heavily armoured tanks delivered by us proved their worth in excellent fashion' (AAPD 1967/214). These tanks, equipped with up-to-date weapon systems, were central to the formation of the Israeli tanks corps and played a vital role in the Sinai ground battle. The shared importance of France and Germany to Israel prior to 1967 can be seen in the ways in which the Arab-Israeli War unfolded. While French Mirage jets won the decisive air campaign, the ground campaign in Egypt was won with German-delivered tanks. Unsurprisingly, representatives of Arab states repeatedly complained to German diplomats that German arms deliveries had greatly facilitated Israel's war effort (see for example PA AA, B130, Bd. 2630, 18 October 1967; PA AA, B130, Bd. 8827, 16 May 1968).

It is against this background that the official West German declaration of neutrality in 1967 needs to be evaluated. That year, the FRG undertook political-diplomatic efforts to appear as a neutral outsider to the Arab-Israeli conflict while secretly extending vital economic and military support to Israel. Israel, however, wanted Germany to openly declare its commitment. It is hard to otherwise understand the following footnote to the war. At the end of May, Israel asked for the delivery of 20,000 gas masks to aid in the protection of the population against eventual

Egyptian attacks involving lethal gas. Friedemann Büttner, formerly a professor of Middle Eastern studies at Berlin's Free University, remarked critically that 't[o] entreat the country which had gassed millions of Jews for gasmasks for the ostensive purpose of preserving the survivors from imminent extinction cannot be considered a serious appeal for help but only a calculated manoeuvre to force the Germans into compliance with Israel's future wishes' (Büttner 1977: 67). German ambassador Pauls was of the same opinion, writing to Bonn that 'the danger of a gas attack seems to me very low'; the motive, Pauls wrote, was 'surely rather to nudge us towards other deliveries with a request that we could impossibly deny' (PA AA, B130, Bd. 2576, 4 June 1967).

The gas mask episode is just one of the myriad instances in which the history of the Holocaust intermingled with the situation in Israel prior to the war. The cruel statements of a number of leading Arab politicians are well-documented: 'We shall hang the last imperialist soldier with the entrails of the last Zionist' (Damascus Radio); 'There will be practically no Jewish survivors' (Shukeiry); 'The Zionist barrack in Palestine is about to collapse and be destroyed' (Ahmed Said, Voice of the Arabs, Cairo) (all cited in Morris 2001: 310). There was a widespread fear of extermination, especially among Holocaust survivors. The Israeli government and army, the United States and NATO states, however, were aware of Israel's military superiority over its Arab neighbours – especially in the event of a surprise attack. As Segev writes, '[t]he threat of 'extermination' had not [...] been real. But the fear of it had been real [...]. More than any other factor, fear had prompted the war – the same fear that had contributed to mass immigration in the 1950s and to the Dimona project. Its roots lay in the Holocaust' (Segev 1993: 392).

In the Bundestag debate on 7 June 1967, parliamentarians of the Social Democratic Party (SPD)/Christian Democratic Union

(CDU) coalition declared that official neutrality did not mean emotional indifference towards Israel. Erhard Eppler of the SPD spoke of an 'inner tension' that was rooted in 'the consciousness of our people that the State of Israel is not a state like any other' (Bundestag 1967). Eppler complimented the German government for having expressed its sympathies with Israel. He noted that, otherwise, the German people and its representatives would have been 'dead on the inside' (*innerlich tot*). He ended his speech stating that Germany 'of course wanted peace in the Middle East', but a peace which 'guaranteed [...] the existence of a state whose coming into existence we Germans were not quite uninvolved with in our history' (Bundestag 1967).

Kurt Georg Kiesinger, chancellor of the 1966-69 grand coalition between the SPD and the CDU, was implicated in Nazism, yet escaped trial and denazification. As a member of a conservative, Catholic student fraternity, he radicalised early and became an Nazi Party member in 1933. Kiesinger expressed his pro-Israeli positioning in the form of a propagandist critique of East Germany:

> On the background of the most recent past of our people, it is truly tragic that those who hold power in the other part of Germany try to flame the conflict in each and every irresponsible manner. They evidently do so in the hope of finding a shred of recognition for their regime. (Bundestag 1967)

Social Democrat Helmut Schmidt, future chancellor and Germany's favourite elder statesman until his recent death, also chimed in on the unavoidable anti-GDR rhetoric, but added that irrespective of the importance of the 'traditional friendship between our people and the Arab peoples, we have to refute their intention, or, more precisely, the intention of their leaders, to annihilate Israel' (Bundestag 1967). Rainer Barzel of the CDU lauded the 'clarity' of German public opinion which 'refrained from showing an indifference of the heart' (Bundestag 1967).

A closer look at the 'clarity' of German public opinion at the time is illuminating with respect to the reconfigurations of German national identity, the repression of the Nazi past and the question of German antisemitism after 1945. A comparative study of East and West German perceptions of the Arab-Israeli War may be a promising undertaking regarding the question of antisemitism in both countries, yet for the usual constraints of time and space, as well as the focus of this work, a short survey of West German reactions and perceptions must suffice. Büttner observed in a 1977 article on the topic that '[t]he particular pro-Israeli bias of the Germans in 1967 [...] was without parallel even in the US' (Büttner 1977: 70ff.). The lack of knowledge about Middle East history, intertwined with the long-standing history of German orientalism, Büttner argued, was insufficient to explain this bias, adding that the 'unwillingness or even outright refusal to accept Middle Eastern realities is psychologically linked to Germany's guilt or, rather, to its repression of guilt' (Büttner 1977: 70ff.). His quoting of Ralf Dahrendorf still rings true. The German liberal thinker described that 'mixture of theoretical humanitarianism and practical inhumanity, which makes Germany so unbearable at times' (cited in Büttner 1977: 76).

This mixture between theoretical empathy and the practical lack of it may be said to be rooted in what Achcar aptly called 'narcissistic compassion' (Achcar 2016: chapter 1). This is a form of identification which only sees an idealised, wishful version of one's own self in the other, while remaining incapable of taking a complex perspective that combines an objectively distanced evaluation of facts with an empathic compassion for human suffering; empathy in the sense of the capacity to adopt, as far as possible, the perspective of those who appear as strangers. While the 'stranger' in this case is represented by the Arab side in the Arab-Israeli conflict, an examination of the German perceptions of 1967 shows rather unmistakably that the Israeli side was also used as a replacement for negotiating the problem of German national identity after 1945.

'SIEG! Dajan – Der Rommel Israels' ran one headline in the tabloid *Bild*, published by Springer (cited in Sontheimer 2012), which probably does not require translation into English. The declaration of victory, written in capital letters, was followed by an equation of Israeli general Moshe Dayan with the *Wüstenfuchs* ('desert fox') Erwin Rommel, Hitler's general in North Africa. Rudolf Augstein, founder of the *Der Spiegel*, an Iron Cross holder for his services in the Wehrmacht and one of the most influential postwar German journalists, also wrote that Israeli soldiers 'rolled like Rommel' (*Der Spiegel* 1967). Augstein knew of the German contribution to the Israeli success: 'An effective tank corps was the prerequisite for the lightning victory in the lightning war (*Blitzsieg im Blitzkrieg*). Germany delivered these weapons two years ago in a triangular trade with the U.S. and Italy' (*Der Spiegel* 1967).

To understand how it was possible to pay Israel compliments by comparing its army to the Wehrmacht, its military campaign to the 1939 invasion of Poland, and Dayan to Rommel, one needs to return to some of the points made in the previous chapters. Postwar West German society saw itself primarily as a victim of the war. Nazi crimes, if explicitly recognised, were generally attributed to a small circle of perpetrators, namely to Hitler and his entourage. While the Wehrmacht destroyed Europe, killed millions and made the death camps logistically possible, postwar Germany generally perceived the Wehrmacht as having a 'clean sheet' with regards to Nazi crimes. This was more or less the case until the Wehrmacht exhibition of 1995 caused a public stir. While Erwin Rommel backed Hitler's power seizure, he was implicated in the 1944 assassination attempt against him and consequently forced into suicide. Thus, Dayan could be 'Germanified' by inserting him into a specifically German 'anti-

Nazi' tradition: that of Nazi supporters who turned against Hitler in 1944 because of looming defeat in the war.

The conflict constellation in the Middle East made possible two intersecting forms of German guilt deferral. The first was the identification of German soldiers with Israeli ones, thus effectively blurring the historical relationship between German perpetrators and Jewish victims. The second was the perceived roles of 'true' Nazis that could be attributed to Israel's Arab adversaries. The trope of 'Arabs as Nazis' holds a particularly salient meaning in the German context, as one cannot escape the suspicion that it is used for the purpose of relief: a transposition of the historical German role of the Nazi perpetrator onto the present-day Arab. Invoking the prior German obedience to Nazism, *Stuttgarter Zeitung* wrote on its title page on 1 June that 'should the German public fail *again*, previous crimes would fall back on it' (cited in Lewan 1970: 77, emphasis added).

On 6 June 1967, *Die Welt* (also published by Springer) spoke of the 'second assassination attempt against the people of Israel in this century.' It explained:

> The world began to remember. Germany did not need to. We know Europe's graveyards, over which no grass has grown in the past 25 years. These days, Germany was petrified. The hateful tirades of Radio Cairo were like a look into the mirror of our most recent past [...]. This could never be allowed to happen: That the survivors of Hitler's massacres were annihilated in their ancient homeland. (cited in Lewan 1970: 87)

The reason why Springer knew 'Europe's graveyards' so well, of course, was because many of the journalists it employed helped to dig them. In 2012, the Jewish Museum of Frankfurt curated a special exhibition about Axel Springer, founder of the Springer publishing house, and his relationship towards Jews and Israel. Drawing sharp criticism from the publishing house's newspapers, the exhibition detailed Springer's policy of employing former

Nazis while pursuing an editorial line that was strongly pro-Israel. For example, journalists working for the publishing house had to sign a 'constitution' whose second paragraph called for the 'reconciliation between Jews and Germans, to which belongs support of the Israeli people's right to exist' (cited in Sontheimer 2012). In fact, Springer's simultaneous, interlinked reintegration of former Nazis and support of the Israeli state is analogous to the orientation of the postwar Federal Republic under Adenauer.

According to *Die Welt*, the war had been like 'a purging thunderstorm' to the 'sultry attitudes' still existing in West Germany (cited in Lewan 1970: 88). This begs the question: did the war 'purge' Germany of its antisemitism, or rather of its burden of an unacknowledged past? The same paper wrote on 19 June 1967:

> [T]he basest infamies have been spread about the Jewish people [...] without national sentiment; never ready for battle, but always keen to profit from somebody else's war effort. Now, however, we speak of the small, brave, heroic, genius people. We need to confess to the Jews of the past two millennia: We have been led [...] to believe in lies and prejudice [...]. We need to revise the intellectual history of the last 2000 years. (cited in Lewan 1970: 134f.)

The *Stuttgarter Zeitung* was of a similar opinion:

> [A]n almost two-thousand years' old image of the type of man of Jewish derivation had collapsed [...]. Naturally, the merchant and the intellectual as types do exist still today; they are outshone, however, by the image of the Jew as military strategist and brilliant soldier who, resolute in the face of death, plunges into the fire of tank-armies and reaches what is the secret yearning of everybody: the victory of the small over the powerful, threatening, merciless. The desire to identify, guilt feelings rooted in history, flow into a wave of sympathy. (cited in Büttner 1977: 80)

Such statements almost do not require analytical scrutiny, given how they readily reveal their intentions. The 'old picture' one had of the 'human type of the Jew' is exchanged for a new picture, yet the structure of antisemitic prejudice remains. This 'new picture' of the Jew, however, sounds like a wishful German self-description: the 'brilliant soldier' who is not afraid of death, the 'military strategist', and so on. German antisemitism did not end, but found relief in the thought that Jews had now also resolved to build a militarised nation state. The media coverage of 1967 is another example of the historically cruel irony that Germany only allowed Jewish assimilation in the Middle East by turning Israeli soldiers into Germans and Arab leaders into Nazis. This had little to do with Middle Eastern realities and much more to do with German discourses about national identity and the Nazi past. The journalist Matthias Walden of *Die Welt* returned to his former self when he wrote that 'there will still be some who sympathize in fossil delusion with the grandiloquent, now grandiosely punished enemy of the Jews, Nasser. But they are mute, stooped away into the corners of their benighted frame of mind [*Gesinnungsnacht*]' (cited in Büttner 1977: 78).

German- and English-language studies of antisemitism have in recent years focused on the question of left-wing antisemitism. In German academia, the study of this phenomenon has almost become a veritable field of its own, which cannot be said for the object of this study, which is the German state's policies towards Israel and the Palestinians. Doubtlessly, however, the mixture of old antisemitism with the brash philosemitism presented above was more relevant to the positioning of the majority of German society towards the Israel-Palestine conflict than the militant anti-Zionism (or even antisemitism) of Germany's New Left after 1967.

The above-mentioned stereotypes (both old and new) of a Jewish 'Other' are obviously also of incomparably higher relevance to the making of German foreign policy, given how they stem from established, mainstream media. Still, historian

Jeffrey Herf, in his recent study of the GDR's and the West German left's policies and positions towards Israel and Palestine, does not problematise these suspicious figurations. Doing so allows him to draw, if only by implication, a simplistic picture in which the GDR and the West German left are presented as anti-Zionist or antisemitic, whereas the majority of West German society is by implication exculpated because of its support of Israel (Herf 2016).[1]

Of course, the point is not to make equally simplistic, parallel counterarguments to such claims. It is beyond doubt that parts of the West German far left after 1967 adopted a worldview in which antisemitism played a defining role.

However, what is today often rather conveniently ignored is that the German New Left initially derived some of its opposition to Zionism from the fact that Israel was supported by those revisionist forces in German society that represented most starkly the continuity of Nazism, against which the German left radicalised in the first place. This was a dilemma which parts of the New Left were unable to resolve (see also Weiss 2005). In July 1967, Ulrike Meinhof, a founding member of the Red Army Faction, wrote clairvoyantly in the popular left-wing paper *konkret* about the 'bloodlust' Israel's victory stirred in the West German press: 'lightning war theories spread, BILD, after 25 years, finally won the battle for Stalingrad in the Sinai desert' (cited in Vowinckel 2004). Meinhof captured the reasons for Springer's identification with Israel well:

> Not the realization of Jewish humanness, but the harshness of the war, not the recognition of Jewish rights to equality, but the use of Napalm, not the comprehension of one's own crimes, but the Israeli Blitzkrieg, solidarity with brutality, with displacement, with conquest, led to questionable reconciliation. (cited in Vowinckel 2004)

Meinhof's moment of clarity, however, was only a brief one. Five years later, she would support the murder of eleven Israeli athletes at the Munich Olympics by the Palestinian organisation Black September. Conflating both the FRG and Israel with Nazi Germany, she framed the attacks as an act of resistance against an axis of fascism spanning from Washington to Bonn to Tel Aviv (Herf 2016: 1919).

But what about the West German engagement with the Palestinians at this point? The 'Arab Palestine refugees' would again play a role in the political calculations of the AA in the aftermath of the 1965 German 'Middle East Crisis', as discussed in the previous chapter. Following discussions with Arab League representatives, German diplomats argued that symbolic financial gestures towards these refugees would be helpful for the swift re-establishment of diplomatic relations with Arab states (see files in PA AA, B130, Bd. 2563). On 20 September 1967, the German cabinet decided upon a 'special German contribution' for the 'Palestine-refugees' to the value of DM50 million. As was noted internally in the AA, this aid was meant to 'express our sympathy with the plight of the Arab refugees and furthermore serve as a gesture towards the whole Arab world in order to facilitate the re-establishment of diplomatic ties with the majority of Arab countries. For this reason, the projects that are to be realized must clearly be recognizable as German ones' (PA AA, B130, Bd. 2797, 7 March 1968). However, the federal government 'should avoid anything that could be perceived by the Arabs as a recognition of a special German responsibility for the Palestine-refugees' (PA AA, B130, Bd. 2797, 7 March 1968). The instrumental humanitarianism displayed by the FRG towards the 1948 refugees of Palestine would soon, however, be forced into a more substantial political engagement. This, along with Germany's attempt to 'normalise' its relations with Israel, is the topic of the next part.

PART III

'Normalisation' and the Palestinian Question in Germany's Israel Policy

THE GERMAN–ISRAELI ALLIANCE lost much of its drama and importance after the two countries established diplomatic relations and after Israel so decisively won the 1967 Arab-Israeli War. Washington had now become Israel's principal backer, allowing the Federal Republic of Germany (FRG) to leave its Middle Eastern *Sonderweg*. While German financial, economic and military support to Israel was considerably less important in both relative and overall terms after 1965, it remained stable. The FRG became Israel's 'second best friend' after the United States and its most important spokesperson in Europe. It remains so to this day. If one were to describe Germany's Israel policy from after 1965 until the 1980s in one word, however, it would be 'normalisation'. A 'normalised' policy towards Israel corresponded with the slogan of an 'even-handed' policy towards the Middle East.

The short time period between the decision to take up diplomatic relations in 1965 and the Arab-Israeli War is key for understanding German-Israeli relations until the end of the Cold

War. In this period, the German government sought to place its relations with Jerusalem on what it regarded as a 'normal' basis. Israel, by contrast, continued to insist on a special, historically rooted German obligation towards the Jewish state.

In Bonn, the Social Democrat and former Nazi resister Willy Brandt assumed chancellorship in 1969, taking over from the Christian Democratic Union's (CDU) Nazi careerist Kurt Georg Kiesinger. The power shift towards the Social Democratic Party (SPD) was understood as an end to the Adenauer legacy in domestic and international terms. Sailing in the winds of Cold War *détente*, the SPD, in coalition with Free Democratic Party (FDP), which by the mid-1950s had edged towards a centre-left political view, launched the *Ostpolitik* from 1969 until 1974 (a period in German-Israeli relations captured carefully and in much detail by Fink 2019). While Bonn had until then combined its orientation towards the West with a confrontational 'politics of strength', towards the East, Brandt's government did not abdicate from the now firmly established western path, but opted for a reconciliatory stance towards Eastern Europe and Moscow (Büttner and Scheffler 1982: 140). Domestically, the student-led revolt associated with the symbolic year '1968' set in motion an important societal confrontation with the immediate Nazi past, a past which, in the eyes of many of the protestors, was still embodied in the repressive institutions of the state (see also Gassert and Steinweis 2006).

The societal and governmental changes associated with the end of the Adenauer state occurred, however, within a structural continuity for which Adenauer had himself laid the foundations, namely that of the rehabilitation and thus normalisation of the postwar West German state. As the need for international rehabilitation was no more comparable with that of the early 1950s, the FRG, now firmly integrated into western Cold War structures, sought a more autonomous, 'normalised' role in global politics – an ambition for which its policy towards Israel proved a test case (Fink 2019).

The Palestine question came to play a key role in the German–Israeli tug of war between 'normal' and 'special' relations. The Palestine Liberation Organisation (PLO), founded in Cairo in 1964, gradually moved towards the centre of the Arab-Israeli conflict arena after 1967, returning the conflict to its pre-1948 Zionist-Palestinian character (Morris 2001: 385). The attack by PLO-affiliated Black September at the Munich Olympics in 1972 violently put the Palestinian problem on the German agenda. However, German engagement with the Palestine question in the 1970s must be understood less in bilateral terms than in the context of European integration and European–Arab relations. After the 1967 Arab–Israeli War, France turned its previous approach to the Middle East on its head, discontinuing its arms sales to Israel and becoming the Western European power most inclined towards Arab interests. For Israel, the FRG consequently became the single most important advocate of its interests in the European Community (EC). While Bonn, mediating between its relations with France, the United States, Israel, Arab states and the Soviet Union, never took the most openly pro-Israeli positions in Europe,[1] any German political-diplomatic weighing in for Israel was curbed by the pro-Arab leanings of Paris (Belkin 2007: 3). Conversely, Bonn was equally able to 'hide' behind France, formulating positions it would have refrained from taking in bilateral relations with Israel (Büttner 2003: 143).

Germany and Western Europe's principal interests in the Middle East, which were to shape engagement with the Palestine question in the 1970s, are still pertinent today. Although it would be reductionist to see European interest in the Middle East as related only to oil, European–Arab relations after the 1950s cannot be properly understood without factoring this in. By the 1970s, the German economy depended on oil, having switched from coal to petroleum in tune with the rest of Western Europe: 'In 1955, coal provided 75 percent of total energy use in Western Europe, and petroleum just 23 percent. By 1972, coal's share had shrunk to 22 percent, while oil's had risen to 60 percent – almost a complete flip-flop' (Yergin 1991: 545). German exports to Arab markets are another factor, as trade with Arab countries had increased significantly even before the oil shock of 1973 (Büttner and Scheffler 1982). Europe needed a stable Middle East much more than the geographically distant United States, not only for economic reasons, but also for fear of spillover from political conflict, such as terrorism, migration pressures or tensions within immigrant communities in Europe. That the United States has never relied on Middle Eastern oil for its own economy also contributed to the superpower's ability to play a much more directly political and imperial role in the Middle East compared with Europe.

Next to those 'hard' interests, one needs to also consider a less tangible change in Western European perceptions. The clichéd phrase of Israel's image turning from a David into a Goliath after 1967 still captures relatively well a shift in Western European governments and in European public opinion. While from a Palestinian perspective, 1948 and 1967 are two dates in a continuous history of dispossession, those dates are clearly demarcated in the perception of a majority of Europeans. Israel was founded in 1948 in the wake of the Holocaust, faced an Arab attack and provided a solution for the pressing problem of Jewish refugees. In 1967, Israel attacked first and dramatically expanded the territory under its control. It is because of this mix of hard interests, the re-emergence of the Palestine question and the shift in perception that the Israel-Palestine conflict gradually came to be seen as solvable in a 'land for peace', two-state scenario.

8

'NORMALISATION BEGINS NOW'
THE GERMAN TRANSITION AFTER 1965

All generations of our people bear the consequences of a politics carried out in the German name between 1933 and 1945. The points of reference for the work of the 5th German parliament and the politics of the federal government shall nevertheless not be the war or the postwar period. The points of reference lie not behind us, but before us. The postwar period is over. (Chancellor Ludwig Erhard in his government declaration on 10 November 1965)

[I]n the case of German–Israeli relations, foreign politics have to take up a forward-looking perspective and cannot be, or cannot be anymore, identified with the concept of reparations. (German ambassador to Israel Rolf Pauls, 26 January 1966)

The previous chapters have understood the FRG's policymaking towards Israel as originating primarily from a postwar need for both rehabilitation and for whitewashing the past. Germany's Israel policy was read not as a thorough confrontation with the past, but as a means of leaving it behind, a way of engaging with it in order to eviscerate from it one's own involvement. By definition, rehabilitation is a finite process; at the end of a process of rehabilitation stands normality. The question of 'normalising' relations with Israel is indelibly linked with the aim to leave the Nazi past behind.

As the official instructions given to the first German ambassador to Israel stated:

> The federal government attaches great importance to the establishment of diplomatic relations with Israel. The exchange of ambassadors between the two countries constitutes a fundamental prerequisite for our goal of the *normalisation* of the relationship between the Federal Republic of Germany and the Israeli state. We hope that this step also opens up new possibilities for reconciliation with the Jewish people. (*Politisches Archiv des Auswärtigen Amtes* [PA AA], B130, Bd. 2635, 8 August 1965, emphasis added)

With the forging of diplomatic ties in 1965, 'normalisation'[1] became a central term in German internal, governmental debates about Bonn's Israel policy. As a political goal, it is linked to two purposes. On the one hand, it expresses the wish to leave the *Sonderweg* of massive, secret support to Israel, as examined previously in this text. On the other hand – and more difficult to pinpoint – the question of 'normalising' ties with Israel also links to domestic discourses on the question of putting the past behind, in the sense of the above quote from Chancellor Ludwig Erhard's government declaration of November 1965.

In direct contrast, Israel perceived diplomatic relations not as a 'normalisation' of bilateral relations, but as one more link in the chain of moral responsibility stretching from the Nazi past into the future that tied Germany to the wellbeing of the Jewish state. On American television, the Israeli Minister of Foreign Affairs Abba Eban expressed the Israeli view on relations with Germany after diplomatic relations in these terms:

> The past still speaks to us with a terrible voice. We have not forgotten the cry of a million murdered children and of six million of our kinsmen done to death. We are haunted by this memory and it does cast a shadow. In our view it imposes responsibilities on

Germany, a negative responsibility, to avoid doing anything which would weaken Israel's security and a positive responsibility to make a contribution to Israel's security and stability. (PA AA, B130, Bd. 2566, 8 March 1965)

The period after 1965 in German-Israeli relations can be read as a tug of war between the two contrasting visions of 'normalised' versus 'special relations'.[2] As historian Carole Fink puts it:

The FRG's goal after 1965 was to establish a *normal* relationship that focused more on the present and the future than on the past. Israel, on the other hand, was determined to maintain its *special* character, insisting that the crimes of Nazi Germany had created a permanent obligation for unconditional support and protection. (Fink 2019; original emphasis)

This difference of perception was, of course, not primarily about which name to give to the bilateral relationship, but what German-Israeli relations would mean in material terms. On the discursive level, the problem was solved during Willy Brandt's 1973 visit to Israel, where he coined the compromise formula of 'normal relations with a special character [*Charakter der Besonderheit*]' (Weingardt 2002: 223).

A first instance of 'normalisation': The exchange of ambassadors

The conflict between 'normalisation' and 'special relations' can be read very clearly from the exchange of ambassadors. Rolf Pauls, the first West German ambassador to Israel until 1968, was a former officer of the Wehrmacht, who had served on the Eastern Front. His deputy was Hungarian-born Alexander Török, who had served in the Hungarian embassy in Berlin when the country was under the fascist, Nazi-installed rule of Ferenc Szálasi from late 1944 to 1945. Both had already aided in the negotiations over the 1952 Reparations Agreement. Unproven allegations existed that Török had not only served the Hungarian government, but that he was an early follower of the fascist Arrow Cross Party and had participated in making his Budapest university *judenrein* (Conze et. al. 2010: 936f.).

So why did Bonn choose two representatives of such a background? Less compromised candidates must have been available. In Israel, the name of Franz Böhm was brought up, who was respected for his role in the Luxembourg Agreement. The German weekly newspaper *Die Zeit* called Pauls' post 'the most difficult and most dangerous' in German diplomacy (*Die Zeit*, 7 January 1966). Pauls' successive postings to Washington and Beijing indicate clearly the relevance of Israel to German foreign policy, as well as Pauls' standing within the diplomatic corps. The Tel Aviv embassy was to be staffed by the best Germany had to offer.

The correspondence between Pauls and his superiors in Bonn makes for an insightful reading into the German conception of its Israel policies and the shifts these were to undergo after 1965. One topic of this correspondence was the critical attitude of the Israeli press towards West Germany. Articles deemed especially unforthcoming yet representative were translated and sent to Bonn. One such article, written by Shlomo Aronson[3] for *Ha'aretz*, deserves to be recounted here at some length, since it connects very well with several arguments brought forth so far. In this article, Aronson wrote that the nomination of somebody like Alexander Török was symptomatic of the German foreign policy establishment's attitude towards Israel and the Nazi past. Aronson argued that Bonn appointed personnel without examining their past, because the Nazi past played no role in the German Foreign Office. He wrote that as long as a candidate was not in the Waffen-SS or a convicted mass murderer, he was suitable for diplomatic service. The article angrily stated that having previously served a criminal, antisemitic, genocidal regime should prohibit employment at the German embassy in Tel Aviv.

Aronson's analysis captured well the German foreign policy establishment's mentality at the time. The writer also pointed out, here re-translated from the German, the 'determination' and 'polite coldness' of Pauls and his superiors which 'could bring the blood of a Jewish correspondent to boil' (PA AA, B130, Bd. 2556, 19 January 1966). It needs to be stressed again that the pervasive complexity of German Nazi criminality at the time was reduced, in the German public and by the German government, to a small circle of perpetrators. The Wehrmacht was not viewed as a criminal organisation and neither was working for the Nazi-allied Hungarian Foreign Office regarded as criminal. This is how Rolf Pauls, who lost an arm and was decorated with the Iron Cross for his service on the Eastern Front, became Germany's first ambassador to Israel. Yet was this not potentially a rather suitable ending of the Adenauer and Ben-Gurion period in German-Israeli relations, which had been marked by a whitewashing of the 'New' Germany? While the obliviousness towards the past rightly criticised by Aronson possibly played a major role, there exists also the possibility that the Auswärtiges Amt's (AA) decision was more intentional than oblivious, a decision linked to the explicit aim of 'normalisation'. As the above-quoted *Die Zeit* article concluded:

> Not only in Israel were there doubts if foreign minister Schröder made the right decision last year to send a former major of the general staff and iron-cross [sic] holder of the Greater German Wehrmacht to be the ambassador in Tel Aviv. Today, these doubts are gone. After hardly five months we already know: If anybody, then Rolf Pauls was the right man to free many Israelis from the prejudice that only the resistance fighters against Hitler were decent Germans. (*Die Zeit*, 7 January 1966)

While the German choice of ambassador expressed a wish for 'normalisation', the first Israeli ambassador to Bonn personified the idea that German-Israeli relations were to be framed in terms of a German obligation brought about by its Nazi past.

In some respects, Asher Ben-Natan came to collect a debt.[4] Born Arthur Piernikartz in Austria, Ben-Natan managed to flee from Vienna to Palestine after the *Anschluss* in 1938, before assisting in the wartime effort to help persecuted Jews flee to Palestine against British immigration restrictions. After 1945 he continued organising *Bricha* activities, the emigration of Shoah survivors to Palestine from the displaced persons camps of postwar Europe. In Israel, Ben-Natan rose fast in the military establishment, occupying the post of director-general of the Israeli Ministry of Defence prior to becoming the first Israeli emissary to Germany. Ben-Natan was key to Israeli weapon procurements in France and Germany, and, as described in the previous chapter, he was also part of the original mission of three to the home of Franz-Josef Strauss in late 1957. The AA consequently feared that his appointment would confirm Arab states' suspicions about the military character of German-Israeli relations. Interestingly enough, the AA also viewed critically the fact that while smuggling survivors out of Europe, Ben-Natan had collected evidence about Nazi war criminals, which would subsequently be used in the Nuremberg trials and which helped in tracking down Adolf Eichmann (PA AA, B130, Bd. 2566, 6 July 1965). However, the AA was aware that it was in no position to turn down the Israeli choice of ambassador. Given the 'difficulties the Israeli government encountered when seeking the parliament's approval for Herr Dr. Pauls, such a refusal would lead to negative reactions by the Israeli public and thus severely strain our relations with Israel. Under such conditions, the Israel government would surely not be able to agree to Herr Dr. Pauls' (PA AA, B130, Bd. 2566, 6 July 1965).

Studying the files, especially those about the negotiations over the future of German financial support to Israel, one sees that Ben-Natan, just like Pauls, was a tough negotiator. He demanded German support to Israel as an obligation because of the Nazi past the German side wanted to 'normalise'. However, while Israel saw German obligations primarily as an obligation to build the Israeli state, it also displayed irritation at German deficits in confronting the past which did not directly affect Israel. For example, after assuming his post, Ben-Natan repeatedly criticised the German hesitation at the time to abolish the statutes of limitations on murder, thus preventing prosecution of Nazi criminals (after lengthy parliamentary efforts, limitations were only fully abolished by 1979).

What did 'normalisation' mean?

In 1965, 'normalisation' included the idea that Israel should support West Germany's claim over the German Democratic Republic (GDR). The desirability of Israeli support for the German goal of unification was often expressed, and was equally evident in the preparatory material given to Pauls:

> The attitude taken by Israel towards the German question after the exchange of ambassadors is of fundamental importance to our approach to this question. Should Israel support our position, it would be demonstrated that our policy of self-determination is recognized also by a state which had before shown great reserve towards Germany [...]. This support would doubtlessly also influence positively the attitude of the public especially in the United States, in Western Europe and in the Commonwealth countries, i.e. those countries where the image of Germany is fundamentally codetermined by the German–Jewish relationship. Pankow's[5] anti-Israel policy hands you the best arguments for the idea that Israeli support of our policy towards the German question is in Israel's interest. (PA AA, B130, Bd. 2635, 2 August 1965)

Again, what we find in this quote is the idea that Israeli–Jewish support is crucially important to the realisation of a central goal of German policy. The 'German-Jewish relationship' is seen as important first of all for the image of Germany that it produces in western publics.

Secondly, the formulaic, state-sponsored anti-Zionist and anti-imperialist discourse of the East German regime was utilised as an argument for the West German claim to sole representation of the entire nation. Of course, this mirrored exactly the GDR's attempts to woo Arab states, by portraying the FRG as being part of an imperialist, anti-Arab axis that stretched from Washington to Bonn to Tel Aviv.

In the context of Israel's position on the German question, the instructions given to Pauls also critically note Israel's view on the postwar German–Polish border as final (PA AA, B130, Bd. 2635, 1 August 1965). The AA criticised Israel for not supporting the West German claim over its prewar Eastern territories.

It is unsurprising that the antisemitic trope of 'Jewish power' also influenced the way the AA considered its Israel policy at the time. Under the heading 'reservations against being overly considerate towards the Arabs in our aid to Israel', Pauls opined:

> It needs to be pointed out again that Israel and the Jews wield decisive influence in the decisive global centres of public opinion making. They will be of great importance for the goodwill extended to us, especially regarding the attitude of the global public towards the German question [...]. The attitude of the *Weltjudentum* towards the German question, which is inseparable from the quality of German–Israeli relations, to my mind weighs heavier for the realization of our most important political goal than the [...] attitudes of a few Arab states. (PA AA, B130, Bd. 8825, 19 October 1965)

As already pointed out in the second chapter, *Weltjudentum* is in German part of the antisemitic jargon, evoking the essentialist notion of a singular, powerful global Jewish figure which exerts considerable influence on global opinion and thus – so it seems to Pauls – on the future of the German nation state.

Pauls, however, was also very critical about the Israeli attitude to Germany. He bemoaned the lack of Israeli 'appreciation of the German goodwill and its practical expressions over the last years, which were a very substantial support for Israel in the struggle for its existence'; he also criticised the tame Israeli stance towards the 'regime in Pankow', whose 'anti-Israelism could hardly be surpassed', as well as Israel's 'repeated denunciations of Nazism' at the United Nations and the global public in general (PA AA, B130, Bd. 2632, 19 October 1965). Pauls found that:

> German–Israeli relations are not at the centre of Israeli political interest. On the contrary, one tries, also after diplomatic relations, to view relations from the perspective of Reparations, which includes the whole complex of German economic aid. Israeli policy towards Germany was and remains inconsistent because it tries to benefit and profit, while ignoring the other side's existence. (PA AA, B130, Bd. 2567, 26 January 1966)

What appears rather clearly in this statement is the aggressive sentiment that Jews only engage with Germans to extract money. This is a key trope of German antisemitism after 1945, evoking an image of Jewish greed in which they exploit the Holocaust for personal enrichment.

As explained in the previous chapters, German reparations and subsequent military and financial support were extended with an expectation of absolution. Yet, when handed this power, Israel was unwilling to use it beyond a degree that was implied in the acceptance of German support itself.

In the same report, Pauls related an incident whereby an Israeli interlocutor had told him that '[w]e are a small country, but versus Germany we are a great power'; Pauls replied: "Don't overplay your hand' (PA AA, B130, Bd. 2567, 26 January 1966). Again, in the same report, Pauls paternalistically defined his view of how to disentangle German-Israeli relations from the aspect of reparations:

[R]eparations and foreign policy are two separate areas. Reparations, by their causality, direct the gaze backwards. Israel needs to learn that 1. reparations between the two states and governments are concluded and individual reparations are reliably paid out in accordance with German law; 2. that foreign policy, in terms of content and goals, must take up a forward-looking perspective and that also in the case of German-Israeli relations, foreign policy must take up a forward-looking perspective and cannot be, or cannot be anymore, identified with the concept of reparations. (PA AA, B130, Bd. 2567, 26 January 1966)

Pauls found that the way to approach this problem was by 'silently supporting those Israelis who support a new relationship with Germany as it is today.' Those Israelis, Pauls found, were a 'minority of young and old people of high quality [*hochwertig*] character and spirit' (PA AA, B130, Bd. 2567, 26 January 1966). Of course, Pauls echoed the instructions of his superiors here as well. The German foreign minister was aware that Israeli public opinion was largely opposed to official relations with Germany. In his instructions to Pauls, he wrote:

[T]he emphasis of your endeavours should be to familiarize the Israeli public with the picture of the new Germany and to improve the personal relations between our two peoples [...]. [A]t first, a careful approach is advisable. Over the longer run, public relations and cultural exchange will be of highest relevance. (PA AA, B130, Bd. 2635, 8 August 1965)

German expenditure on 'public relations' and 'cultural exchanges' in Israel up to the present day is astonishing (see Belkin 2007): Israel is a prime destination for youth exchanges of political, historical or sportive nature; Germany also funds research institutes on German history and culture, translations of the canons of German literature; and so forth.

Next to the above-mentioned specific German–Israeli dimension of the Nazi past, Israel also continued to be perceived in terms of a general western interest. To foreign policy officials, this was an obvious point in little need of much elaboration. The instructions given to Pauls speak of a general western, strategic interest in a stable Middle East, considered to be of central geostrategic importance due to its location connecting Europe to Africa, the Indian Ocean and East Asia, as well as being an 'important source of oil' (PA AA, B130, Bd. 2635, 8 August 1965).

The ambassador echoed '[o]ur obvious interest in the consolidation of the economic and political condition of Israel as a factor of the free world in the Middle East.' In his estimate, '[t]he next seven to ten years will be decisive in this regard. If Israel is given the opportunity to build up in the same speed and with the same results as until now, it will then be able to stand on its own two legs' (PA AA, B130, Bd. 8825, 19 October 1965).

The question of German support after 1965

While the aim of 'normalisation' made necessary a cessation of secret support, the importance attached to Israeli and Jewish 'goodwill' seemed to make continued high levels of support recommendable, as did the continued strengthening of Israel as a western frontier state in the Middle East. This set of German interests and perceptions translated into the form of military and financial support of Israel that the country would take after 1965.

As discussed in the previous chapter, the first question on the German–Israeli agenda after the decision to enter diplomatic relations was the question of military support. Israel wanted to see this support continued, whereas for Germany, the main point of diplomatic relations was to put German-Israeli relations into the open and stop the weapons deliveries which had led to the German 'Middle East Crisis' of 1964–65. The result was a changing of the guards, with the United States taking over the crucial delivery of the tanks, as explained earlier.

The next question was that of German financial support. Israel's opening position was that Germany should continue with the secretive 'Operation Business Friend' loan along with additional official development aid as 'compensation' for the loss of German weapon supplies. Bonn wanted to discontinue secret support, both military and financial. As discussed in the previous chapter, 'Operation Business Friend' was originally planned to amount to a payment of 2 billion Deutsche Mark (DM) over the course of 10 years, with yearly instalments of DM200 million. By 1965, DM644.8 million had been paid out. With less than half of the initially envisaged payments made, the operation was discontinued – a break from the Adenauer policy of secret support. However, what was paid afterwards as official development aid continued to be very substantial. According to numbers given by the federal government, between 1965 and 1997, Germany loaned Israel the equivalent of €2.306 billion under highly favourable conditions. Long-term repayment and low interest rates meant that the 'business friend' and subsequent 'development aid' were more akin to a grant then a loan (Bundestag 2012).

The negotiations over the military and financial support that lasted from March 1965 until May 1966 were lengthy, tedious and harsh. Their detailed reconstruction may be found elsewhere (see for example Hansen 2002). It is the harshness of tone, the certitude with which both sides presented their positions, and the cool, superior, at times arrogant tone of the German negotiators that is the point here, for it runs counter to a commonly held view of German-Israeli relations in which the roles are clearly divided: between a morally repentant Germany and an Israel demanding historical reparation. Germany actually negotiated from a position of strength (*Aktenedition zur Auswärtigen Politik der Bundesrepublik* [AAPD] 1965/173; cf. Hestermann 2016). In these negotiations, 'morality' was seen by the German side as an Israeli bargaining chip that was to be dropped from the negotiating table. As German special envoy Kurt Birrenbach wrote to Chancellor Erhard early on:

> As the massive demand for injecting morality into the financial aid was not repeated today, it seems that the opposite party has backed down on this question as well. Yet even here, we only want to use the word 'seems', because this general clause will surely always be a diplomatic instrument of this country towards the Federal Republic. (AAPD 1965/172)

Carl Carstens, the influential state secretary in the AA and later president of the FRG, was also concerned with the Israeli evocations of morality: 'I am bothered by the repeated use of the term 'moral responsibility'. What should we be morally responsible for? Surely not for the problems Israel has with its Arab neighbours' (AAPD 1965/173). According to Carstens, Germany met its obligation for 'making good the injustice inflicted on the Jews' already with the Reparations Agreement of 1952, as well as with the laws regulating individual reparations (AAPD 1965/173). He engaged a legal argument, insisting that the 1952 Reparations Agreement included a clause that Israel would thereafter not evoke demands based on Nazi persecution. German ambassador Pauls reported from Israel in the same terms: 'We should [...] make clear to the Israelis that we see through their constant appeals to our moral obligation: That they say morality, but mean money, without being ready to give us the slightest bit of relief' (PA AA, B130, Bd. 2567, 26 January 1966).

Golda Meir, a long-standing critic of Ben-Gurion's 'New Germany' policy and who was emotionally distrustful of postwar West Germany, was of the opinion that:

> [...] one could cooperate without obscuring the past. However, there could never be a balancing of the accounts. It was not only the six million that were missing from Jewry and from Israel, but also all of their offspring [...]. If the Germans denied what they owed to Israel only so that the country's mere existence could be

upheld [...] she would tell Ben Natan to break off negotiations. (AAPD 1965/420)

Again, Germany was well aware of the obvious fact that in these negotiations, it was Germany that had something to give, not Israel (AAPD 1965/172). What seemed to be standing in the way of 'normalising' relations, then, as already demonstrated, was not least a fear of 'Jewish power' rooted in an antisemitism that was at times also uttered in the language used by a previous Germany: Ambassador Pauls feared that should negotiations with Israel fail, '[t]he Jews will unleash the dogs from Jerusalem to London to New York' (AAPD 1965/439).

In 1966, Adenauer visited Israel, a visit which, despite him not being the German chancellor anymore, had all the appearances of a state visit (Schwarz 1997: 787). Whilst there, he publicly declared that 'I too, was a member of the Zionist movement' (Braach-Maksvytis 2011: 300). This was true in the literal sense: Adenauer had joined the *Komitee Pro Palästina* ('German Pro-Palestine Committee') in 1927, a German organisation in support of Zionism (Braach-Maksvytis 2011: 299). Adenauer's statement was also true in the much stronger sense, as the former chancellor had possibly been the most important western politician for Israel in its early and formative years.

During a table dinner in Adenauer's honour, however, Israeli Prime Minister Levi Eshkol insulted the chancellor by making statements to the effect that the FRG's confrontation with the past and way to reacceptance into the international community were still far from finished. To this Adenauer replied: 'If goodwill is not acknowledged, nothing good can come out of that,' and threatened to leave immediately (Schwarz 1997: 790). What Hans-Peter Schwarz, Adenauer's biographer, did not add was what Adenauer also said on the occasion: 'National Socialism killed as many Germans as it did Jews', a rather peculiar reading of history already expressed vis-à-vis Ben-Gurion in the 1960 meeting (cited in Jelinek and Blasius 1997: 321). Rolf Pauls, correctly described by Schwarz as 'an Adenauer man from the very beginning' (Schwarz 1997: 788), was satisfied: 'The coincidence of the Adenauer visit and the conclusion of the negotiations over economic aid signify the end to an episode in relations [...] the actual process of normalisation begins now' (cited in Jelinek and Blasisus 1997: 323).

9

'EVEN-HANDED'?
GERMANY, ISRAEL AND THE MIDDLE EAST (1969–82)

In 1969, Willy Brandt, a former antifascist, became the first Social Democratic chancellor of postwar Germany. Viewed in terms of a 'working through of the past', the Brandt chancellorship was a progressive development in the FRG.

The SPD not only looked back on a recent history of anti-Nazism, it was also, after the founding of the FRG in 1949, the party most outspokenly supportive of Israel. After all, the Reparations Agreement had been ratified only because the SPD voted unanimously in its favour. Since the mid-1950s, the Social Democratic opposition in the Bundestag had argued for full diplomatic relations with Israel, which the governing CDU opposed for the reasons outlined in Part I. A certain romanticised perception of Israeli 'Kibbutz-Socialism' also played a part in the early siding of the non-communist West German left with Israel. Furthermore, the SPD and Israeli Labor Party, which presided over the country until 1977 in its various incarnations, were linked within the Socialist International. One could thus expect that the chancellorship of Brandt would have instituted an era of deepened German-Israeli ties. However, this was not the case.

While on a material level, German-Israeli relations were to remain stable, with Germany continuing to provide Israel with the above-mentioned annual loan of DM140 million and military cooperation evolving in new forms, Germany distanced itself from Israel on the political-diplomatic level over the question of Middle East peace in general and the Palestine question in particular. The German distancing from Israel that lasted from the late 1960s until the early 1980s was principally shaped by deeper, political-economic interests, which the SPD, as the ruling party, was compelled to follow (Büttner and Scheffler 1982: 145).

Ironically, one could even argue that the fact that the Bonn government was less visibly staffed by former Nazis contributed to growing irritations from Israel. An episode like that of the Eichmann trial, in which Israeli silence over murky figures in the German government was traded for military and financial support, seemed much less probable now in a government that featured fewer former Nazis. As Egon Bahr, Brandt's foreign-policy advisor and co-architect of *Ostpolitik*, bluntly told the Israeli ambassador Ben-Natan, the new German government had no personal links to the Nazi era and therefore no sense of 'collective guilt' towards Israel, and thus would stop its 'exaggerated' levels of support (cited after Fink 2019: 121f.).

Today, Brandt is a politician many Germans can agree upon regardless of party identification; yet the reasons for the latter-day respect accorded to his persona are the same which during his time led to his bedevilment by the political right (Münkel 2013). The height of anti-Brandt campaigning was reached in the 1961 and 1965 general elections, which Brandt lost against Adenauer and Erhard, respectively. Brandt's years in Scandinavian exile – a direct consequence of his persecution by the Nazis – were then the principal target of attack. As the German historian Daniela Münkel succinctly put it in an article for *Die Zeit*:

142

Brandt's opponents could be sure that their slander of his emigration to Scandinavia resonated well, since it spoke to firmly embedded prejudice against exile and helped to whitewash the perpetrator and fellow-traveller biographies of many Germans. Denunciation of Brandt as a 'traitor to the fatherland' linked up with the historically well-known denunciation of the SPD as the party of nationally rootless vagabonds [*vaterlandslose Gesellen*], categorically questioning its ability to govern. (Münkel 2013)

One of Brandt's fiercest opponents was Franz Josef Strauss, the instrumental German figure behind the military support of Israel. As he famously charged in the run-up to the 1961 elections: 'We must be allowed to ask Mr. Brandt one question: What did you do during these twelve years outside? We know what we did inside' (Münkel 2013). Strauss surely knew what he did 'inside': pursuing his career under the Nazi regime and in its institutions, while also being a soldier of the Wehrmacht on the Eastern Front. Konrad Adenauer, the other principal figure behind the German build-up of Israel, liked to refer to Brandt's original name, Frahm, which he changed in Scandinavia, in order to point towards these years in exile. Pressure on Brandt did not come only from the political right, but from the non-parliamentary radical left as well. In fact, even the *Jusos* ('Young Socialists'), the SPD's party youth, had after 1967 turned towards the Palestinians and southern liberation struggles.

Before examining the role of the Palestine question in German-Israeli relations during the 1970s, it is useful to look into Brandt's attitude towards Israel and the Palestine question. This is important given the centrality of Brandt's legacy to the SPD and beyond. In a speech on the occasion of the Christian–Jewish 'Week of Brotherhood' in Cologne in March 1971, Brandt formulated his position on Israel and the Palestine question in these terms:

Israel is – and the slogans of radical groups can do nothing to alter this – the magnificent attempt to create a secure homeland for a long homeless people. It is bitter that the birth of this state had as its price new victims, and new suffering. Who would wish to deny this? Who would wish to deny the misery of the Palestinian Arabs? But in this as well, we have no right to appear as the arrogant moralists of the world. Rather, we must follow the chain of causality of suffering and injustice back to its origin: here in the heart of Europe. The Federal Republic, the more fortunate of the two German states that rose from the wreckage of the year 1945, acknowledged its obligations to the survivors. The reparations agreement reached then with Israel is an accomplishment of Konrad Adenauer and the Social-Democratic opposition of the time that we view as a cornerstone of our self-image as a state. (cited in Schmidt 2014: 77f)

In this speech, Brandt acknowledges the discursive influence of the German New Left, seeing a need to defend Israel against the 'slogans of radical groups'. He acknowledges the 'misery of the Palestinian Arabs', who have emerged as the 'new victims' as a direct consequence of the founding of Israel. Brandt also acknowledges German obligations towards the State of Israel, a responsibility which, in the form of the reparations agreement, is a 'cornerstone' of the German 'self-image as a state'. However, he concurrently negates an indirect form of German responsibility for the 'new victims' (the 'Palestinian Arabs') as a form of modesty: 'we' have to focus on where the 'causality of suffering' originated, 'the heart of Europe'. Brandt's refusal 'to appear as the arrogant moralists of the world' surely sounds reasonable from an inner-German perspective, but from a Palestinian perspective, it must appear as unjust, for the simple fact that Palestinians bear no fault for Jewish suffering in Europe, which Brandt places at the beginning of the 'chain of causality of suffering'.

One may also add that the FRG also quite simply saw no interest in appearing as 'the arrogant moralists of the world' in this particular instance. So far, Bonn had sought to avoid giving the impression of taking 'indirect' responsibility for the

144

Palestinian refugees of 1948. This would have opened the doors to Arab demands for equity in German political and economic support of Israel and the Palestinians – an unthinkable scenario even in the context of an 'even-handed' Middle East policy.

The Palestine question in Germany: The 1972 Munich Olympics

On the morning of 5 September 1972, eight members of the al-Fatah-linked Palestinian organisation Black September entered the athletes compound of the Munich Olympics, killing two Israeli athletes and taking nine hostage. The next morning, after a botched German rescue operation, all Israeli hostages were dead, having been killed by the Palestinian terrorists. One German police officer and five of the eight Palestinians had also died in the shootout at the Fürstenfeldbruck airfield near Munich.

The hostage crisis placed the Palestine question on the domestic German agenda, and, for the first time, it came to play a central role in German-Israeli relations. The Munich attacks and the Israeli retaliation mission in its aftermath have been covered in several documentaries (see especially the Oscar-winning *One Day in September* by Kevin McDonald, 1999), a Steven Spielberg movie (*Munich*, 2005) and much academic writing (Fink 2019; Herf 2016; Large 2012; Schiller and Young 2010).

The 1972 Munich Olympics were minutely orchestrated to demonstrate to the world the novel, open, democratic and liberal character of West Germany, a demonstration which took place on the level of architecture, sloganeering (*Die heiteren Spiele* ['The Joyous Games']) and, ironically, extremely lax security measures (Large 2012). The Games, similar to awarding Brandt the Nobel Peace Prize a year earlier, bestowed legitimacy on Germany; they were also a symbolic act of reintegration into the circle of 'civilised' nations. Clearly, they sought to form a counterpoint to the 1936 Olympics in Berlin, which had been used to show the world the strength of the Nazi regime, while simultaneously assuaging fears of Nazi aggression.

It is easy to read historical symbolism into the games. Munich considered itself 'the capital of the [Nazi] movement' (Large 2012: 2). Dachau, the longest-running concentration camp of Nazi Germany, was just outside the city gates. However, in Israel, participation in the Games was not a topic of public debate. As the Israeli team entered the Munich stadium under the Star of David banner, the stage was set for a display of the New Germany, including its 'normalisation' with Israel (Large 2012).

Inevitably, the Palestinian terror attack was also an attack on the political rationality behind the Games. Black September named the operation 'Ikrit and Biram', after two Palestinian villages whose inhabitants were expelled in 1948. Palestine, then, violently pushed itself into the frame of German–Israeli and German–Jewish relations. The attacks suddenly brought Ikrit and Biram, Munich and Dachau, into the same equation, a brutal conjoining of historically different events and ensuing narratives. Translated into the German context, the terror attack that originated from the Israel-Palestine conflict took on a different meaning: Jews were murdered in the New Germany.

Black September and the PLO's aim behind the attack was to place the Palestine question on the global agenda. As the last remaining member of the squad, al-Gamashy, stated: 'I am proud of what I did in Munich, because it helped the Palestinian cause enormously. Before Munich, the world had no idea about our struggle. But on that day the name of Palestine was repeated all over the world' (cited in an interview in the documentary *One Day in September*, 1999).

The Israeli government was shocked by the disastrous German handling of the hostage crisis. Zvi Zamir, chief of the Israeli intelligence agency Mossad, was present at the at the Fürstenfeldbruck shootout. He reported back that the German police 'didn't make even a minimal effort to save lives' (Israel State Archives 2012). Zamir found that the German priority was to continue the Games as quickly as possible. In fact, they had remained uninterrupted for the most part of the hostage crisis (Israel State Archives 2012). While the Israeli public sentiment was boiling at this point, official Israeli anger at Bonn was still largely kept behind the scenes. Israeli cabinet protocols show that the government wanted to avoid a diplomatic fallout with Germany. According to the commented document collection by the Israel State Archives, published on the fortieth anniversary of the hostage crisis in 2012, Golda Meir sought to maintain good relations with Brandt, whom she saw 'as a friend and supporter of Israel in present and future political strategies' (Israel State Archives 2012). Israel relied on Bonn to convey messages to Moscow regarding the question of Jewish immigration. While Israel was sceptical about Brandt's *Ostpolitik*, fearing that a more conciliatory stance towards Moscow could translate into softer Arab policies, Jerusalem needed to use to its advantage its hitherto close relations with a country whose importance on the international scene was growing. Moreover, Bonn's influence in the EC was needed to deepen Israeli economic relations with the European Common Market. Lastly, the Meir government wanted to avoid tensions in order to avoid harm to Brandt's re-election chances in the upcoming general elections.

On 20 November 1972, Black September hijacked a Lufthansa plane en route from Beirut to Munich. Refuelling in Nicosia and Zagreb, the hijackers threatened to fly the plane to Munich and explode it there unless the three Palestinian terrorists were allowed to go free. Israel, which had in fact warned Germany about the possibility of such a hijacking, urged the Brandt administration not to give in to the hijackers' demands. Contradicting Israel's counterterrorism policy, Bonn did the opposite. It allowed the three Palestinians to go free; they went on to receive a hero's welcome in Libya, and Germany never demanded their extradition from Tripoli. At this point the initially reserved Israeli anger burst. Politicians and the press linked the events to the Nazi past. Brandt, personally offended, wrote a letter to Meir protesting the drawing of parallels to the Nazi era. In the Israeli cabinet, one minister picked up on suspicions uttered in the press, angrily wondering whether there was a 'conspiracy here between the German authorities and the terrorists, in order to be swiftly rid of the murderers who weighed, not on the Germans' conscience, but on their peace and quiet and on their interests' (Israel State Archives 2012). This idea of a staged hijacking sounds fantastic, but it was in fact not ruled out by Meir (Israel State Archives 2012), nor was it ruled out by German officials. Ulrich Wegener, who worked for the German Interior Ministry at the time, founded the German special forces GSG 9 in response to the Munich attacks. Closely involved in all stages of the events, Wegener stated in *One Day in September* that the hijacking was indeed premeditated: Bonn would free the Palestinians, and in return the PLO would refrain from further attacks on German territory. That Bonn never tried the three last attackers and attempted to wash the whole affair off its hands so quickly was the topic of an investigative report by *Der Spiegel* in 2012, which sourced the relevant archives and was co-written by the in-house historian Klaus Wiegrefe. The article speaks of West German 'appeasement' towards Black September and the PLO. As Herf shows, the German secret service was clearly aware that Black September was linked to al-Fatah and the PLO (Herf 2016: 172), and reveals that officials of the AA met with members of Black September in the weeks following the Munich attack. For the PLO and Black September, even unofficial contacts with West German authorities meant an upgrading of their status, an important step towards more official forms of recognition. According to *Der Spiegel*, the AA even struck a deal with Arafat directly: in return for a cessation of terror attacks on German territory, Bonn would allow Arafat to have a personal envoy in the FRG. While this envoy would clearly not be given any form of official status, it was important for Arafat to secure PLO influence over Palestinian workers and students present in the FRG (*Der Spiegel* 2012). Interestingly enough, both within the AA (Spiegel 2012) and the German Interior Ministry (Slobodian 2013: 207), Palestinian groups under the PLO umbrella were generally referred to as 'resistance' groups, a remarkably positive term.

According to Herf, who cites the public annual report of the *Verfassungsschutz* (Federal Office for the Protection of the Constitution), 3,000 Palestinian workers and students resided in West Germany at the time. Historian Quinn Slobodian suggests 800 Palestinian students lived in the FRG, with Palestinians thus representing the largest Arab population at West German universities (Slobodian 2013: 209). Palestinian workers were organised into the General Union of Palestinian Workers (GUPA), and Palestinian students into the General Union of Palestinian Students (GUPS). Both unions were subordinated to al-Fatah (Herf 2016: 173). Many among the Palestinians in Germany hailed from Jordan, having fled the country after the bloody anti-Palestinian crackdown from which Black September derived its name.

The conclusions drawn by *Der Spiegel* regarding a German-PLO deal seem historically plausible, but they cannot be verified here. The question of sub-official FRG-PLO relations from 1967 until the onset of the Oslo process in 1993 warrants further empirical research. However, speaking of German 'appeasement' of the PLO, as the authors of the report do, seems exaggerated in light of the German clampdown on Palestinian individuals and organisations following the attacks. Hans-Dietrich Genscher, then interior minister and later long-standing foreign minister, signed a banning order of GUPA and GUPS shortly after the

Munich attacks. Indications exist that Abdallah Frangi, leader of the GUPS, was knowledgeable about the attacks and that Palestinians living in the FRG were connected to the Munich attackers. Publications distributed by the GUPS endorsed guerrilla warfare and certainly opened themselves to the German Interior Ministry's charge that '[GUPS and GUPA] political activity threatened the inner security and public order of the Federal Republic' (Slobodian 2013: 212; see also Herf 2016: 173-89). Next to banning these two organisations, the FRG expelled almost 200 legal Arab residents from the country, with 2,400 Arabs already barred from entering the FRG in the month after the attack (Slobodian 2013: 211-13). Official documentation does not detail how many of the roughly 13,000 illegal Arab residents in the country were deported.

Outraged responses from within Arab states included the occupation of German diplomatic buildings and an 8,000-strong protest in Lebanon. Parts of US news media even drew parallels between the FRG and the Nazi state (Slobodian 2013: 214-15). The banning order against GUPA and GUPS read that these organisations 'understand violence as a means for political contestation, and they bring international issues occurring outside the space of West Germany into the Federal Republic' (Slobodian 2013: 213). Palestinian migration to the FRG engendered the transnationalisation of the Israel-Palestine conflict and Palestinian narratives of the conflict, which had not been part of societal discourses in the FRG prior to 1967. The Palestine question had thus entered domestic German politics and had done so mainly via the student left. As Slobodian shows, the 'interior ministry's conflation of foreigner political violence with anarchism and Maoism sought to reinforce a narrative link between foreigners and the hundreds of German Communist groups [...] that had emerged with the fragmenting of the leftist student movement after 1969' (Slobodian 2013: 207).

The Palestinian question as posed within Germany after 1967 is linked to the question of antisemitism within the German New Left. In Germany, this latter question fills several bookshelves, while the topic of Germany's Israel policy does not. As the German New Left never influenced the formulation of Germany's Israel policy, the question of its antisemitism is not addressed here.[1]

Brandt in Jerusalem and the Arab-Israeli War of 1973

In June 1973, Willy Brandt became the first German chancellor in office to visit Israel, following an invitation extended in January 1972. This was an invitation that could not be declined, not least because it was made official by Israel without prior consultation with Bonn (Schmidt 2014: 14). For Germany, there was no obvious gain to the visit during a time in which it seemed to be successfully mending its relations with Arab states, re-establishing diplomatic relations with them all between 1971 and 1975 (Büttner and Hünseler 1981: 133).

Israel's interests in deepening ties with the FRG were more evident than vice versa, despite the bilateral crisis over Munich and its aftermath. Israel looked for political backing by a country that was by then the leading economic power in Europe and which, due to Brandt's *Ostpolitik*, also appeared as a much more independent and self-confident global political actor than ever before in the Cold War (Fink 2015; Fink 2009). Jerusalem counted on Bonn to provide an inner-European counterweight to France after its pro-Arab turn, as explained in the introduction to this part. Lastly, in this context, we may also safely assume that Israel was interested in disturbing the German–Arab soothing of relations.

Brandt found the visit to have been one of his 'most difficult tasks'. His aim, however, was 'to put paid to Israel's demand that the past play a major role in West Germany's present and future policies' (Fink 2015: 513).

The similarity (or continuity) between the 1966 visit of ex-chancellor Adenauer and that of Brandt seven years later is that both were not visits of penitence, but of German national self-assertion (a difference in this regard being that Brandt, on a personal level, was not prone to the crude equations between German and Jewish suffering that Adenauer liked to make in the presence of Israeli counterparts).

An indication of the role the State of Israel held within the Brandt government's overall foreign policy, and, relatedly, of how the German government at the time positioned itself towards the Holocaust in the context of its reconciliatory policy towards Eastern Europe and the Soviet Union, was the difference between Brandt's famous genuflection in front of the Warsaw Ghetto memorial in 1970 and the absence of such a gesture in Yad Vashem in 1973. Israeli hosts and spectators worldwide had hoped for an act of similar magnitude. Brandt's symbolic gestures in Yad Vashem, however, followed the policy of 'normalisation'. After laying down a wreath of roses wrapped in the German national colours, Brandt solemnly recited, in German, verses from Psalm 103 of the Bible: 'Merciful and gracious is the Lord [...]. Not forever will he retain his anger [...]. As far as day is from night, so hath he relieved us from our transgressions' (cited in Fink 2015: 509). The visit was without lasting consequences for the Middle East, which a few months later became enmeshed in the next round of Arab-Israeli warfare.

The 1973 war and the question of German neutrality

The 1973 Arab–Israeli War, which brought Israel to the edge of catastrophe, was won with the help of crucial American supplies, delivered from air and sea during the fighting (Morris 2001:

433ff). As in 1967, Germany declared neutrality in the conflict, the Netherlands being the only European country officially in support of Israel, which was attacked by Syria and Egypt. German societal support for Israel in 1973 was less enthusiastic than in 1967. Brandt repeatedly underlined, however, that there could not be a 'neutrality of the hearts' and rebuked Arab oil 'blackmail' (Fink 2019: 253).

Beyond declarations, what did German neutrality mean in practice? At the time, the Israeli daily *Ma'ariv* stated: 'This is a neutrality that indirectly encourages genocide in order to secure the uninterrupted delivery of oil from Libya. Once they have murdered for ideological reasons, this time for oil. The difference is not big' (cited in Büttner 2003: 145). There was a wider and not entirely unfounded perception, in Israel and beyond, that Germany had now ridded itself of its historical obligations towards Israel in exchange for Arab oil (Büttner and Scheffler 1982: 139). Bonn's 'stumbling and inconsistent' (Fink 2019: 252) political responses to the 1973 war continue to be the stuff of historical contention. Late opponents of the Brandt government argue that 'the FRG under Willy Brandt did not allow American armed forces to use their military bases in the country to supply Israel with weapons' (Jander 2017; see also Wolffsohn 2018 for a broader political attack on the Brandt government's Middle East policies). What Martin Jander, lecturer at the Free University of Berlin, seems to suggest here is that since the FRG did not *want* Israel to be supplied with crucial arms from German territory, the United States was also *unable* to do so. Both assumptions are misguided. In fact, as the available historical literature on this episode shows (Schmidt 2014; Blumenau 2010; Gerlach 2006) and as the official document collection of the AA archives for the year 1973 also clearly demonstrates, Bonn protested the shipment of weapons from the port of Bremerhaven only after the first ceasefire was declared on 22 October. However, the German government knew of American resupplies from its territory by 16 October, when German Minister of Foreign Affairs Walter Scheel was informed about the matter by the American diplomat Martin J. Hillenbrand, to whom Scheel expressed understanding, but underlined that Arab states should not be informed about the resupply operations (Blumenau 2010: 127). In the words of German Middle East scholar Helmut Hubel, '[t]he protest thus had no practical significance but served as a conciliatory political gesture toward the Arab states' (Hubel 2004: 72). In fact, an official protest was issued by the AA on 25 October, when two Israeli-flagged ships 'had been loaded with U.S. equipment by a company in German government ownership and the media had gotten wind of the story' (Schmidt 2014: 60f.).

An open German consent to the military supply of Israel from German ports would have undermined the German claim to 'even-handedness' in the Arab-Israeli conflict. Already faced with the threat of an Arab oil embargo, a public charging of Israeli freighters would have cost Bonn 'what shred of credibility' it still possessed in the eyes of Israel's Arab opponents (Schmidt 2014: 61). Brandt was especially piqued by the carelessness – or else – of the Americans using vessels that were openly discernible as Israeli. After this episode, American supply of Israel continued unabated via Bremerhaven (Schmidt 2014: 61).

In the course of the 1973 war, officials in the AA and Brandt himself complained internally of having been treated like a 'colony' by Washington (Blumenau 2010; Schmidt 2014: 64). This impression was partly caused by Washington's unilateral moves in the conflict. It had been rather lax in informing Bonn about the resupply operations on its territory, and on 25 October it put all its North Atlantic Treaty Organisation (NATO) troops on highest alert without prior consultation, including its nuclear forces, thus threatening to escalate a regional war into direct superpower confrontation. German exasperation with the United

States also reflected the disappointment of a state which, in the course of its *Ostpolitik*, had gained political manoeuvring space on the international scene. The 1973 war reminded Bonn that this space was ultimately defined by the United States.

A major factor that explains the differing US and German positions on the 1973 war is that the FRG depended on Arab oil supplies, while the United States did not. As an internal report from the AA summed up at the time:

> We have a big interest in an early end of the Middle East Conflict also since we import approximately 71% [...] of our oil from Arab producers including Libya and Algeria, which are parties to the conflict. We share this dependence with other Western European states and Japan while the US only imports 6% of its oil from Arab countries. Europe and Japan, thus, depend more on an arrangement with the Arabs than the US. This is another reason why we and our EC partners are trying to convince the Arabs that Europe takes a neutral stance in this conflict and expects not to be hit by oil reductions. (cited in Blumenau 2010: 125)

Whereas German neutrality in 1973 was primarily an instrument in relations with Arab states, the question of neutrality and of the policy of overall 'even-handedness' must be posed also in light of German-Israeli military relations. The move towards Arab states especially after 1973 is related to the end of the German role in the arming of Israel in 1965 and the making of the US-Israeli alliance afterwards, as discussed previously. However, this altered constellation did not mean that German–Israeli military relations were discontinued, but that they were transformed. After the 1973 war, Brandt confided to British Prime Minister Edward Heath, without further specification, that 'the actual degree of support was greater than could be publicly admitted' (Schmidt 2004: 63). The German historian Wolfgang Schmidt alludes to a somewhat mysterious 'important electronic device' delivered by Germany on short notice that was helpful in the Israeli war effort (Schmidt 2004: 63). According to Shpiro, it was the German-designed 'revolutionary new type of missile boat', produced in the French wharf of Cherbourg, which 'formed the backbone of the astounding Israeli naval successes in the 1973 war' (Shpiro 2003: 321).

From the 1970s onwards, German-Israeli military relations moved, to mutual benefit, into the sphere of research and development. Shpiro details how, after the 1973 war, Israel was able to capture intact the latest Soviet T-62 tanks. Through Mossad-Federal Intelligence Service channels, exemplars of these tanks were secretly delivered to Germany, with German tests showing that they could not be penetrated by standard NATO cannons. Thus, the new German standard tank, the Leopard 2, introduced in the early 1980s, was built using a 'non-NATO-standard 120mm smooth-bore cannon'. This requirement, which caused consternation at NATO headquarters and was protested by the United States, was a direct result of the technical evaluations of the Soviet armour provided by Israel. This development, in turn, informed the production of the Israeli Merkava III tank afterwards: 'Thus a circle was closed, in which Israeli designers, who assisted Germany in the development of its main battle tank, adopted the German gun design into their state of the art armour system' (Shpiro 2003: 323). The United States' protested against the joint German–Israeli development for reasons of economic competition: with the joint development of these central weapon systems, Israeli and German companies extended market shares against American competitors.

Both German and Israeli experts on the matter (Nassauer and Steinmetz 2003; Shpiro 2013; Shpiro 2003) place great importance on a project codenamed CERBERUS, behind which lay the Israeli development of a still-secret system of radar jammers, a key element in the development of the European Tornado aircraft, which Brandt's successor, Helmut Schmidt, called 'the biggest armaments project since the birth of Christ' (Shpiro 2003: 323). Developed without any parliamentary knowledge, Germany invested into CERBERUS about DM2.2 billion (roughly €1.1 billion; Nassauer and Steinmetz 2003: 8). Shpiro describes the significance of this project in terms of NATO strategy in Europe. The technological innovation of this project was to enable the Tornado aircraft to overcome the Soviet anti-aircraft missile defences, penetrating deep behind the Iron Curtain with minimal losses in order to make possible the discharge of 'tactical' nuclear warheads (Shpiro 2003: 324). The CERBERUS system would thus have played an important military role in the worst-case scenario of all-out war in Europe. Shpiro explains that 'the technological advances of CERBERUS later formed the basis for Israeli airforce successes against the Syrians during the 1982 Lebanon campaign, when sixteen Syrian missile batteries were destroyed on one day and over 120 Syrian aircraft shot down without a single Israeli loss' (Shpiro 2003: 334). Israeli 'electronic warfare systems' were also used in Germany's bombing campaign in the Balkans in the mid-1990s, and German tanks used Israeli-designed ammunition in the Kosovo campaign in 1999 (Shpiro 2003: 334). Thus, German–Israeli military cooperation played a part, ironically yet fittingly, in Germany's first war after 1945, a war that was legitimised in the name of Auschwitz, rather than in spite of it. As Shpiro argues, the stability and mutual importance of military relations has 'contributed significantly to normalisation of relations in other fields' (Shpiro 2003: 306) throughout the history of German–Israeli relations.

To the continuity of military relations, so important to both countries' military-economic sectors, we need to add German support for Israeli economic integration with Europe. Due to its isolation in the Middle East, trade with Europe is crucial to Israel. The 1970 preferential trade agreement was replaced in

1975 with an agreement regulating further trade liberalisation. Tariffs on Israeli industrial goods exported to Europe were gradually dropped in consequence, while tariffs on agricultural produce significantly reduced. Bonn put its weight against the interests of countries like Italy, a direct competitor of Israel for Mediterranean agricultural produce. As tariffs for European goods exported to Israel were reduced at a slower pace than vice versa, the Israeli economy was allowed to adjust itself to further trade liberalisation. This and other provisions in the treaty beneficial to Israel were realised due to German support (Weingardt 2002: 267f.). It is not a secret that the FRG has been seen and continues to be seen as the most important advocate of Israeli interests in the EC and subsequently in the European Union.

The stability and continuity of economic and military cooperation allows risking tensions on the political-diplomatic level. Yet, without doubt, the tensions of the early 1970s would only increase until 1982. It was over the Palestine question that Germany encountered the limits of 'normalising' ties with Israel and adopting an 'even-handed' approach to the Middle East.

Declaring Palestine? Germany, Europe and the Middle East after the 1973 Arab–Israeli War

The 1973 Arab-Israeli War opened the way to the Egyptian-Israeli settlement six years later. It allowed Egyptian President Anwar al-Sadat, portrayed as the 'hero of the crossing', to reach a compromise with Israel. Hit hard by the war, a 'land for peace' scenario became desirable to the majority of the Israeli public (Morris 2001: 437). Sadat went to Jerusalem in 1977, and in 1979, the Israeli Likud-led government under Menachem Begin exchanged the Sinai Peninsula for peace on the Egyptian front. To European dissatisfaction, this 'separate peace' sidelined the Palestinian question, preventing a more comprehensive settlement of the Arab–Israeli and Israeli–Palestinian conflicts.

From the aftermath of the 1973 war until 1980, the EC engaged with the Palestine question within their European Policy Cooperation (EPC) foreign policy mechanism. This diplomatic declaratory engagement had no tangible effects on the Middle East conflicts. One of its main results was to transform the Arab-Israeli conflict into a Israeli–Palestinian one in official Western European perception (Büttner 2003).

The six EC countries produced their first non-official Middle East paper in 1971. Known as the 'Schumann paper' after its main author, Maurice Schumann, who was French minister of foreign affairs at the time, it was based on the French text of UN Security Council Resolution 242, stipulating that Israel should retreat from all territories captured in 1967, without, however, explicitly mentioning the Palestinians. Germany backed away from the paper after Israeli protests, thus rendering it ineffective, much to French chagrin. After the oil boycott of the 1973 war, however, Bonn toughened its position. The declaration issued on 6 November 1973, in the war's aftermath, was, in line with the recent, relevant UN Security Council resolutions on the conflict, based on the principle of land for peace. Reiterating the 'inadmissibility of the acquisition of territory by force', it called on Israel to 'end the territorial occupation' of 1967. It recognised Israel's 'right to live in peace within secure and recognized boundaries' and, crucially, added that 'in the establishment of a just and lasting peace account must be taken of the legitimate rights of the Palestinians' (cited in Büttner 2003: 145). This time, Bonn did not step back. Quite the contrary, in 1974, the German ambassador to the UN, Rüdiger von Wechmar, spoke of a Palestinian 'right to self-determination' in the UN General Assembly, the first representative of a western state to do so (Weingardt 2002: 276). This statement should be understood in light of the 'right to self-determination' the FRG demanded for itself, namely, the claim over the GDR (Jäger 1995: 3f.). In 1974, Brandt's chancellorship ended. Along with Austrian Chancellor Bruno Kreisky, Brandt met Yasser Arafat in Vienna in 1979 during a meeting of the Socialist International. While Brandt, now party chairman of the SPD, took part in the meeting not in a governmental capacity, the encounter was celebrated by the PLO as a major breakthrough in its diplomatic efforts for recognition in Western Europe.

The London Declaration of 1977 and the Venice Declaration of 1980 marked further shifts among EC states towards the Palestinian question. The 1977 document spoke repeatedly of a 'Palestinian people', stating that 'the legitimate right of the Palestinian people to give expression to its national identity' would need to 'take into account the need for a homeland' (Büttner 2003: 146f; see also Persson 2015: 89). The historical allusion to the Balfour Declaration, drafted sixty years earlier by the British Empire, promising a national home to the Jewish people, was not lost on anybody. The Venice Declaration, generally understood as a response to the US-sponsored Egyptian-Israeli Camp David Peace Treaty of 1979, went one step further. It stated:

> A just solution must finally be found to the Palestinian problem, which is not simply one of refugees. The Palestinian people, which is conscious of existing as such, must be placed in a position, by an appropriate process defined within the framework of the comprehensive peace settlement, to exercise fully its right to self-determination. (European Council 1980)[2]

Furthermore, and most provocative to Israel, the declaration stated that the PLO needed to be associated with future negotiations. Based on archival research in the AA, German political scientist Hubert Leber, in a study on German-Israeli relations during the premiership of Begin, found that the FRG 'was neither a restrained nor a particularly pro-Israeli actor' in the drafting of the declaration. While Bonn prevented a stronger pro-Palestinian wording as espoused by France (for example, demanding the inclusion of a recognition of Israel's 'right to exist'), the FRG backed criticism of Israel's settlement project in the territories occupied in 1967 and opposed unilateral changes to the status of Jerusalem (Leber 2015). Israel's de jure annexation of Jerusalem with the 'Jerusalem Law' of 1980 can also be read as a response to the Venice Declaration (see also Leber 2015).

In response to the Venice Declaration the Israeli cabinet produced a 'harsh' communiqué which compared the declaration to 'a Munich surrender, the second in our generation' (Greilsammer and Weiler 1987: 49). The framing of the PLO as a reincarnation of the Nazis and the Europeans as latter-day Chamberlains blind to the dangers of Jew hatred was a clear indication of what European diplomatic advances towards Palestine meant to many in Israel: an anti-Israel policy in which growing recognition of the Palestine question was exchanged for the flow of Middle Eastern oil, an exchange greased by the deep history of European antisemitism. Mistrust of Europe, a special mistrust of Germany and constant Nazification of the Palestinians and the PLO was, of course, a hallmark of Menachem Begin's Likud (formerly Herut) government which came to power in 1977.

The power shift in Israel to the right significantly strained European–Israeli relations in general and German-Israeli ones in particular. However, the Venice Declaration was equally opposed by the Labor Party, while the reaction of the Israeli public ranged from indifference to contempt (Greilsammer and Weiler 1984: 145).

Interestingly enough, the PLO also reacted critically to the Venice initiative. Since the declaration did not accept the PLO as the representative of the Palestinian people, and since it did not rebuke the Camp David agreements as inadequate to a just solution of the Israeli–Palestinian conflict, the PLO saw in Venice not an alternative to the Camp David agreements, but a way of salvaging them. Washington was in fact not at all displeased with the Venice Declaration precisely because it saw in it a basic affirmation of Camp David (Greilsammer and Weiler 1984: 145f).

Which effect, then, did European diplomatic engagement with the Middle East have on the question of peace? The short answer is: none, or very little indeed. It would be easy to sweep this whole episode aside simply by pointing to the pivotal role played by the United States and the 'primarily derivative' (Garfinkle 1983: 17) interest the Europeans held in the Palestine question as a means to ease relations with the oil-producing Arab states. The US government had early delineated to the Europeans the limits to their Middle East engagement. As US President Richard Nixon said in 1974: 'we are not going to be faced with a situation where the nine countries of Europe gang up against the United States – the United States which is their guarantee for their security. That we cannot have' (cited in Persson 2015: 77).

In a recent study on the subject, political scientist Anders Persson argued that viewing the European approach towards the Palestinians as derivative of oil interests is 'too simplistic', given that the EC 'had expressed a genuine disapproval of Israel's continued occupation and particularly of the construction of settlements on occupied territory' (Persson 2015: 76). This may be so, but then the question remains as to why this disapproval was translated into international engagement precisely when the oil-exporting Arab states decided to flex their muscles.

David Allen and Alfred Pijpers closed their 1984 edited volume on European foreign policy towards the Middle East (a volume offering much deeper research than many of the more recent works on the topic) with a few sobering remarks. They noted that, at their time of writing, regardless of national orientation, there were four basic interests which the West European states held in common vis-à-vis the Middle East, and all of these are still in place today: firstly, what the authors took to be the obvious commercial interest, namely access to Arab oil and markets; secondly, Europe's stake in a stable Middle East, and the prevention and settlement of conflicts; thirdly (less tangibly but equally important), the commitment to the survival of the Israeli state, a commitment that does not, however, extend to Israel beyond its pre-1967 borders; and fourthly, the European interest in maintaining the transatlantic alliance.

Allen and Pijpers found the EPC declarations between 1973 and 1980 to have stood in contrast to these goals, notably those of Israeli security and of stable relations with the United States. The authors note that the declarations seemed to have placed the Israeli and the Palestinian right to a secure existence within mutually recognised state borders on a footing of equal political and moral importance. Yet, they cautioned, it would be 'fallacious' to think that the EPC declarations truly meant an even-handed recognition of both the Israeli and Palestinian right to a safe existence. While the existence of a Jewish state in the Middle East has been, for Europe, an end in itself, a Palestinian state has not. Proof of this was provided during the Israeli invasion of Lebanon in 1982. The *déconfiture* of the PLO was not met with European disapproval, as Allen and Pijpers write, arguing that such a cool reaction would be 'completely unthinkable' in a reverse scenario of Israel being invaded in the same way (to say nothing, one may add, of something similar to the Sabra and Shatila massacres happening to Jewish-Israeli citizens) (Allen and Pijpers 1984: 243).

Recognition of Palestinian rights, the authors wrote, has always been 'instrumental' and derivative of more 'fundamental' interests (Allen and Pijpers 1984: 242ff.). This chimes with much of the analysis laid down so far. As we have seen, the FRG consistently recognised the Palestine question only as means towards other ends. In the postwar period, when German reparations helped in building the Israeli state, the FRG was, of course, aware of the fact that the state they helped to construct was created on the basis of the displacement of another population. However, in a time of population transfers all over the colonised world and postwar Europe, there was no incentive to recognise the plight of a displaced people which did not have the means to make its situation heard. The first moves towards the Palestine question, in terms of publicised humanitarian aid to refugees, were a function of the FRG's interest in mending relations with Arab states after 1965. And so it was for Western Europe after the 1973 Arab–Israeli War. The gradually evolving position towards the recognition of a Palestinian right to 'self-determination' in a 'homeland' was shaped primarily in the context of European–Arab relations after the oil boycott. That these goals are still awaiting their realisation must not least be explained by pointing to the deeper, shared European interests in a stable Middle East, the pivotal role of the transatlantic relations, and an interest in safeguarding Israel as a key ally in the region, interests which ultimately shape the European engagement with the Palestine question.

10

REALIGNMENT
THE GRADUAL SOOTHING OF GERMAN–ISRAELI
TIES AFTER 1982

Throughout the 1980s, we can observe a soothing of German-Israeli ties and German realignment with US policy in the Middle East, which occurred within broader political changes in the region. The Iranian Revolution of 1979 led to a shift away from the Israel–Palestine conflict arena, while the effects of the Second Oil Shock in 1979 were gradually offset, for Europeans, by the diversification of oil imports. Oil prices stabilised as both Tehran and Bagdad increased output to finance the Iran–Iraq War. The Palestine question would only impose itself again on the United States and Europe with the Palestinian uprising, the Intifada, in 1987. Nevertheless, the calming of German–Israeli relations was not a smooth process.

The Begin-Schmidt controversy

Following the turmoil of the Venice Declaration, the so-called 'Begin-Schmidt controversy' rocked German-Israeli relations from 1981 to 1982. During his chancellorship (1974–82), Helmut

165

Schmidt refrained from reciprocating Israeli Prime Minister Yitzhak Rabin's visit to the FRG in 1975. Schmidt's declared intention to follow a German Middle East policy 'no longer [...] overshadowed by Auschwitz' (Wolffsohn 1993: 33) found expression in German plans to sell Leopard II tanks to Saudi Arabia. In the course of the controversy, Begin framed Schmidt as an unrepentant Nazi. German public opinion, sometimes in problematic terms, stood behind the chancellor, who himself refrained from escalating the war of words. However, the tank deal with Saudi Arabia was never realised. According to historian Shlomo Shafir, this was partially due to SPD opposition in the Bundestag. The principle of German commitment to Israel played a key role in this opposition (Shafir 2008; see also Leber 2015).

Schmidt's personal change in position towards Israel is representative of a wider German shift. Schmidt's attitude towards Israel after the 1967 war was positive, not least because he saw Israel as a staunch defender of western interests in the Middle East. As such, Schmidt's favourable inclinations cooled with the duration of Israel's occupation of the territories captured in the war (Shafir 2008).

The Begin-Schmidt controversy is generally remembered as a personal animosity. Begin remains the only prime minister in Israeli history with personal experience of the Shoah (Wolffsohn 1993: 32). He had lost his parents in the genocide and fought the German army as a member of the Free Polish Army. Moreover, Shafir pointed to Schmidt's suppression of his own biographical involvement in the Nazi past. Throughout his life, Schmidt clung to the legend of the Wehrmacht's clean sheet. Shafir remained diplomatic when pointing to the hardly credible nature of Schmidt's insistence that he 'could not have known'. In 2014, German journalist and scholar Sabine Pamperrien published a book, based on sound archival study, which established that Schmidt 'was partly contaminated by Nazi ideology' (Pamperrien

2014). A previous leader of the Hitler Youth and career officer of the Wehrmacht must have known of the war of annihilation and the Wehrmacht's involvement in the Holocaust. That it took until 2014 for a German scholar to assess the relevant files reveals a societal hesitancy in tarnishing a figure so important to postwar national identification.

It is of course almost impossible to disentangle trauma from instrumentality in political speech. Clearly, Begin's emotional antipathy towards Schmidt was driven by the fact that the latter had actively supported a regime which had killed Begin's family and exterminated his people. Trauma formed part of Begin's politics, and his opposition to Schmidt stood in continuity with his opposition to the Reparations Agreement of thirty years earlier. It is, however, difficult to say how Begin would have dealt with the question of German reparations had he been in power at the time. It is probable that the needs of consolidating the state and integrating it into the West would have overridden his personal convictions. And while during his premiership Begin retained a sharp rhetoric towards Bonn, he never endangered the substance of the political and military relationship with the FRG (Leber 2015). Still, in 1952 as well as in 1982, his historical-psychological anti-German stance was based on a somewhat more realistic view of German postwar society than the erstwhile views represented by Ben-Gurion.

The 1982 Israeli invasion of Lebanon

German–Israeli relations reached a new low on the societal level in the context of Israel's 1982 Lebanon invasion. The massacres against Palestinian refugees in the camps of Sabra and Shatila, perpetrated by Christian Phalangists under the Israeli army's oversight, led to a deterioration of Israel's image in the German public. To the degree to which images of Israel were already based on projections, they could easily be reversed for purposes of guilt relief. The 'Nazification' of Israel by parts of the German public in 1982 is regularly cited as illustrative of antisemitism on the German left and the political mainstream. The perceptions of Israel which came to the surface in the FRG at the time indeed testified to an inability to cope with the past (Büttner 2003: 114f.; see also Kloke 2008 or Wetzel 1983). Begin's need to depict Arafat as a latter-day Hitler hiding in his Beirut bunker, and an existing need in Germany to identify Israeli Jews as Nazis, correspond insofar as historical memory leaves alone neither victims nor perpetrators, or their succeeding generations (see also Segev 1993: 400).

The Venice episode and the Begin-Schmidt controversy showed that the policy of 'normalisation' had now truly run its course. The diplomatic fallout of the Venice Declaration demonstrated that Israel's toleration of German political moves towards Palestinians ended when it came to the crucial questions of Palestinian self-determination and the political legitimacy of the PLO. Israel's reactions against the German crossing of these limits consisted fundamentally of scandalisations drawing their ammunition from the Nazi past (see also Büttner 2003: 152f.). European positioning on the Palestine question from the aftermath of the 1973 Arab-Israeli War until the Venice Declaration crystallised a shared European view that a two-state solution, based upon a division of the territory along the 1967 demarcation, would be the desirable outcome of the Israel–Palestine conflict. However, Bonn's declaratory engagement came without the corresponding substantial actions. For example, in contrast to France, Austria or Italy, the FRG had not given any significant diplomatic concessions to the PLO until that point (Jäger 1995: 5). The PLO would become an acceptable diplomatic actor for the FRG only after the mutual recognition between Israel and the PLO as per the Oslo Accords.

German memory culture and politics: From closure to redemption?

The SPD lost power to the Conservatives in 1982, with Helmut Kohl's CDU/CSU-FDP coalition going on to govern until 1998. In its framings and political usages of the Nazi past, the era of Kohl marked a return to that of Adenauer. In contrast to the postwar period, however, Kohl's policies of how to remember and how to forget the past were the stuff of public contention in a democratically matured republic.

Born in 1930, Kohl claimed for himself a *Gnade der späten Geburt* ('grace of late birth'). Although a member of the Hitler Youth, he was too young to have taken part in the war and genocide. To the embarrassment of the left of centre segment of the German public, he repeatedly spoke of this 'grace', even during his first visit to Israel in 1984. Kohl's delegation on this trip included Kurt Ziesel, a former Nazi and extreme right-wing journalist in the postwar republic.

The irritations Kohl provoked in Israel were no clumsy mistakes, but politically calculated discursive acts meant for a German home audience. However, Kohl's policy of making peace with the past showed itself most clearly not in Israel, but in the German soldier cemetery of Bitburg. On 5 May 1985, Kohl and US President Ronald Reagan laid down floral wreaths at the concentration camp and cemetery at Bergen-Belsen. Bergen-Belsen was only included in the program visit at the last minute, following protests in the United States. The majority of the German public stood behind Kohl. The shared US–German ceremony to mark the fortieth anniversary of German capitulation to the (western) Allies led Reagan into a grave political crisis. Next to soldiers of the Wehrmacht, members of the Waffen-SS were also buried in Bitburg. These had participated in one of the worst civilian massacres in occupied France in the village of Oradour-sur-Glane. The leader of the CDU faction in the

Bundestag, Alfred Dregger, escalated tensions with a letter to US senators opposing the visit, in which he argued that the Wehrmacht and the Waffen-SS had fought a common western war against the Red Army (Rabinbach 1988: 1821f.).

Brandt's key foreign policy act concerning the Nazi past was the genuflection in Warsaw. Schmidt's chancellorship was less iconographic, with no comparable event to mark it. The Bitburg visit, in contrast to Brandt's genuflection, was an act of normalisation, not expiation. The gesture of US-German reconciliation turned Wehrmacht soldiers, Waffen-SS members and American soldiers into equal victims of war. In other words, those who were murdered in Bergen-Belsen were symbolically put on par with the Waffen-SS.

In the Bundestag, only the newly-formed Green party opposed the visit to Bitburg. The party's emergence from the 1970s new social movements was also reflected in its views of the Israel-Palestine conflict. A visit by a Green party delegation to Israel and the Palestinian territories created an outrage, as it took an unequivocally pro-Palestinian position (Weingardt 2002: 314-15). The visit was heavily criticised in both Israel and Germany, marking the party with the stain of antisemitism, which it has since managed to wash off, in tune with its gradual political de-radicalisation and move towards the centre of German parliamentary politics.

While Kohl was blurring the lines between victims and perpetrators, a societal shift had already begun to take place – a shift that would gradually put the Holocaust into the centre of a newly emerging German memory culture and politics.

In his bestselling book about the year 1979 in global history, the German historian Frank Bösch allocates one of his ten chapters to the German reception of the American TV miniseries *Holocaust*, which aired in West Germany that year, and was watched by over a third of the German population. They were confronted, many for the first time, with how the Holocaust was perpetrated with the helping hands of ordinary Germans, not by a small, criminal elite. After the airing of each episode, a panel of historians answered viewers' questions live on television. Callers expressed their surprise, outrage and sadness. For the first time in postwar German history, a national debate about the Holocaust took place. In 1979, *Holocaust* became the 'word of the year' in Germany and part of the national vocabulary.

It is not entirely without coincidence that a German translation of historian Raul Hilberg's monumental study *The Destruction of the European Jews* was published shortly after the airing of *Holocaust*. And it speaks volumes about West German defence mechanisms that this first study of the Holocaust had not seen the light of day in Germany for almost thirty years. Hilberg finished the first version of his work in 1955, but it took him five years to find an American publisher. Ironically or not, it was then the Munich Institute for Contemporary History, founded under postwar Allied rule, which prevented translation of the book at least twice (Aly 2017). When it did appear in 1982, it was under a fringe press of the New Left and ignored by German historians and the public. Only in 1990, thirty-five years after Hilberg first completed his study, was the book published in a three-part paperback edition of the renowned Fischer Press.

The long, arduous publishing history of Hilberg's study came to an end almost simultaneously with the *Historikerstreit* ('historians' quarrel') in the German public sphere about the singularity of the Holocaust. To the right stood historian Ernst Nolte, the debate's instigator, claiming that the Holocaust was not of a different quality than the crimes of the Soviet Union and, moreover, interpretable as a pre-emptive measure against possible similar crimes by the Soviet Union against Germany. For Nolte's provocations to have been successful, it would have required a society in denial about its past. That this had by then less been the case is evidenced by the fact that Nolte's left-liberal opponents around the philosopher Jürgen Habermas, at least in retrospect, decisively carried the day. Today, one may say that almost the polar opposite to Nolte's argument predominates in publicised opinion: that the Holocaust was both singular and German.

However, looking at 1980s West Germany, another event stands out as probably the most consequential one for the subsequent development of German memory culture and politics, namely the influential speech by German President Richard von Weizsäcker on 8 May 1985, three days after the Bitburg visit. Meant not least as a counterpoint to the Bitburg affair, it was received positively internationally, including in Israel. Weizsäcker's speech was accepted throughout German society because it addressed groups of diverse political and cultural affiliation, serving an integrative function (Beljan and Lorenz 2015). Its greatest importance lay in calling 8 May not a day of defeat, but of liberation. This was of course untrue: the majority of German society did in fact experience the end of the war as a defeat. Ex post facto reframing it as liberation, however, was a rhetorical move with a double effect. First and most important, it established unequivocally the criminality of the Nazi regime. Weizsäcker also made clear that the crimes of Nazism were visible to the German public at the time. In doing so he refuted the ever familiar excuse that one 'could not have known' – a step of major importance. Secondly, however, reframing 8 May as liberation could also be interpreted as a subtle opening for new forms of victim identification – how, after all, do you liberate a perpetrator? Accordingly, Weizsäcker only named as perpetrators the Nazi leadership. The majority of German society appears as guilty only because it chose to ignore the crimes, not because it actively or tacitly helped in committing them.

Yet the core of Weizsäcker's speech was something else. Quite literally, it was an offer of national redemption through memory. It was an offer not to be refused, and an offer which has more recently become the subject of critical interventions into German memory culture (see especially Czollek 2018; Jureit and Schneider 2010). Weizsäcker's promise of redemption, which he sought to derive from a rabbinical tradition, presaged the shape of German memory culture to come:

> The Jewish nation remembers and will always remember. [...] 'Seeking to forget makes exile all the longer; the secret of redemption lies in remembrance.' This oft quoted Jewish adage surely expresses the idea that faith in God is faith in the work of God in history. Remembrance is experience of the work of God in history. It is the source of faith in redemption. This experience creates hope, it creates faith in redemption, in reunification of the divided, in reconciliation. (Bundespräsident 2015)

27 January 2015 marked seventy years since the liberation of Auschwitz. On that day, one of Weizsäcker's successors, former German President Joachim Gauck, said in his commemorative speech that 'there is no German identity without Auschwitz' (Bundespräsident 2015). That this statement had by then become the new normal in Germany is rooted in Weizsäcker's speech of thirty years earlier. Following unification, the rationality of redemption would ground Germany's Israel policy as well.

PART IV

New Commitments and Failing Prospects

Germany, Israel and Palestine from Unification Until Today

IN THE DECADES following unification, Germany intensified its political and military commitment to Israel. In 2008, Chancellor Angela Merkel declared in front of the Israeli Knesset that Israel's security is part of the German *Staatsräson* ('reason of state'). The years after unification also saw the rise and fall of the Israeli-Palestinian Oslo peace process, into which Germany had invested considerable hope and financial support. Germany still adheres to the language of the Oslo process, despite the fact that the 'reality on the ground' is now far removed from it.

The general picture of German–Israeli relations after unification is one of ever-closer cooperation in all fields. Trade between the two countries increased in volume over the whole period studied in the following chapters, with Germany remaining Israel's second-largest trading partner (after the

United States) until 2009, when this position was taken over by China. Reflecting the size of both countries' economies, Israel was less important to Germany, moving from fortieth to forty-seventh place on the list of German importing countries (Asseburg and Busse 2011: 699 & 705). Scientific cooperation is another important factor in bilateral relations, one that overlaps with the field of military relations. To this picture we may add the various forms of youth exchanges, organised predominantly from the German side. The more recent Israeli hype about Berlin has also attracted some scholarly attention (see Oz-Salzberger 2016). Overall, the Federal Republic of Germany (FRG) remained Israel's second-most important ally after the United States. The German involvement in the Oslo process (1993–2000) and its afterlife needs to be analysed with this in mind.

Both Germany's recommitment to Israel and its role in the peace process occurred within a wider frame of international relations, transforming as they did after the Cold War from superpower competition to American global hegemony. This hegemony was starkly impressed upon the Middle East in the 1991 Gulf War, which re-established a permanent, direct American military presence in the region, asserting American control over Gulf oil flows. The FRG hesitated to participate militarily, preferring instead to help payroll the war effort.

The incorporation of the German Democratic Republic (GDR) and the lifting of the Iron Curtain returned Germany from a hyper-dependent western frontline state to its position of Europe's quintessential 'middle power', prompting fears of German nationalism and power ambitions abroad.

In the first instance, the FRG's deepening of relations with Israel should be read as a means to express continued adherence to 'the West'. German political elites felt this need not least in order to demonstrate their distance from the Nazi past, following European misgivings about unification (see also Barkawi and

Laffey 2006: 341). That Germany opened its doors to post-Soviet Jews in the 1990s needs to be explained also in this light (see also Brenner 2010).

Maybe more importantly still, Germany's recommitment to the Jewish state needs to be understood also with regard to the changes in German national identity after unification. Over the years following unification, German efforts at publicly commemorating the Holocaust have greatly increased, eventually becoming integral to liberal constructions of German national identity. As the introduction to this book already described, to the German political elite, close relations with Israel serve as an indicator for a 'mastering of the past'. The following chapters first assess the German recommitment to Israel and then turn to the question of how this recommitment played out in the Israeli-Palestinian conflict.

11

RECOMMITTING
GERMANY'S ISRAEL POLICY AFTER UNIFICATION AND THE COLD WAR

Nationalism is a modern phenomenon pretending to be rooted in the eternal depths of history. The term 'reunification' conveys such a quasi-natural sense of belonging, suggesting the coming together of what had previously only been artificially separated. Had it been up to the rest of Europe and the crumbling Soviet Union, German separation may well have continued. After all, incorporating the GDR would again turn the FRG into Europe's dominant power. Due to organised pressure from expellees, Chancellor Kohl even stalled on the question of Germany's Eastern borders. Poland, lying economically shattered on the other side of the Danube, was disquieted.

Just as nobody in the 1980s would have predicted the fall of the Berlin Wall anytime soon, nobody expected unification to be completed less than a year after 9 November 1989. Washington approved of unification on the condition that the enlarged Germany was to remain in the North Atlantic Treaty Organisation (NATO), for which, interestingly, there was only some 20 per cent support among the West German population.

The Soviet Union, busy managing its demise, was ultimately won over in a humiliating exchange for a German development loan. The rest of Europe, meanwhile, had no choice but to acquiesce (Wiegrefe 2010).

Unification and the Gulf War: Impact on German-Israeli relations

In Israel, the unification of East and West Germany evoked the spectre of the past. Continuing the rhetorical anti-German line of his party, Likud Prime Minister Yitzhak Shamir was one of the few politicians to utter his reservations in public: 'The great majority of the German people [...] decided to kill millions of Jewish people' and if it becomes 'the strongest country in Europe, and maybe in the world, they will try to do it again' (Wiegrefe 2010: 2). Israeli apprehensions concerned the possible revival, as clearly indicated by Shamir, of rabid German nationalism and antisemitism. Secondly, it feared that the anti-Israeli political stance of the GDR would affect Germany's future foreign policy (Hestermann 2014).

With regards to the latter issue, the GDR had gradually softened its adversarial position since the mid-1980s. This development was accelerated under its last governments led by Hans Modrow and Lothar de Maizière. After the March 1990 elections, the newly constituted GDR parliament asked 'the Israeli people to forgive us the hypocrisy and hostility in the GDR's official policy towards the State of Israel, to forgive us the persecution and degradation to which Jewish citizens were exposed in our country even after 1945' (cited in Voigt 2008). With unification occurring soon after, this change, accompanied by a distancing from the Palestine Liberation Organisation (PLO), was ultimately of little import. As unification occurred on western terms, Israeli misgivings about East German influence turned out to be unwarranted. And although the question of

German nationalism after unification is more complex, it ultimately turned out in Israel's favour too.

Contrary to Israeli apprehensions, a united Germany on western terms showed itself to be more beneficial to the Jewish state than two countries locked in a systemic opposition, of which the question of Israel–Palestine formed part. The Kohl government initially displayed irritation at Israeli misgivings about unification; a flurry of visits by German officials sought to calm the turmoil, and Bonn promised increased support (Pallade 2005: 136). However, much more than unification, it was the 1991 Gulf War which placed the Holocaust squarely back into the centre of German–Israeli relations.

Several German companies had previously contributed to Iraq's chemical weapons program. Scud rockets fired on Israel during the first days of the war, combined with Saddam Hussein's rhetoric of annihilation, unavoidably fused into a Holocaust–Germany gas association. Tom Segev, who finished *The Seventh Million* in 1991, describes the image of Israelis with gas masks in sealed rooms as an alienating, traumatic experience, closing his book with this sentence: 'Never before had so many Israelis shared so Jewish an experience' (Segev 1993: 507).

As immediate redress for German industrial participation in Iraq's ballistic and chemical weapons program, the German foreign minister travelled to Israel and signed a cheque for humanitarian aid to the value of 255 million Deutsche Mark (DM; approx. €82 million today). Two American Patriot missile batteries stationed in Germany were also delivered. Israel handed Germany a detailed wish list of military goods. The most important items delivered in the Gulf War context were eight Fuchs tanks, a grant for an improved Patriot battery and three Dolphin-class submarines, which were delivered at the end of the decade (Pallade 2005: 151-5). Israel had in fact already planned to buy these specifically designed submarines in the 1980s, but needed to pull out of a signed deal for financial reasons. The Dolphins were to radically transform the capabilities of Israel's navy.

Israeli military analyst Reuven Pedatzur summed up the whole episode well:

> Ironically enough it was the ruler of Iraq, Saddam Hussein, who rescued the navy by attacking Israel with Scud missiles during the Gulf War of 1991. This assault, which occurred on the background of information about the massive German assistance to Iraq in developing its missiles and also in building its chemical and biological arsenal, led the German government to try to 'compensate' Israel, and improve Germany's image in the West, by agreeing to build Israeli submarines in a German shipyard in the summer of 1991. (Pedatzur and Shiek 2002)

The Dolphins also bridged a production gap in Germany. With domestic orders lacking due to unification and Gulf War costs, deliveries for Israel were still justifiable, thus helping maintain production stability in the naval sector of the German arms industry (Nassauer and Steinmetz 2003: 21). The importance of keeping production steady should be seen not only in purely economic terms of preventing unemployment or indirectly subsidising an important sector of German industry. The German arms industry is also politically relevant. The stronger the German arms industry is, the higher Germany's potential degree of military independence. Moreover, arms exports are an instrument of German foreign policy. Lastly, large-scale projects such as the Dolphin submarine construction allow for the testing of new technologies, helping Germany to keep its qualitative, competitive edge in the naval-military sector.

Military relations after unification: An overview

As German political analyst Leandros Fischer observed, the Dolphin episode during the Gulf War marked a return to the original quid pro quo character of German–Israeli relations under Adenauer and Ben-Gurion (Fischer 2019: 30). Delivering submarines to Israel in order to offset German companies' participation in the Iraqi missile program is indeed comparable to buying Israeli silence over former Nazis in the German administration, as happened, for example, during the Eichmann trial (see above). According to German military analysts Otfried Nassauer and Christopher Steinmetz, the delivery of the first three Dolphins constituted the most costly German arms export to Israel up to that point. The costs cannot be calculated with absolute certainty; however, Nassauer and Steinmetz are sure that the FRG took over at least 85 per cent of the production costs for the three submarines, amounting to about DM1.1 billion. They estimate that the remaining 15 per cent was paid in kind by German arms procurements in Israel, thus sparing Israel from touching its state budget (Nassauer and Steinmetz 2003: 20). International affairs scholar Yves Pallade estimated German aid to Israel in the Gulf War context to total DM2 billion, only coming second to that extended to the United States, which received German contributions to the value of DM8 billion, roughly equivalent to €2.58 billion today (Pallade 2005: 153).

In 2005, on its last day in office, the Red-Green coalition government signed a deal for two more submarines, following the three submarines delivered in the 1990s after the first Gulf War. In 2006, the delivery of a sixth was agreed upon. Germany contributed a third of the costs to those latter three Dolphins. One of the main purposes of the submarines was deterrence against the Iranian nuclear program: it is an open secret, ritually denied by Germany, that the submarines can be equipped with nuclear missiles, having been especially equipped with enlarged cannon tubes for this purpose (Nassauer and Steinmetz 2003). Germany, by providing the submarines, is simultaneously able to ease eventual pressures of being dragged into direct military confrontation with Iran during a potential Iranian–Israeli war (Aruch 2012: 16).

At the time of writing, a deal over three further submarines is pending due to a corruption scandal reaching all the way into Israeli Prime Minister Benjamin Netanyahu's office. It is unlikely that the deal will be cancelled, however. In 2015, Berlin agreed to the sale of four corvettes, which will be used to protect Israeli gas extraction off the Gazan and Lebanese coast. Initial considerations of making this sale dependent on Israeli concessions regarding settlement construction were dropped, with Berlin carrying 27 per cent of the costs (Bergmann and Stark 2017; Nassauer 2017).

One auspicious characteristic of large-scale projects such as these is that Germany either practically pays for them, as in the case of the first three submarines, or substantially contributes to their financing, as in the case of the subsequent submarines and the corvettes. A popular explanation for this would be that Germany subsidises the arming of Israel out of historical guilt. It is true that German subsidies are partly identified with an idea of 'reparations'. This is the case especially for the first three submarines delivered after the 1991 Gulf War. Much more explicitly from the Israeli side, German subsidies for the submarines are also seen as being in continuity with the 1952 Reparations Agreement (Aruch 2012: 17). As political scientist Oz Aruch demonstrates on the basis of Wikileaks files, the Israeli government sought to link the submarine deliveries to what it saw as outstanding reparations from East Germany, which had refused payment in 1952 (Aruch 2012: 17). However, as should already be clear from the above, there is no single, causal explanation for the German military commitment to Israel, whose gains, even if not always on a directly observable material level, are generally mutual.

Another factor one needs to consider in this context is the pivotal military relationship between Washington and Jerusalem.

Israel's military budget depends to a crucial degree on US contributions. Since the mid-1980s, annual US military and economic aid to Israel has stood at about $3-3.5 billion (Odlum 2002: 2). Israel is the highest recipient of US military aid, and the only nation among those recipients that is allowed to invest part of this aid into its own military industries. Since Israel's military coffers are mostly filled with American dollars, buying arms from Germany would be akin to an indirect American purchase of German arms. This is part of the reason why Germany is largely responsible for financing large projects such as the Dolphins. The towering nature of the American–Israeli military relationship also means that German–Israeli military relations tend to operate in the spaces not filled out by the former relationship, such as the naval sector.

Other forms of military cooperation

In 1991, the German Federal Ministry of Defence replied to a parliamentarian's request that 'since the beginning of our cooperation with Israel, it has been the practice of all governments to keep this cooperation informal, out of the public eye' (cited in Nassauer, Steinmetz and Pallade 2002), a statement some believe to be exemplary of the whole duration of military cooperation. Available information is difficult to verify, however, as only leaks and political scandals brought much of the current knowledge about the more recent military relations to light (Nassauer and Steinmetz 2003: 5).

The confidentiality of German–Israeli military relations frustrates descriptive and analytical ambitions. Furthermore, the problematic characteristics of German public discourse turns this into a particularly unwieldy topic, enabling facile scandalisation on a perforce thin and unreliable empirical basis. Mordechay Lewy, a former Israeli ambassador to Germany, commented drily on

Pallade's somewhat bulky 2005 study that had the author focused on intelligence and military cooperation only: 'such a work might even have been a commercial success, given the public's insatiable appetite for anything associated with the Mossad and secrecy' (Lewy and Newman 2007: 138). The question, of course, is whether this is the sort of success one wishes to look for, especially in Germany. On the basis of the available empirical evidence, authors such as Shpiro, Nassauer or Pallade all take care to emphasise the mutual benefits of military cooperation, in order not to feed into perceptions whereby Germany constantly gives and Israel ceaselessly demands.

Apart from the large-scale submarine deliveries covered above, military and intelligence cooperation occurs on a steady, everyday basis. Military, intelligence and scientific exchanges are closely interlinked. Pallade, who is very supportive of what he has observed, has provided an exhaustive account of this cooperation throughout the 1990s and early 2000s. He finds military and intelligence to be stable, built on mutual trust, and working 'quite independently of the current political situation and changes in government in both countries' (Pallade 2005: 243).

Building upon the empirical work of Shpiro (as discussed in the previous chapters), Pallade places high importance on intelligence cooperation, which, as with military relations, he finds to be on par with intra-NATO cooperation (Pallade 2005: 128), with Mossad known to have operational freedom on German territory (Pallade 2005: 244). The Federal Intelligence Service, for example, has played a mediating role in prisoner and corpse exchanges with Lebanon's Hezbollah (Pallade 2005: 90-101). Overall, intelligence relations have covered information exchange about third countries (for example, on armament levels) and, as Pallade writes, '[j]oint actions against terrorism and rogue states', such as the German banning of the Hamas-linked al-Aqsa charity in Germany in 2002 (Pallade 2005: 86-8).

Military cooperation between the two countries covers joint research and development, armament provision and production, as well as training between the two armies (Pallade 2005: 136-240, Nassauer and Steinmetz 2003). As one example of joint development and research, Nassauer and Steinmetz, who emphasise the importance of Israel's delivery to the FRG of Soviet-made weapons for inspection after the 1967, 1973 and 1982 wars, recount how, in a reciprocal gesture, Israel was given large stockpiles of GDR weaponry and military material after unification. These camouflaged deliveries, which were accidentally uncovered by the Hamburg coast guard, proved helpful to research and development, leading to the German and Israeli modernisation of their air-to-air missiles (Nassauer and Steinmetz 2003: 12).

The delivery of components for integration into larger weapon systems is another dimension of cooperation. For example, Israel's Merkava 4 tanks are equipped with German 400 MTU motors (Nassauer and Steinmetz 2003: 23). As component deliveries do not appear in Germany's official arms export statistics, published since 1999, they can easily be kept secret.

Relations also deepened regarding the more direct industry-to-industry cooperation. As Pallade writes: 'On an industrial and commercial level, partnerships with German arms producers allowed the Israelis to get a foothold in the [European Union's] industrial defence sector, which was largely closed to outsiders through bilateral agreements and internal alliances' (Pallade 2005: 241f.).

As regards cooperation between the two armies, training of Israeli soldiers on German weapons is, of course, a corollary to the German production of these weapons for Israel, yet the interlinking of the Bundeswehr and Israel Defence Force (IDF) is deeper and more complex than that. In a rare occurrence, leading figures behind this cooperation partly lifted the veil in a German radio interview in 2002. Israeli general Reuven Benkler, who at the time worked as the military attaché at the Israeli embassy in Berlin, stated in the interview:

> There are few secrets between the two armies. Everything is on the table and we almost permanently and directly share everything with the German army about what we learn from the practical experiences of our army. And we are an army with very rich experience. The German army is one of the few which gets a comprehensive picture of us: how we fight, what we do, what we learnt from our missions and what we did right. As a result, the Bundeswehr takes part in everything we develop [...] in all insights and consequences derived from praxis. (cited in Deutschlandfunk 2002)[1]

Benkler's German counterpart, Helmut Willmann, had previously served as the inspector of the Bundeswehr and counted among his many medals an 'honorary citation' from the IDF, the first non-IDF soldier to receive one, for his efforts in bringing the two armies closer together. Willmann explains his ambitions also in historical terms. For example, a tour of Yad Vashem is obligatory for German army delegations visiting Israel. After having 'experienced Yad Vashem', German soldiers were then to 'also experience the Israeli army':

> I was [...] fascinated by the [Israeli] army. This is an army that is always in action. This is a country that basically always fought for its physical existence. This means: We, who were at that moment, in the 1990s, changing the German army from a peacetime army to a combat army, were of course looking for contacts with armies that had more experience than we did. And from a professional point of view, I was very impressed with the Israeli army. And I knew that cooperating with the Israeli army is of course of professional benefit to us. (cited in Deutschlandfunk 2002)

Not wanting to disclose more precisely what this cooperation entailed, Willmann stated that it is comparable in level only with that of the American, British or French armies, estimating the

Bundeswehr to be the 'most important partner of the Israeli army after the U.S. army.' Benkler confirms the impression of close relations: 'Relations are on a daily basis. Without disruption. These are working relations between allies' (cited in Deutschlandfunk 2002).

At the time of this interview (spring 2002), media reports surfaced claiming Germany was withholding the delivery of important material to the IDF because of the Israeli crackdown on Palestinians during the Second Intifada (2000-05). In contrast to France or Britain, this was an act not legitimised by the German government in terms of human rights or its own federal export laws, which would have made an embargo necessary. Chancellor Schröder, however, ended the debate early in the Bundestag in April 2002: 'I want to say it very clearly: Israel gets what it needs for maintaining its security, and it gets it when it needs it' (cited in Nassauer, Steinmetz and Pallade 2002). That the Israeli defence minister had openly threatened Germany with a new Holocaust debate may have helped (this, after all, is the flip side to the rehabilitation or whitewashing argument). Yet, as the statements of Benkler and Willmann quoted above indicate, the German military establishment seemed to have by then already acquired a sufficient self-interest in military relations and in seeing the IDF 'in action'.

12

MEMORY POLITICS AFTER UNIFICATION
HOW ISRAEL BECAME PART OF THE GERMAN *STAATSRÄSON*

Shortly after unification, a RAND analysis for the US army on German post-Cold War foreign policy noted that the question of Germany's 'geopolitical maturation' was related to historical-psychological and cultural factors. These factors explained Bonn's military abstention from the 1991 Gulf War (Asmus 1992: vi). In a tone of surprise, the study observed:

> [...] the almost total lack of any discussion about German strategic interests in the Gulf and how they should guide policy. Instead, the terms were set by such issues as whether Germans 'owed' the United States political support in the Gulf in return for American support during the unification process, or whether Germany's historical obligation toward Israel required it to act in a specific fashion. German policy was often passive – a sharp contrast to Bonn's role in Europe when vital German interests were at stake. (Asmus 1992: vi)

This observation also applies today. The question of German power has received renewed attention since the 2008 financial crisis led to the Eurozone crisis. When imposing tough austerity measures on Greece, Germany ignored Greek protestations over perceived German harshness and arrogance. Berlin also brushed off reparation demands for the German occupation of Greece during World War II. While the Nazi past plays no role in Eurozone policy (at least not for Germany), it looms large in German public debates about the Middle East, which are dominated by the sense of historical commitment to the Israeli state.

To understand the deep recommitment to Israel, in terms of both words and action, which occurred in German foreign policy over the course of the 1990s and early 2000s, it is helpful to look at the changes in German memory politics and accordant national identity changes.

The Nazi past as a patriotic project?

Flag-waving Germans, pogrom-like anti-foreigner violence, the national anthem chanted in the Bundestag – it is hardly surprising that unification evoked a Nazi imagery in the eyes of more critical onlookers, especially from outside of the country. As in the German left-wing polemic Eike Geisel wrote at the time, the fall of the Berlin Wall erased the last reminder of what was experienced as defeat in World War II (Geisel 2015: 44), with German nationalism asserting itself more confidently after unification. However, it would be wrong to assume that German nationalism had been dormant prior to the early 1990s. It is much more helpful to look at the transformations of German ideology. The ferocious national identity debates continuing unabatedly after unification still evinced an unaccounted-for, repressed postwar guilt, demonstrating that the question of how to construct a German national identity vis-à-vis the Nazi past remained unsettled (Zuckermann 2004; Evans 1997).

One prominent answer to this question was given by Martin Walser during a prize ceremony at the Paulskirche in 1998. The

German novelist spoke out against what he saw as the 'moral cudgel' of Auschwitz, and braced himself against the 'permanent presentation of our shame' (Walser 1998). Receiving much public support for his call to put a closure to the Nazi past, Walser was valiantly opposed by Ignatz Bubis, then president of the Central Council of Jews in Germany.

Looking back, the will to bury the past has not become the defining feature of German memory politics after unification. True, in recent years, calls for closure have made a loud and raw re-emergence from the private to the public sphere with the rise of the far-right Alternative for Germany. Yet, at least for the time being, German memory politics has taken a different route, one that harks back to the Weizsäcker speech addressed previously. Remembering the Nazi past, or, more specifically, remembering the Holocaust, has become key to how the German nation imagines itself as a community.

The initial debates about the Berlin Holocaust Memorial indicate how 'Auschwitz' can be integrated as a positive part of German national identity. Gerhard Schröder, the German chancellor who oversaw the memorial's construction, wanted it to be 'a place where one likes to go' (Leggewie and Mayer 2005). The German historian Eberhard Jäckel, one of the key figures behind the memorial, publicly said on the fifth anniversary of its construction that 'some in other countries envy the Germans for this memorial' and that it helped Germans 'to walk upright' again (cited in Thünemann 2013). These comments may sound absurd. Yet what they express is a somewhat crude, dialectically tinged phenomenon that gradually emerged after unification: that of German national pride in how the country was confronting its past.

During the 1990s, German integration of the Holocaust into governmental purposes reached a peak in the Red-Green coalition's justification for German participation in NATO's intervention in Kosovo. As Foreign Minister Joschka Fischer famously argued during a Green Party convention in January 1999, Germany was to participate not despite of Auschwitz, but because of it. According to Fischer, the Balkan wars transferred upon Germany a responsibility to combat fascist and Nazi tendencies not only at home, but also to act militarily against similar such phenomena when they made their return to Europe. That the first German military intervention since 1945 was legitimised in the name of Auschwitz by the Green Party's foreign minister, who had similarly based his prior pacifism on opposition to the Nazi past, may be seen to demonstrate how this past could be turned from an obstacle into a vehicle for military 'normalisation' (see also Hawel 2007). However, interventionism in the name of Auschwitz was not an exclusively German affair. As security studies scholars Tarak Barkawi and Mark Laffey note, western-liberal interventionism of the 1990s defined its legitimacy very much against the historical example of Nazism, reinforcing an 'image of the West as the preventer of genocide and the punisher of violators of human rights' (Barkawi and Laffey 2006: 341). As such, German participation in NATO's intervention and its justification for it was a further form of western integration.

The origins of Staatsräson

There is no direct line between German memory and Middle East politics. The notion of *Staatsräson* illustrates the complex connection between the two. Some years before Merkel's well-known speech to the Knesset in 2008, this notion was originally developed by the Social Democrat Rudolf Dreßler, then German ambassador in Tel Aviv during the Second Intifada. The way in which he lays out this notion in a short essay is representative of a dominant perspective on Israel and Palestine within the German political elite, so much so that it merits a more detailed reconstruction here. Dreßler begins his essay by detailing the horrors Palestinian suicide bombings inflicted on Israeli society. Extrapolating the Israeli death toll, he asks his readers how Germany would have reacted to a comparable situation on its own soil. Dreßler mentions Palestinian deaths during the Second Intifada in only one sentence. The ambassador then moves directly to the Nazi past, explaining that it was the Holocaust which had led him into politics. He then situates his plea for a continued confrontation with the past into the context of German-Israeli relations, which were 'never closer, never better' (German Federal Agency for Civic Education 2005). Dreßler informs his readers that he was the first German ambassador ever to have been invited to the Holocaust Memorial Day ceremony in Yad Vashem. He continues by writing about military relations, recounting how German marine soldiers trained with their Israeli counterparts in a 'friendly' atmosphere, and how he personally acquainted himself with the Israeli military's view of the intifada.

Summarising German-Israeli relations in all fields, Dreßler notes that Israel considers Germany its closest ally after the United States. Even in the military sphere, he adds, relations are as close as with any NATO ally. He ends with an emotional appeal as to why Israel's security should be made part of the German reason of state:

> Never in my life did I have to think about my country's right to exist, even though Germany twice brought the world to an abyss in the past century [...]. No daily threat! No denial of the right to exist! No fight for one's own state! This is why I use the word 'security' as the key term for a constructive rebooting of the Middle East process. The community of states must work for Israel's security [...]. *The secured existence of Israel is in the national interest of Germany, it is therefore part of our reason of state.* (German Federal Agency for Civic Education 2005, emphasis added)

Dreßler's essay takes the Second Intifada as an entry point for his actual topic, which is German responsibility for Israel's security due to the Nazi past. He then proposes to make the security of the strongest military power in the Middle East part of the German *Staatsräson*, a move deeply embedded within Germany's strategic outlook on the region. The Israel-Palestine conflict is historically complex and morally ambiguous; in contrast, there is no ambiguity about the absolute evil of the Holocaust. *Staatsräson* means viewing the Israel-Palestine conflict through the lens of German Holocaust memory.

Staatsräson and the German public

The ritualised ways in which the German government talks about its historical commitment to Israel contrast with the emotive, troublesome debates in the public and private sphere about Israel and Palestine. The majority of German society does not seem to share its government's commitment to the Israeli state. All of the more recent major studies on this subject – from those of the Anti-Defamation League to the Bielefeld-based studies on 'group-focused enmity' – indicate that German support for the 'special responsibility' towards Israel is waning. Moreover, roughly 15 to 20 per cent of respondents in these studies hold more easily identifiable antisemitic attitudes. Referring to the available large-scale surveys, Asseburg and Busse summarised in 2011 that less than half of the German population feel Germany should be specially committed to Israel. This attitude can be found especially among the younger generations, East Germans and voters of the left. Given the German framing of Israel's security as being part of the reason of state, it is interesting to note that the image of Israel deteriorates especially when Israeli violence escalates, such as in the wars on Gaza (Asseburg and Busse 2011: 711).

This divide between societal attitudes and governmental policy at least partially harks back to Adenauer's decision to pay reparations to the Israeli state, which similarly was not demanded for by the majority of German society. Any explanation of the government/public divide today has to take German antisemitism after 1945 into account. However, this divide is not particular to Germany alone, but can be observed across western countries, including the United States.

In this light, one problem with the predictable German governmental framing of its relations with Israel is that it evades basically all of the thorny political questions the relationship raises. German officialdom does not address the cognitive dissonance that seems to trouble rather a lot of Germans, but rather accentuates it. The German government's basic image of Jews and of Israel is a passive one: it is that of 'the Jew as victim'. The core idea of Zionism was to overcome this image and its underlying European historical reality. The images produced by the Israel-Palestine conflict, however, are those of occupation, siege and warfare between the powerful and the powerless.

German postwar societal attitudes towards Jews and Israel and how these relate to the questions of *Aufarbeitung* and national identity is a fascinating topic, but one for another book (and already much discussed elsewhere anyways). It is quite clear, however, that exoneration can find many forms in Germany. As is often noted, it showed itself very transparently in the anti-Zionism of parts of the earlier German left. It also reveals itself in rather embarrassing over-identifications with Israel and all things considered Jewish – a phenomenon much more widely spread in Germany than anywhere else in the West (see Stern 1992).

At the end of the day, the most important realm of memory is not international relations, solemn governmental pledges or even public rituals. The work of memory hits hardest where it hurts most: the family (Frie 2017). The pronounced public memory culture since unification contrasts sharply with the long-standing absence of introspection in many German families (Welzer, Möller and Tschuggnall 2002). At the end of the day, the problematic relationships Germans have with their past will not be solved in the Middle East, as much as many would like them to.

Staatsräson in action: The Iranian nuclear program and deterrence made in Germany

In her 2008 speech to the Israeli parliament, Angela Merkel spoke more about Iran than the Palestinians. This is understandable given that Israel can rather easily manage the military threat Palestinians are able to pose, whereas the story of the Iranian nuclear program is a different, potentially existential one. The chancellor admonished Iran's 'threats' and 'slander' against 'Israel and the Jewish people', saying that the Iranian nuclear program is foremost a threat to the safety and existence of Israel (Merkel 2008).

At the time of Merkel's speech, then Iranian President Mahmoud Ahmadinejad provoked international outrage by engaging in Holocaust denial and openly talking about ending Israel's existence. In 2006, Tehran convened an international conference to 'review' the Holocaust, starring an array of lunatics, including the French Holocaust denier Robert Faurrison, a German member of the modern Nazi Party, the National Democratic Party of Germany, and ex-Ku Klux Klan leader David Duke.

Iran's nuclear program, particularly under Ahmadinejad's presidency, had put Germany into an uncomfortable position, as it has relatively strong economic interests in Iran. According to the Auswärtiges Amt (AA), 30 per cent of Iranian industrial infrastructure is German-made, and German exports to Iran far outweigh Iranian imports. For economic reasons alone, Berlin has been interested in a multilateral and negotiated solution to the nuclear program, putting its weight behind the nuclear deal negotiated in 2015 chiefly by the previous American administration under Barack Obama (as well as the European Union [EU], China and Russia). When the Trump administration pulled out of the agreement in May 2018 and reinstated economic sanctions, German-Iranian trade was slashed by 50 per cent. Current German unhappiness with the confrontational approach of the United States is not due to economic considerations alone, however. Officials in Berlin do believe in the need for de-escalation, as well as a negotiated and multilateral, long-term and peaceful solution to the nuclear problem.

Looking at German–Israeli relations in the context of Iranian nuclear ambitions raises the following question: why did Israel so vociferously oppose the Obama administration during the negotiations leading up to the 2015 agreement, but largely refrained from criticising policymakers in Berlin at the time, who were very invested in the deal? Part of the answer lies in the fact that the United States is their more important ally, while another part lies in the submarine deliveries described above. The German military commitment to Israel should be understood as giving material expression to the German commitment to Israel's security, as officially expressed by Angela Merkel in her 2008 speech. This impression was also related to me in a number of background talks and by two German interviewees wishing to stay anonymous. These interviewees were intimately involved in German–Israeli relations: both worked in Israel, one in an official function for the German government.

Indeed, nothing exemplifies better the idea that the FRG stands in for Israel's security than by providing it with nuclear-capable submarines, given that they provide Israel with immediate second-strike capacity against Iran: if Iran were ever to attack

Israel with a nuclear strike, there would be swift retaliatory answer from the sea. To use the language of the Cold War, destruction would be mutually assured. As is further shown above, there is a relatively high likelihood that the FRG helped finance Israel's nuclear program. In this light, providing Israel with the means of deterrence against Iran would simply mean continuation of German support for Israel's nuclear capacities.

The resolve with which newly founded Israel pursued its always unlikely nuclear program cannot be explained without the trauma of the Holocaust. It is little wonder then that Germany's contributions to Israel's nuclear capacity are viewed by many in Israel as forms of making amends. As a *Jerusalem Post* editorial in 2006 stated on the occasion of the second submarine agreement:

> The stance of the German government underlines a radical transformation for that country's people. While their grandparents' generation perpetrated the Holocaust, and the previous generation paid for the Holocaust with reparations to its victims, the current generation is helping prevent a second Holocaust by providing the [IDF] with some of the most important defensive weapons systems in its arsenal. As far as corrective steps go, that's a huge one. (cited in Achcar 2010: 395).

While this obviously does not represent the overall Israeli view on the question, the editorial nevertheless radicalises the logic espoused by Ben-Gurion in his 1960 conversation with Adenauer, when he argued for German help in building the Israeli state as one step towards the 'impossible' goal of repairing the damage of the Holocaust. Here, however, it seems as if reparations for the 'original' Holocaust in the form of arms deliveries is possible, since they are seen to prevent a 'second Holocaust'.

By contrast, the German government seeks to avoid public debate about military ties with Israel (see also Nassauer and Steinmetz 2003). One reason for this is a German culture of relative military restraint as it evolved after the experience of defeat in two world wars. However, the issue is more complicated in the case of weapons deliveries to the Jewish state. The controversy about the late author Günter Grass' poem *Was gesagt werden muss* ('What must be said') illustrates these complications well.

The poem, which appeared in 2012 in the *Süddeutsche Zeitung*, as well as being published in Italy and Spain, was about the German submarine deliveries, Israel and Iran. It ostensibly sought to criticise German weapons deliveries to Israel which would enable it to 'destroy an Iranian people'. Grass' poem was swiftly criticised by the majority of German public commentators as antisemitic, his genocidal attributions to Israel read as a form of perpetrator/victim inversion by somebody who had only shortly before admitted his participation in the Waffen-SS during the last moments of World War II. Critics of Grass found his depiction of Israel as a danger to 'world peace' to be antisemitism in code form, while his allusions to a German taboo on the critique of Israel was criticised as summoning the idea of a Jewish lobby powerful enough to stifle German debate. Frank Schirrmacher, co-publisher of the *Frankfurter Allgemeine Zeitung*, a liberal-conservative German newspaper, wrote possibly the most eloquent and convincing critique of Grass (Schirrmacher 2012).

It is unnecessary to revisit an altogether predictable debate over Grass' memory, especially one which integrates seamlessly into similarly structured pre-existing discussions. Grass' heavy-handed, moralistic poem, which is difficult to read without an acute sense of embarrassment, had nothing new to add to the questions it purportedly sought to tackle, and could easily be interpreted in terms of what in Germany and Austria is referred to as 'guilt-defensive antisemitism'. More interesting than the poem were the reactions it stirred in German public debate. If subsequent reactions are one indicator of the quality of a critique, the poet was unable to pass the minimal threshold of avoiding applause from the extreme and neo-Nazi right, as well as, one may add, from the Iranian regime. However, while Grass was largely ostracised in the public sphere, he received support from private citizens. This is another indication of the complicated divide mentioned above: that between ritualised public commitment to Israel and an emotive public debate about Israel and Palestine.

What the Grass controversy ultimately shows once more is that debates about German foreign policy in the Middle East are often started from, or if not immediately move towards, the terrain of national identity and the Nazi past. While Grass found that German submarine deliveries made possible a genocide against the Iranian people, *The Jerusalem Post* editorial thanked Germany for aiding Israel in preventing an Iranian genocide of the Jews in the Middle East. In other words, projections and politics prevent a more rational debate.

Chancellor Merkel refrained from commenting on Grass' poem, preferring not to enter the debate it provoked. By contrast, it is revealing to ask what types of debates the German government actually wants concerning its relations with Israel. The year 2015 provides a good illustration in this regard. That year saw both the fiftieth anniversary of German-Israeli diplomatic relations, as well as the seventieth anniversary of the liberation of Auschwitz and German surrender to the Allied forces. It was for the anniversary of diplomatic relations that celebrations and events were organised in Germany throughout that year, despite the event only resonating with a small minority of the German public. Moreover, the anniversary did not arouse any interest in Israel beyond that which was demanded by diplomatic courtesy. Events in Israel were co-organised with Germany and paid for with German money. Indeed, as disclosed by a number of anonymous interviewees, including German government officials involved in the matter, the anniversary was a rather German affair in Israel, too (see also Zimmermann 2016: 49). As the above quotes from *The Jerusalem Post* editorial indicate, the dynamic is opposite in the case of the submarines, which are openly and publicly framed as a continued form of German reparation. Indeed, this opposite dynamic shows rather well what Germany also seeks to invest in when contributing to Israel's military force: Jewish gestures of absolution. This German desire gives birth to notions such as 'friendship' and 'reconciliation', so preponderant in the German governmental framing of bilateral relations, yet so absent from Israeli discourse.

13

GERMANY IN THE TERRITORIES
PERPETUATING THE OCCUPATION?

This chapter is about how the German recommitment to Israel, in terms of national identity and political-military support, played out in the arena of the Israel-Palestine conflict. Following secret negotiations, the Oslo Accords, signed in 1993 and 1995, aimed to set in motion a peace process in line with United Nations Security Council Resolution 242. The PLO explicitly acknowledged Israel's right to exist, while Israel recognised a Palestinian 'right to self-determination', accepting the PLO as a legitimate partner in the negotiations over the 'final status issues', most importantly borders, settlements, Jerusalem and Palestinian refugees. Those final status issues were supposed to be solved within five years, yet the parties did not come to an agreement on any of them. The first Oslo Accord created the Palestinian Authority (PA) in 1994, a body that still exists today, which was tasked with Palestinian 'self-governance' in the limited, densely populated areas under its control (Areas 'A') in occupied Palestinian territory (oPt).

Looking back at the Oslo Accords today and what came of them, it is easy to forget the initial euphoria and hope they gave rise to. Germany threw itself into the peace process with great relief. It is fairly clear that a vision of Palestinian statehood, albeit underspecified, existed in Germany and Europe. And despite the fact that the Oslo Accords never stipulated such a result, the European view at the time was that a Palestinian state would be the 'necessary, desired, and inevitable outcome of the peace process' (Pardo and Peters 2010: 17).

An initial problem one confronts when writing about the German role in the Oslo Process (1993–2000) and its afterlife is that the two-state discourse the German government upholds is detached from the reality of Israeli sovereignty over the oPt. This divide incidentally relates to a methodological problem encountered when researching for this book. German aid workers and political representatives interviewed in both the Palestinian territories and 'Israel proper' generally offered me two options for the interview. I could either have an 'official' version, which I was allowed to record, or an 'unofficial' one, which I was not. This indicates the heightened sensitivity around the topic, as interviewees hesitated to risk transferring locally generated knowledge to the German public sphere. Although the Oslo framework officially guides German foreign policy towards the conflict, interviewees displayed irritation or laughed when I mentioned the Oslo terminology as though it still held any meaning.

The methodological problem of transparency, incurred by always having opted for the 'unofficial' interview version, is somewhat offset by the fact that after direct Israeli–Palestinian negotiations under the auspices of former US Secretary of State John Kerry failed to produce a result in 2014, only few illusions about the prospects for a two-state solution continued to exist in the academic and policy-advisory literature (see for example Asseburg and Busse 2016; Lovatt 2017; Thrall 2017). In this light, it is interesting to take note of a German-language introductory overview of the Israel-Palestine conflict, published in 2016. The book's two authors work for the Stiftung Wissenschaft und Politik (SWP), a major German foreign-policy think tank which advises the Bundestag and the federal government on international politics. Interestingly enough, there seemed to have existed a demand in the German book market for such an overview. Clearly, the facts the authors present are not really central to the German public debate about the matter. In their last chapter, they describe what they see as a 'one state' reality of unequal rights in Israel and Palestine. Aware that there are presently no prospects for a two-state solution, they outline the current situation, well-known to any observer of the conflict, of direct and indirect Israeli control over the Palestinian territories. While short on the grossly unequal access to economic resources, the authors describe the system of unequal civil rights to have developed in the oPt, a system which they suggest fits the definition of apartheid in international law (Asseburg and Busse 2016).

Nevertheless, the Christian Democratic Union (CDU)/Social Democratic Party (SPD) coalition treaty of early 2018 reiterated the German commitment to a two-state solution. Echoing the Oslo Accords, the coalition parties called for all final-status issues to be 'solved in negotiations'; the treaty also repeats the traditional criticism of further settlement construction, viewed as contradicting international law and the two-state solution (Christian Democratic Union of Germany 2018).

The German relief

Why does Berlin still speak in the language of Oslo, when reality has long surpassed it? Has Germany played a distinct role in the Oslo process, and if so, how can we understand this role?

The mutual recognition between Israel and the PLO afforded considerable relief. As CDU parliamentarian Karl Lamers put it at the time, Germany's 'special relations with Israel' had on occasion led to a 'painful discrepancy' because 'it seemed as if the wellbeing of Israel was connected to the continued homelessness of the Palestinians' (Bundestag 1993). A cross-party consensus existed suggesting that in order to maintain the historical momentum, proponents of the peace process would require generous support and detractors needed to be discouraged. The only voice that was more cautious about the Oslo process was that of Hans Modrow of the Party of Democratic Socialism (PDS), one of the last overseers of the Eastern German regime's demise, under whom, as described above, the GDR's anti-Israel stance was partially reversed: 'We understand the worries of those who fear that the compromise now achieved will be set as the status quo, blocking further steps towards a comprehensive peace agreement in the Middle East' (Bundestag 1993). In order to signal German support for the Oslo process, Minister of Foreign Affairs Klaus Kinkel accordingly announced German support for Israel's association with the EU, and a willingness to further deepen bilateral relations.

As a consequence, Germany was to become the driving force behind the 1994 Essen Declaration, which defined EU-Israel relations as 'special' (Wildangel 2018: 50). According to political scientist Patrick Müller, Bonn's engagement was 'critical' for the drafting of the EU-Israeli Association Agreement in 1995, whereby Germany 'functioned as Israel's chief advocate regarding preferential trade and access to research and technology programs in the EU' (Müller 2011: 393). The Association Agreement was a direct reward for the Oslo Accords, which seemed to create positive movement in a key area of European foreign policy (see also Hollis 1997: 20).

Kinkel then spoke of the need to further increase German aid for the oPt, which was already exceptionally high in per capita terms. This financial aid, discussed below, was supplemented by bestowing some of the symbolic insignias of statehood on the

PLO. Arafat was invited to an official visit, the PLO representation in Bonn was upgraded to diplomatic status, and the FRG was one of the first western countries to open a representative office in the Palestinian territories (Müller 2011: 393f.; Frangi 2002).

The European and German role in the Oslo process

With the onset of the Oslo process, Europe was invited as a funder into a course of action it did not decide upon. Indeed, funding the Oslo process was the only role Europe was able to play in what was then the Middle East's central conflict arena. The American and Israeli policy of keeping the Europeans out of political negotiations between Arab states, Israel and the Palestinians extends from the 1978 Camp David Agreement up until the 2014 negotiations under the auspices of US Secretary of State John Kerry. Instruments such as the 'Middle East Quartet' (composed of the United States, Russia, the UN and Europe) are the exception that proves the rule, primarily created to absorb European political ambitions (see also Persson 2015: 119).

By putting Europe on the political sidelines of the Oslo process, the United States sought to reserve the role of an 'honest broker' to itself. Israel, quite rightly, expected a much more forthcoming stance from its American ally than from the EU countries. As Rouba al-Fattal summarised, Europe's role as a funder 'was not only needed but also welcomed by all parties. For their part, the Palestinians were in dire need of assistance to kick-start their economic activities, whereas the Israelis and Americans were happy that the 'Old Continent' would pay the bill while being alienated from further political aspirations in the region' (al-Fattal 2010: 7; see also Hollis 1997: 21). It is rather telling that Germany had phased out its annual 'development loan' paid to Israel by 1996 and re-channelled it, with Israeli approval, towards the newly formed PA.

This financial nature of Europe's role has led to the now clichéd characterisation of Europe as a 'payer' and not a 'player'. The German government's conception of the role it should play in the 'peace process' was formulated by Chancellor Gerhard Schröder upon assumption of office in 1998 as such:

> We cannot play the role of godfather in the peace process between Israel, the Palestinians and the neighboring Arab states [...]. This role falls to the U.S. and to the international organizations. However, we Europeans can and should contribute to making the peace process irreversible by targeted economic aid, by opening the markets and by providing infrastructure. This is how we can meet our historical responsibility – especially and directly for Israel and for peace. (Bundestag 1998)

While Schröder's description of the German role neatly mirrors Anne Le More's often-quoted characterisation of donor engagement that 'the US decides, the World Bank leads, the EU pays, the UN feeds' (Le More 2005: 995), it also conveys a specifically neoliberal understanding of political progress. Here, economic aid, provision of basic state structures and market openings are, so it appears, expected to quasi-naturally lead to economic growth, which in turn would make peace 'irreversible'. It is neoliberalism with a German touch, as Schröder embeds this market-based approach to peace within German historical responsibility.

Accordingly, Germany has been a key driver within the EU for an 'economic' approach to peace- and statebuilding (Müller 2011). The EU has been the largest donor to the Palestinian territories since the Oslo process and during the post-Oslo period of Palestinian 'statebuilding', with Germany having contributed most to EU aid (Müller 2011: 393). The FRG is also a major bilateral donor, with the occupied Palestinian territories having received some of the highest German per capita distributions: to date, German aid has amounted to €1.1 billion (German Ministry for Cooperation and Development 2016).[1]

By the mid-1990s, the majority of EU aid to the territories had already shifted towards covering the PA's running costs and providing humanitarian relief (Le More 2005: 992). Between 2000 and 2006, support for the PA and humanitarian aid (including contributions to the United Nations Relief and Works Agency [UNRWA]) together dwarf annual disbursements for infrastructure or institution building (Musu 2010: 132-3).

Contrary to Schröder's vision, economic aid did not make the peace process 'irreversible'. What it effectively did was to uphold the institutions of Oslo, without realising the expected aims of the peace process. It is fair to say, based on numerous talks with German political representative and aid workers 'on the ground', that economic aid has so far only propped up a process and not led to peace. As a result, the focus on humanitarian relief and upkeep of the PA effectively means subsidising the Israeli occupation.[2]

The Oslo process started to derail in the mid-1990s with the Goldstein massacre in Hebron, the assassination of Israeli Prime Minister Yitzhak Rabin, and suicide attacks by Hamas targeting Israeli civilians. The return to government of the Likud in 1996 led to European frustrations about the discontinuation of the peace process. This corresponded with Germany markedly increasing its commitment within the EU towards this process, emphasising the importance of Israeli security and close alignment with both Washington and Tel Aviv (Müller 2011: 394).

Increased German engagement in the late 1990s also sought to counteract wider European frustrations with the first Netanyahu government, and 'to avoid a situation in which Berlin would face pressure to adapt to an increasingly ambitious European policy that did not reflect its national preferences and that did not pay sufficient attention to its special allegiance to Israel' (Müller 2011: 395). It is in light of the German government's goal to preserve the status quo and to keep alive the process that one needs to read the 1999 Berlin Declaration, in which Europe openly stated its support for the creation of a Palestinian state for the first time, albeit in a somewhat non-committal wording: 'The European Union reaffirms the continuing and unqualified Palestinian right to self-determination including the option of a state and looks forward to the early fulfilment of this right' (European Parliament 1999). Drafted in close cooperation with Washington and accompanied by the strong backing of Germany, which held the EU presidency at the time, the main aim of the declaration was in fact to prevent Arafat from unilaterally declaring a Palestine state, with the text emphasising that any such avowal must be the outcome of negotiations. Viewing the declaration as one step that could actually be forthcoming for a Palestinian state in the future, Israel nevertheless protested harshly against it, evoking the Holocaust in doing so (Pardo and Peters 2010: 17).

After Camp David: Consequences of the Second Intifada

As demonstrated above, it was during the Second Intifada that the FRG elevated its commitment to Israel to the level of *Staatsräson*. There are concrete political consequences to this intensified commitment. Following the Second Intifada, Germany would adopt the Israeli line on the question of security, and would start to engage in Palestinian 'statebuilding' after the American expression of support for a Palestinian state in 2002. Developments after the 2006 Hamas victory in the elections of the Palestinian Legislative Council (PLC), the PA's parliament in the oPt, illustrate this double-strand of German policy. Hamas' win at the ballot box has different sources, reflecting increased funding, improved organisational capacity and, importantly, the boosting of the Islamic fundamentalist variant of militant anti-Zionism following Israel's unconditional retreat from Lebanon in 2000 in the face of the Lebanese Hezbollah. It is important, however, to also read the victory as a rebuke to the failed model of liberation that the PLO stood for in the eyes of the majority of the oPt population – a corrupt PA, engaged in policing its own population on behalf of the occupier, from which it was unable to wrest even minimal concessions (see also Haddad 2016: 273f.). Having deemed the elections free and fair, the EU chose not to recognise their outcome, a move which unsurprisingly dealt further blows to its credibility in the region (Wildangel 2018: 53). The FRG adopted almost verbatim the Israeli position on the electoral victory of Hamas (Asseburg and Busse 2011: 703), and was 'a key advocate within the EU of isolating the Hamas-led government' (Müller 2011: 396f.). Moreover, during the first Gaza War (2008–09), the Merkel government adopted the Israeli line, drawing criticism from the opposition in the Bundestag, and consequently also rejected in its wake the Goldstone Report, which found both sides responsible for war crimes.

Thus, instead of entertaining the idea that the rise of Hamas may be related to the failure of the Oslo process to bring about viable economic and political change to Palestinians, Germany became a driver for salvaging this very process by sidelining Hamas and focusing on the 'West Bank first' approach, in which there was still a 'partner' with whom to do 'statebuilding' (Asseburg and Busse 2011: 708).

How is one to evaluate European statebuilding efforts after Oslo, given that a Palestinian state seems more unrealistic than at any point since the end of the Cold War? The perennial critique levelled against European engagement in the Palestinian territories, which can be heard in everyday development discourse 'on the ground', as well as in the policy advisory literature, is that the declared European commitment to a Palestinian state is not backed up by more concrete political measures. While the EU does not fail to regularly reiterate its support for a Palestinian state, so the criticism goes, it certainly does not use its political and economic leverage to enforce it. René Wildangel, a former director of the Ramallah office of the German Green Party's Heinrich Böll Foundation in the West Bank, has summarised this gap between declaration and action in a 2018 SWP analysis. He illustrates it with four examples: the European approach to Palestinian reforms under the Fayyad government; its approach to Israel's claims over Area C; the differentiation question; and the Gaza blockade.

After the West Bank and Gaza split, the EU became a staunch supporter of PA Prime Minister Salam Fayyad's government (2007–13) in Ramallah. The former official of the International Monetary Fund embodied the European approach to 'technical' statebuilding along neoliberal lines. Yet, while the EU was ready to lavish Fayyad with financial support, it was not prepared to politically recognise a Palestinian state, even after the UN deemed the PA's governance institutions fit for statehood (Wildangel 2018: 53f.).

As for Area C (representing 60 per cent of the West Bank's territory which fell under Israeli 'interim' control in the second Oslo Accord of 1995), a 2011 EU report was cognisant of the fact that without this territory, a Palestinian state could only consist of 'islands' (see EU Directorate-General for External Policies 2013). Likewise, the World Bank asserts that the Palestinian economy is losing $3.4 billion annually by not having access to Area C (cited in Wildangel 2018: 56). The majority of Area C is closed to Palestinian access, with only 1 per cent of the area theoretically open for Palestinian construction (although the approval rate for building permits is practically zero). Moreover, sections of the Israeli right have become vocal about officially incorporating large parts of Area C into Israeli state territory (Wildangel 2018: 57). According to the UN Office for the Coordination of Humanitarian Affairs, Israeli destruction of Palestinian buildings peaked in 2016, including destruction of some EU-funded projects (United

Nations Office for the Coordination of Humanitarian Affairs 2016). It is thus no surprise that most German development work focuses on the 'islands' of Areas A and B.

It is whilst the Israelis demolished EU-funded structures in Area C that the EU debated preventive steps. In the background, the AA prepared a 2012 working paper that developed a number of benchmarks for Palestinian development in Area C, yet concluded by emphasising that 'these ideas should be developed with Israel' and that Germany intends to promote a 'non-confrontative approach' towards Israel over the area (Wildangel 2018: 56). The results of such an approach are clear: EU practice amounts to statebuilding without a contiguous territory on which the Palestinian state is supposed to be built.

With regards to the question of differentiation, while the EU had always formally distinguished between the territories Israel occupied before and after the 1967 Arab–Israeli War, no practical political consequences have so far followed from this. This was seen to change in 2013 when the EU published 'guidelines' for differentiation, which barred Israeli settlements in the oPt from EU funding. Persson (2018) shows how the guidelines led to a shock within the Israeli government, which saw them as potentially leading towards a full-blown anti-Israeli boycott policy. However, a return to diplomatic normality soon followed. One example suffices: the 2013 guidelines were linked to Horizon 2020, an extensive EU program for scientific cooperation, from which universities and research institutions beyond the Green Line would have to be excluded. Interestingly enough, the Horizon 2020 agreement allowed Jerusalem to insert a clause stating that Israel did not have to recognise the guidelines. This, of course, defeats the purpose of the exercise of differentiation, effectively turning occupied territories into disputed ones.

As regards Gaza, the ever-deteriorating conditions of life in the sealed-off strip are not in dispute: only a few hours of electricity per day, a dysfunctional sewage system leading to a severe shortage of potable water, an aid-dependent economy, regularly re-destroyed in wars since 2008–09, an entire generation growing up without experience of life outside. In a report written in 2012 (in other words, before the last Gaza War of 2014), the UN predicted Gaza to be 'uninhabitable' by 2020. A further UN report written in 2017 found that living conditions for the 2 million inhabitants of the strip were worsening 'further and faster' than originally predicted in 2012.[3]

While the Bundestag called for a lifting of the blockade in 2010, and although the EU and the FRG have pledged €568 million for Gaza's reconstruction after the devastations of 2014, there have been no attempts to ease the restrictive import regulations, let alone a lifting of the blockade (Wildangel 2018: 61f.).

Following from the above, an often-heard recommendation in the European policy-advisory literature is that Europe should back up its dedication to a Solomonic division of the land with some of the economic instruments at its disposal. For example, the above quoted SWP analysis from 2018 argues that Germany and the EU should act more forcefully towards differentiation at the Green Line, while simultaneously extending security guarantees to 'Israel proper', trying to assuage Israeli apprehensions and pre-empt the charge of antisemitism (Lintl 2018; see also Hollis 2004). An unconvincing and rather skewed argument one can sometimes hear in this context is that because Germany commits to Israeli security, it should act against Israel's will to force the two-state solution into reality, as such a solution would be the best guarantee of Israeli security.

However, enforcing differentiation along the Green Line (for example, by economic sanctions or boycott measures) would mean a direct confrontation with a close ally over a Palestinian population which has nothing to offer in return. The FRG has repeatedly made clear that it rules out anti-Israeli sanctions, most notably boycotts. It is practically impossible to imagine a scenario wherein Germany would engage in punitive measures against Israel to keep open the possibility of a Palestinian state in the West Bank and Gaza. It is equally improbable that Germany would step to the head of the negotiating table with parameters for a two-state solution. Evidently, if Germany would back up its declaratory commitment to a Palestinian state with economic measures, it would incur the harshest Israeli protest, which would paint Germany in the very same colours it has tried to wash off in its relations with Israel, namely those of its Nazi past. Secondly, the clear preference Germany has shown for its relations with Israel over those with Palestinians throughout the Oslo peace process is equally linked to Berlin's interest in securing a key western ally in the region. This, in turn, seamlessly integrates into the FRG's overriding transatlantic orientation. On the other hand, German economic and political withdrawal from the Palestinian territories would mean defunding Palestinian governance structures and effectively dissolving the Oslo framework. This would starkly expose the underlying reality of Israeli control over the territories, as well as the system of unequal political and economic power this entails. Germany does not want to be seen supporting such a situation. For lack of better options, then, the German government upholds the idea of a 'negotiated two-state solution' and engages in Palestinian 'statebuilding'. Doing so under the unaddressed conditions of the occupation and the settlement project, however, rather serves to entrench those conditions than working towards Palestinian self-determination in an independent state.

CONCLUSION

Germany's relevance to modern Jewish history is existential. Germany meant death to European Jews; it also meant life to Israel. This is written with a descriptive purpose and not in a balancing, redemptionist sense. The Federal Republic of Germany (FRG) played a key role in the early consolidation of the Israeli state. West German support to Israel was at its most crucial when the FRG was still most immediately marked by the Nazi past. This fact is largely explicable by the structure of exchange that is specific to the relations between these two countries: that between whitewashing and statebuilding. This structural convergence of interests, which those two states were so compelled to fulfil for one another, explains what seems incomprehensible on a different, individual level: namely the fact that the state which integrated so many survivors and relatives of victims and the state which incorporated so many Nazi criminals and countless enablers in its institutions could forge such important relations at such an early point. Indeed, when viewed from this perspective of mutual statebuilding, both symbolic and material, current German evocations of a 'miraculous reconciliation' appear as posterior embellishments of a political exchange, embellishments which are, in fact, already part of this very exchange.

The West German state, a creation of the Cold War, relied on the 'reintegration and amnesty' of former Nazis into its administration as well as into the functional elites of society. Overall societal functioning rested not least on mechanisms of repression and guilt evasion. Thus, the turn to Israel forcibly blurred the structural continuities of the Nazi era in postwar Germany. Its primary function was to signal the existence of a 'new' Germany that could not yet exist, one that had repudiated its immediate Nazi past.

The carefully delimited forms of contrition the postwar FRG engaged in were primarily a function of foreign policy, oriented towards regaining German sovereignty by firmly embedding it in the 'West'. This means that without tacit American pressure, and without Israeli insistence on some form of making amends, much less would have come out of Germany in terms of reparations, restitution and confrontation with the past.

On the Israeli side, the question of why Israel sought relations with the FRG and the question of German support are almost synonymous. One third of Israel's founding population consisted of Holocaust survivors. Most Israelis were related to or knew others who perished. This was a country built by traumatised refugees from Europe; by those who Nazi Germany would have killed had it had the chance to do so. What other reason than obtaining the means for its consolidation could this state have had for entering relations with the FRG, the state in which the majority of the perpetrators lived unscathed? It is the fact of German economic, financial and military support – about which the German political discourse tends to remain remarkably silent – which explains the 'miracle of reconciliation', a trope that, by contrast, is so prominent in German political discussions about Israel. Beyond the question of material interest, the Israeli rationale for accepting German support can be summed up as such: if antisemitism is an ever-persistent fact of history, and if building the Israeli state constitutes the best (or only) effective response against antisemitism and persecution, then it is possible to accept substantial support from the postwar FRG, a state that had incorporated war criminals, countless Nazi Party members, profiteers and enablers in its institutions and society.

Until 1965, the FRG was the only country among the western powers to extend to Israel all three forms of support: economic, financial and military. The Reparations Agreement of 1952 was a crucial contribution to Israel's economic modernisation. The 'Operation Business Friend' loan, extended until 1965, was an important financial injection to the value of 644,8 million Deutsche Mark. After the 1956 Suez War, Germany became a key military ally of Israel. In contrast to French weaponry, equally important to Israel's military build-up, the weapons and correlated material provided by the FRG came free of charge.

During this formative period of the Arab-Israeli conflict, the FRG was thus more important to Israel than France, Great Britain or even the United States. The military force displayed by Israel in the decisive Six-Day-War could not have been developed to this level without the FRG's prior support. The United States fully took over its role as Israel's pivotal external backer only after 1967, when the latter's status as a regional hegemonic power had already been demonstrated, due to German help.

While whitewashing was a specifically German reason for supporting Israel, one should not forget that the Cold War informed Germany's Israel policy in a more concrete sense as well. The archival evidence shows clearly that Israel, especially after the 1956 Suez War, was supported as a bulwark against Arab nationalism and Soviet influence in the Middle East. Israel, to reiterate the words of Adenauer to Ben-Gurion in March 1960, was a 'fortress of the West' (cited in Blasius and Jelinek 1997: 337).

The fact that German support lost its crucial nature for Israel after 1965–67 can be seen in the ways in which the next round of Arab-Israeli warfare unfolded. In the 1973 war, as FRG territory was used for American resupplies of Israel and German military support contributed to Israel's naval superiority, the war's outcome was more or less determined by the two global superpowers. The loss of German importance to Israel thus needs to be understood relative to the exceptional nature of the US-Israeli military alliance. After the 1965–67 transition period, the FRG assumed the role of Israel's 'second-best friend', which it holds until today. The 'Operation Business Friend' loan was transformed into a more regular annual development loan, which later merged into German support for the Oslo process. The FRG became Israel's most important backer within an integrating Europe, notably in terms of trade relations. Military and intelligence cooperation was institutionalised, while joint research and development, component deliveries, information exchange about Soviet weapon systems and other forms of cooperation formed a stable undercurrent of bilateral relations.

After unification, German commitment to Israel increased. The comparatively well-known submarine deliveries, decided upon in the context of the 1991 Gulf War and still ongoing until the time of writing, have dramatically enhanced Israel's naval military strength. The 2015 decision to supply Israel with four corvettes to protect its Mediterranean gas extraction, moreover, demonstrates Germany's commitment to upholding Israel's military and economic power status in the region. Like the growth in memory culture, this renewed commitment needs to be read as one means to exorcise the Nazi past in the context of dramatic German power expansion.

The question of German power in international politics remains tied to the question of how Germany positions itself towards the Nazi past. This linkage between power and memory, created with the 1952 Reparations Agreement, remains the deeper nexus from which Germany's Israel policy derives its purpose and orientation.

In conclusion, scholarship and public debate about the Arab-Israeli conflict and international relations of the Middle East need to pay more attention to the German role in the region. The historical importance of Germany to the Middle East is usually hidden from view. The renewed relevance of the 'German question' in international affairs suggests that it might not only be of academic interest to make this importance more visible.

Antisemitism, racism and whitewashing

The postwar foundations on which German-Israeli relations rest to this day are shaky. The earlier history of the relationship raises the question of how and to what extent antisemitic thinking influenced Germany's Israel policy. While Adenauer's ideas about 'Jewish power' are perhaps better known, such thinking influenced German foreign policymaking at least until 1967. During the short transition period of Germany's Israel policy between 1965 and 1967, the FRG sought to 'normalise' its relationship with Israel. The communications between Rolf Pauls, the FRG's first ambassador to Israel and a former decorated Wehrmacht officer on the Eastern Front, and his superiors in Bonn, revealed at least two aspects of antisemitic thinking during this important transition phase. Firstly, Jews tended to be imagined as a powerful, collective, singular figure yielding inordinate power over Germany's position in the world and thus over the German ability to realise key foreign policy goals, such as the claim to sole representation over the territory of both German states. Secondly, and not in contradiction to this perception, German foreign policymakers aimed to 'liberate' their policies towards Israel from the reparations paradigm. This striving was mixed with impatience, even anger, at the Israeli insistence upon German special obligations to it because of its Nazi past.

Moving further, the potentially more interesting question to ask is how the FRG reframed its Jewish 'Other' in its relations with Israel. Amnon Raz-Krakotzkin has written that '[p]aradoxically, the exodus of the Jews from Europe enabled their assimilation into Europe' (Raz-Krakotzkin 2015: 294). The paradox is historically accurate: the FRG allowed Jewish assimilation only after the Jewish exodus from Europe, an exodus for which Germany bears the greatest responsibility. The West German public's reactions to Israel's 1967 victory in the Arab-Israeli War or the admiration of 'Jewish' military power along Prussian-Aryan lines seem bitterly ironic in this light.

Zionism was and remains not least an attempt to emulate European nationalism in order to defend Jews against it. In other words, by adopting the model of the nation state, much like the later anticolonial movements of the twentieth century, Zionism appropriated the tools of Jewish national emancipation from the instruments of its oppressors. Post-Nazi Germany was able to incorporate Zionism into its own national identity not least because the Jewish state resembled so little the Jewish victims of Germany in the Nazi period.

Germany accorded to Israel the power of absolution, and the Israeli state used that power to acquire material support for its own consolidation. As was discussed notably around the issue of the Eichmann trial, the symbolic exculpation of Germany corresponded with the 'Nazification' of Israel's Arab adversaries. This double-move is well entrenched today. There is no doubt that worrying levels of antisemitism in the Arab world attest to a long-term political, economic and cultural crisis of countries comprising the Middle East and North Africa. Nevertheless, the fact that the far right in Germany as well as the wider 'West' can oppose Palestinian opposition to Zionism by declaring it as principally driven by antisemitism is a darkly absurd joke. The trouble is that the German mainstream lacks the adequate sense of humour to fully comprehend it. The 'Nazification' of Arabs and its accordant trivialisation of historical Nazism reached a grotesque peak in 2015, when Israeli Prime Minister Benjamin Netanyahu declared publicly that Hitler had not initially intended to kill the Jews, but that it was the Palestinian Mufti al-Husseini who inspired him to perpetrate the genocide. Had the German chancellor said this (albeit a truly unlikely scenario), she would rightly have been accused of the crudest form of Holocaust distortion and of excusing Nazism. Instead, the German government officially reminded Israel, not without a hint of pride over how well Germany has confronted its past sins, of who the original perpetrator was.

While the Merkel government renounced Netanyahu's statement, the Israeli prime minister's comment was quickly picked up by the far right in Europe and Germany. This is far from surprising, as for the far right to pose as Israel's great defender against 'Muslim antisemitism' is an elegant way of killing two birds with the same stone. Not only does it allow the whitewash of historical guilt and present-day antisemitism, it also legitimises racism against Muslims. It is a transparent operation, but it's working well – which reveals a lot about German society at the present moment.

In May 2019, the German parliament condemned the Boycott, Divestment and Sanctions (BDS) movement against Israel as antisemitic. The Alternative for Germany (AfD) abstained in its vote on that resolution, but only because the party felt it did not go far enough. As the draft resolution put to the floor by the AfD shows, instead of condemning BDS, the party wanted to legally ban it from Germany altogether, and instead of linking it 'only' to antisemitism in general, it wanted to pair it with eliminatory Nazi antisemitism in particular. A rather Orwellian case of antisemites deciding who the antisemites are.

Historical subconsciousness is a tricky thing and there are good reasons for many Germans to invest their political energies elsewhere than in the boycott of the Jewish state. Yet Germany's stance against the BDS movement, a fringe phenomenon in German politics in any case, should not be confused with an infinitely more demanding effort that is still waiting to happen: the concerted fight against the resurgence of *völkisch*-authoritarian fascism in the heart of German politics. In October 2019, an armed German Nazi tried to storm a synagogue in Halle that was unprotected on the highest Jewish holiday of Yom Kippur. Miraculously, the door withheld the gunman for long enough, sparing the seventy worshippers from being massacred. Whilst escaping, the terrorist shot two bystanders. What happened in Halle is the shocking but unsurprising result of allowing the far right back into the centre of German politics.

Overall, the current far-right trend in Europe and the United States points towards the more complex ways in which the majority of German society creates its figurative Jewish and Muslim 'Others'. In Europe, antisemitism and anti-Muslim racism are rising. However, the common struggle against both forms of hatred is a marginal phenomenon. As scholars of antisemitism and racism Ben Gidley and James Renton write, '[a]ntisemitism and so-called Islamism – not Islamophobia – are twin and, in the Western official mind, connected enemies of the West.' They point to the heart of the matter when they ask: 'How can it make sense to talk about a relationship between antisemitism and Islamophobia in this context, in which the figures of the persecuted Jew and the political Muslim are on opposite sides of a war waged by the West?' (Renton and Gidley 2017: 4).

Germany is often applauded and likes to applaud itself for its work of memory, of *Aufarbeitung*, of confrontation with the past.

It may be true that the levels of shame and seriousness with which the Holocaust is publicly debated in Germany compare favourably with the more complacent attitudes towards past crimes that can be found in other western nation states, not to speak of states in full denial of their past atrocities, such as Turkey. However, Germany's memory work has failed to immunise German society against fascism. Whereas German society after 1945 was evidently still marked by National Socialism, the thoroughness of defeat, Allied occupation and the fact of American hegemony over Europe ensured that the FRG would develop along liberal-democratic lines. Of course, history does not simply repeat itself, yet its returns can be worse than farcical. The rise of the far-right AfD has eclipsed the electoral relevance of open neo-Nazism. The thin layer of bourgeois respectability that the party dons to its authoritarianism and *völkisch* racism seems to be enough to turn it into the third-largest party in Germany and a contender for power in the federal states of East Germany. The AfD could yet emerge as the greatest threat to the inner peace of Europe.

Germany, Israel, Palestine

It is difficult to imagine a set of relationships more sensitive than that between the Shoah, Israel and the Palestinian dispossession of 1948. When considering the historical links between Germany, Israel and Palestine, it should be firstly made clear that the 'victims of the victims' trope is problematic in a German context. It seems to suggest a comparability or even equation between Jewish extermination in Europe and the Palestinian dispersal. This trope thus forms part of what in the German context is denoted as guilt-deferring 'secondary antisemitism'.

Israel was not founded because of the Shoah. However, unlike any other event, the rise of Nazism and the Shoah accelerated immigration to the Jewish community in Palestine, increased the

Zionist determination for statehood and confirmed the need for a Jewish state.

For many readers the issue of Palestine within Germany's Israel policy today would first seem to raise moral questions about the extent of historical responsibility. Does German responsibility, assumed for the Jewish state, reach downwards towards those who had to make room for its creation? If you ask the German government, the answer is clearly negative. In her 2008 speech to the Israeli Knesset, Angela Merkel praised Israel's achievements without even once mentioning the occupation.

Looking back, the German government was of course aware of the Palestinian refugees, yet, unsurprisingly, they did not feature in German considerations about the Reparations Agreement of 1952. After all, if the turn to Israel was not due to 'moral' considerations in the first place, why should there have been a moral linkage forged further downwards? Prior to the Israeli occupation of the 1967 territories, West German engagement with the Palestine question can be subsumed under the rubric of 'instrumental humanitarianism'. As such, the 'Arab Palestine-refugees' were not regarded as a political collective. Financial contributions to UNRWA, dating back at least to the mid-1950s, were limited. Aid was given to create goodwill among Arab states and to offset the negative effects of Germany's support of Israel to German–Arab relations. Care was taken, however, to avoid any impression of a German assumption of 'indirect responsibility' for the 1948 refugees.

The unresolved Palestine question forcefully entered Germany with the 1972 attack on the Munich Olympics. The German handling of the Palestinian terror suggests that the FRG's priority was to keep the Israel-Palestine conflict outside its territory, a priority over which Bonn was willing to risk grave diplomatic tensions with the Israeli government. During the remainder of the Cold War, the FRG undertook declaratory moves towards the

CONCLUSION

Palestine question in the context of European attempts to find a common foreign policy stance in the Middle East distinct from that of the United States. The Oslo process (1993–2000) led to palpable German relief, promising to dissolve the 'dilemmas of even-handedness' (Büttner 2003) incurred by needing to navigate between Germany's Israel policy and its wider Middle Eastern interests. The FRG has been a main funder of the Oslo process and of subsequent Palestinian 'statebuilding'. Overall, however, both the 'peace process' and statebuilding efforts have led away from, rather than towards, a two-state solution. Germany continues to invest in its footprint in Palestine, but without making any serious political moves in favour of Palestinian statehood.

For now, it looks as if Germany will continue to play its part in sustaining an untenable situation between Israelis and Palestinians, one it has historically contributed to in so many ways, some of which were examined in this book.

NOTES

FOREWORD TO THE PAPERBACK EDITION

1. London School of Hygiene and Tropical Medicine, 'Gaza: 64,000 deaths due to violence between October 2023 and June 2024, analysis suggests', 10 January 2025, https://www.lshtm.ac.uk/newsevents/news/2025/gaza-64000-deaths-due-violence-between-october-2023-and-june-2024-analysis (last accessed 11 June 2025); *The Economist*, 'How Many People Have Died in Gaza?', 8 May 2025, https://www.economist.com/interactive/middle-east-and-africa/2025/05/08/how-many-people-have-died-in-gaza (last accessed 11 June 2025).

PREFACE

1. The original speech was held in German, but quotes are taken from an official German translation.
2. Countless similar examples could be given. This particular example, however, circulated within international media and in Israel, too. See *Times of Israel* (2018).
3. I owe much of this insight and indeed the formulation of the phrase to my colleague Jan Rybak.
4. See Pallade (2005), Hansen (2002) and Wolffsohn (1993), but also Markus Weingardt's more balanced narrative chronology of

German–Israeli relations, published in 2002. For examples of the 'moral bias' in English-language literature, see Lavy (1996) and Gardner-Feldman (1984).

5. When conducting research on Germany's Israel policy in the AA's archives, it is necessary to pay attention to Nazi continuities in the German foreign policy establishment. The historical enquiry by Conze et al. (2010) on this topic is relatively sparse about Germany's Israel policy. However, their findings on the continuity of Nazi personnel, while unsurprising, are sufficiently disquieting in order to work on the assumption that antisemitic thinking has influenced the formulation of Middle East policy in the AA. One may think in this context of the notion of the 'traditional German-Arab friendship'. It seems plausible to assume that former Nazi regime adherents have found it easy to engage in a more Arab-leaning foreign policy not simply for reasons of 'plain' strategic or economic interests. Indeed, compared with the 'Arabists' of the AA, the German Federal Ministry of Defence and the chancellor's office were much more positively inclined towards Israel. However, as the problem of Nazi continuity (in terms of personnel and traces of ideology) extended to all sectors of the FRG's state institutions, it is difficult to create a binary equation in which an Arab-leaning stance is automatically suspected of antisemitism and an Israel-leaning one is not.

1. THE COST OF WHITEWASHING

1. The interview itself was conducted by Günter Gaus on 29 December 1965 and aired on 4 January 1966. See also Stern (1992: 383).
2. Personal interview with Tom Segev. See also Tempel (1995).
3. Earlier and more critical contributions include those of Lewan (1975) or the edited volume by Abdel Hadi (1973). These works tend to overemphasise the American role, neglecting the space of autonomy the FRG created for itself. For an opposite account which clearly overstretches German autonomous decision-making, see Wolffsohn (1988).
4. Giora Josephtal, who led the Israeli negotiations, wrote to his wife: 'It is all unreal. The Germans are unreal, too, for they represent the best aspects of the Weimar Republic and not the Germans of the past twenty years. And I do not know how much influence they have

in Bonn' (cited in Deutschkron 1970: 57). This encounter between Israelis and Germans in a small suburb of The Hague was indeed surreal. In order to avoid provoking Jewish resistance and outrage at the negotiations any further, the parties had agreed that, for 'optical' reasons, English would need to be the official language of negotiation, knowing that German would quickly be used. As Deutschkron illustrates, during the first negotiations, Felix Shinnar and Otto Küster found out that they both were brought up in Stuttgart, having even attended the same school (Deutschkron 1970: 57). Giora Josephtal and Felix Shinnar were both German-born Jews, escaping the country in 1938 and in 1934, respectively, to settle in Palestine. Like Küster and Böhm, Shinnar was part of the educated upper middle class, holding a PhD in law. Küster and Böhm did not follow the Nazi regime, opposing it to varying degrees. After 1945, both were highly active in the domain of restitution.

5. Translation by Tooze (2011: 68), who cites the letter from Michael Wolffsohn. Erhard's letter is a key document, and also published in the AAPD (1952/108).

6. Voting records can be found at Bundestag (1953).

2. BUILDING ISRAEL

1. The German–Israeli Reparations Agreement may also be seen in the context of the cooperation between the Zionist movement and Nazi Germany prior to the Holocaust. The most far-reaching and contentious form of cooperation, which included occupational retraining and community education (among other things), was the Ha'avara Agreement (Transfer Agreement). In place from 1933 until 1939 (formally 1941), this was a complex mechanism by which capital owned by German Jews could be exported to Palestine in the form of German goods. Zionist cooperation with the Nazi regime stood against a wider Jewish boycott of Germany at the time. Breaking this boycott and creating a less radically anti-Jewish image were the main factors with regards to German cooperation. Prior to full-scale extermination, the Transfer Agreement was one means to make Germany *judenrein*. For the Zionist movement, the agreement was in line with prior policies, whose aim was to build a Jewish state in Palestine. This was (and still is) seen as the only possible defence against antisemitism. Thus,

cooperating with the devil himself was possible as long as it furthered the aim of building the state. The transfer was crucial to the settlement of about 60,000 German Jews in Palestine. The capital provided by the agreement and the fact that German Jews were much wealthier than immigrants from Eastern Europe meant an important contribution to economic development and agricultural settlement at the time. The Ha'avara Agreement is best read as a temporary convergence of interests between the small, essentially powerless Zionist movement and the German state. In other words, Nazi Germany considered Zionist Jews useful for a limited period of time prior to the Holocaust (Nicosia 2008).

3. THE AGREEMENT AND THE ARAB STATES

1. Archival files of the AA tentatively confirm the picture drawn by the above authors. For example, in 1956, Israeli representatives approached a company based in Hamburg which specialised in the salvage of vessels in order to express interest in sunken German World War II submarines. In the same year, the metal and steel company Klöckner reported to the Foreign Office that it was selling 'material' to Israel to which it was not eligible under the Reparations Agreement. Transactions were undertaken via third parties in order to evade open breach of the treaty. The company also stated that it was producing 'very specific weapons' for Israel (PA AA, B130, Bd. 3739, 29 March 1956).

4. AFTER SUEZ

1. The document collection edited by Vogel, which has partially been translated into English (Vogel 1969), illustrates very well that historical sources are rarely neutral. Other works, for example those of Weingardt and Hansen, also make extensive use of this collection, but without noticing what Trimbur called its 'very hagiographic' character regarding the persona of Konrad Adenauer (Trimbur 2003: 267, fn. 14). In fact, Vogel was not merely a journalist, but also temporarily employed by the German secret service when observing the Eichmann trial in Jerusalem. Vogel was highly active in publishing books and movies that propagated Adenauer's version of German-Israeli 'reconciliation'.

5. SHIFTING IMAGES

1. A first step towards polishing the German image was Adenauer's consequent visit to the Bergen-Belsen concentration camp, along with Nahum Goldmann, who advised him to make this visit, in February 1960. Adenauer's hagiographer, Hansen, documents how he heroically undertook the visit even against the advice of his doctor (Hansen 2002: 541). The German weekly *Der Spiegel* reported more soberly at the time: according to the newspaper, the West German government organised the trip to Bergen-Belsen in response to the bad press provoked by the ongoing antisemitic incidents. Reporters of the foreign press were driven to the camp on German army trucks. However, the truck drivers adhered to the regulations of not driving faster than 60 kilometres per hour. As a result, they arrived too late for Adenauer's wreath ceremony (*Der Spiegel* 1960).

2. This translation is based on the one provided by the translator, who gave *Aufarbeitung* as 'coming to terms with'. I have used the term 'working through' here because it is seen to capture better the psychological connotations of *Aufarbeitung* (see also the discussion of the term by Hartman himself). Furthermore, *Aufarbeitung* suggests a process that is constant. As such, it should not be confused with the terms 'mastering' or 'overcoming' the past, which imply closure.

3. The German version states the same, appearing as slightly less blunt due to the indirect form in which the German interpreter stenographed the dialogue: 'Der Herr *Bundeskanzler* sagte, er habe von Anfang an die Bestrebungen der zionistischen Bewegung mit aufmerksamer Anteilnahme verfolgt. Er wies ferner darauf hin, daß durch das Ausfallen dieser Schicht von Juden und durch das Ausfallen einer ähnlichen Schicht Menschen in Deutschland zwischen dem Schicksal der Juden und der deutschen Entwicklung in mancher Beziehung Parallelen bestünden. Auch in Deutschland seien gewisse gute Persönlichkeiten einer bestimmten Lebensperiode ausgefallen, und daher habe er soviel Verständnis für das, was der Herr Ministerpräsident gesagt habe' (Jelinek and Blasius 1997: 333, original emphasis).

6. CHANGING THE GUARDS

1. Hannfried von Hindenburg argued that the German decision to

enter into diplomatic relations with Israel in 1965 was due to popular pressure from below (Hindenburg 2007: 3). However, this argument is not supported by the available archival files. Hindenburg's argument is an incorrect historical simplification, as also demonstrated by William Glenn Gray in his scathing review of Hindenburg's 'beguilingly simple and heroic story' (Gray 2010: 145). While by the 1960s, German silence on the Holocaust and World War II partially gave way to a limited acknowledgement of responsibility and the opening of a more honest debate, it is certainly not the case that a moral drive for reconciliation became dominant in German postwar society, and that this supposed moral drive translated into the FRG's decision to take the relationship with Israel to an official diplomatic level (Gray 2010).

7. TANKS AND FANTASIES

1. Because of its politically charged nature, Herf's analysis runs dangerously close to involuntarily belittling National Socialism, when he asks in his introduction 'whether the East German Communist regime was the second anti-Semitic dictatorship in Germany's twentieth century, whether parts of the West German radical Left constituted an anti-Semitic movement' (Herf 2016: 9). It is certainly a little overstretched to liken the petty dictatorship of the GDR and the West German student movement to Nazi Germany and the Nazi Party.

PART III: 'NORMALISATION' AND THE PALESTINIAN QUESTION IN GERMANY'S ISRAEL POLICY

1. During the period covered in this part, this role was assumed especially by the Netherlands and Denmark. For obvious reasons of political relevance, their support of Israel was much less significant than the often more subtle German support.

8. 'NORMALISATION BEGINS NOW'

1. In the following, the term 'normalisation' will be used with quotation marks to signify analytical distance, as this term points to a specific and often problematic usage, context and self-understanding.
2. This analytical frame undergirds the more recent work of German

historian Jenny Hestermann (2016), who studied the visits of German officials to Israel. While her nuanced, careful critique of German visions of 'normalisation' corresponds to some of what is said here, she retains a largely descriptive level of analysis that focuses on the 'feeling' of individual German–Israeli encounters.

3. Aronson moved towards academia and has continuously been a relevant voice in Israeli public debate. He could not, however, recall this particular article.

4. Based on an anonymous expert interview with an Israeli historian of Israel's foreign relations and a contemporary witness.

5. The name 'German Democratic Republic' or, by its acronym, 'GDR', was taboo in official West German parlance, which referred to the 'other Germany' by various names, one of them being Pankow, the Berlin district where the East German government was seated, or SBZ (short for 'Soviet Occupation Zone').

9. 'EVEN-HANDED'?

1. The question at stake is to what degree the radical fringe of German society articulates more widely held yet tabooed/repressed issues. The anti-Jewish violence committed by fringe elements of the German New Left after its splintering has recently been minutely described by Herf (2016) for English audiences. This violence included, but was not limited to, a failed attempt to bomb a Jewish community centre in Berlin on the thirtieth anniversary of the November pogroms, and the infamous 'separation' between Jews and non-Jews by German terrorists during the 1976 Entebbe hijacking. What can these chilling individual acts by German left-wing extremists tell us about the context from which they emerged? In a text that became important to the (self-)critique of the German radical left, Moishe Postone convincingly criticised those perceptions of National Socialism that treated antisemitism not as a core aspect of Nazi rule, but as peripheral to it. Postone argued that the reduction of Nazism to a form of extreme capitalist normality made it possible to see Nazism everywhere. By tending to see the old Nazi state reincarnated in the FRG's institutions, the New Left exaggerated the structural continuities which the right both ignored and represented. This reduction allowed members of the New Left to identify with a whole host of struggles, identifications

too easily branded as a learning from the past. The history of the German left after 1945 is, until this day, also a history of extreme and easily shifting identifications either with Israel or with Palestine. As Postone wrote: 'No western Left was as philo-Semitic and pro-Zionist prior to 1967. Probably none subsequently identified so strongly with the Palestinian cause. What was termed 'anti-Zionism' was in fact so emotionally and psychically charged that it went far beyond the bounds of a political and social critique of Zionism. The very word became as negatively informed as Nazism, in the one country where the Left should have known better' (Postone 1980: 103; see also Claussen 1986).

2. The Venice Declaration is the only declaration that is still available on the EU's website, suggesting it is still considered to be the most concise, elaborate statement of the EC countries prior to the Oslo process and still holds validity (see also Büttner 2003: 147, fn. 89).

11. RECOMMITTING

1. See also Pallade (2005: 240-3), whose selection, translation and interpretation of quotes from the interviews differ from those given above.

13. GERMANY IN THE TERRITORIES

1. EU aid to the oPt currently averages €300 million per year (Wildangel 2018: 51). Interestingly enough, while the EU's role as the main payer is not in doubt, there are no generally agreed numbers in the literature. The standard estimate is that the EU has provided about half of overall aid to the territories (Persson 2015: 130). According to Persson's research, judged plausible by Hollis (2015), European aid to the occupied territories in the framework of Oslo has totalled about €10 billion (up to 2010), including individual contributions by member states. This number fits well with the data provided by Constanza Musu (2010: 132-3).

2. US and EU development of the PA's internal security and policing capacities is carried out by the United States Security Coordinator and the European Union Coordinating Office for Palestinian Police Support. While the United States focuses on the PA's armed security

forces, the EU focuses on policing, its work including 'rebuilding prisons, detention centers, and police stations. Other types of assistance include providing the Palestinian police with IT equipment, training prison officers, holding gender workshops with the Palestinian police, and study trips to various places in Europe for judges, lawyers, prosecutors and police officers' (Persson 2015: 127).

3. For the press release of the report compiled by the UN country team in the oPt, see UN News (2017).

BIBLIOGRAPHY

As explained, interviews with experts were in the main anonymous. When used explicitly as sources, they are also referenced in the notes.

Main primary sources

Politisches Archiv des Auswärtigen Amtes – PA AA

Aktenedition zur Auswärtigen Politik der Bundesrepublik – AAPD

Abdel Hadi, H. (ed.), *BRD, Israel und die Palästinenser: Eine Fallstudie zur Ausländerpolitik*, Köln: Pahl-Rugenstein, 1973.

Achcar, G., *The Clash of Barbarisms*, London: Routledge, 2016.

———, 'Eichmann in Cairo: The Eichmann affair in Nasser's Egypt', *Arab Studies Journal*, 20, 1 (2012), pp. 74-103.

———, *The Arabs and the Holocaust: The Arab–Israeli War of Narratives*, New York: Saqi, 2010.

———, 'U.S imperial strategy in the Middle East' (2003) in *Eastern Cauldron: Islam, Afghanistan, Palestine, and Iraq in a Marxist Mirror*, London: Pluto, 2004, pp. 9-45.

———, 'The Washington Accords: A retreat under pressure' (1993) in *Eastern Cauldron: Islam, Afghanistan, Palestine, and Iraq in a Marxist Mirror*, London: Pluto, 2004, pp. 189-205.

———, 'Zionism and peace: From the Allon Plan to the Washington Accords' (1994) in *Eastern Cauldron: Islam, Afghanistan, Palestine, and Iraq in a Marxist Mirror*, London: Pluto, 2004, pp. 205-23.

BIBLIOGRAPHY

Adenauer, Konrad, 'Interview with Günter Gaus', https://archive.org/details/AdenauerInterview, last accessed 2 Dec. 2019.

Adorno, Theodor W. 'What does coming to terms with the past mean?' in G. H. Hartman (ed., trans.), *Bitburg in Moral and Political Perspective*, Bloomington: Indiana University Press, 1986, pp. 114-29.

Adorno, T. W. and M. Horkheimer, *Dialektik der Aufklärung: Philosophische Fragmente*, Frankfurt am Main: Fischer, 2012.

al-Fattal, R., *The Foreign Policy of the EU in the Palestinian Territory*, Brussels: CEPS, 2010.

Allen, D., and A. Pijpers (eds), *European Foreign Policy-Making and the Arab-Israeli Conflict*, The Hague & Lancaster: M. Nijhoff, 1984.

Aly, G., 'Angst vor der Wahrheit', *Süddeutsche Zeitung*, 17 Oct. 2017.

Anderson, B., *Imagined Communities: Reflections on the Origin and Spread of Nationalism* (rev. ed.), London & New York: Verso, 2006.

Arlosoroff, M., 'When Ben-Gurion saved Israel's economy at any price', *Haaretz*, 23 Mar. 2018.

Arendt, H., *Eichmann in Jerusalem: A Report on the Banality of Evil* (rev. and enl. ed.), Penguin: New York, 1994 [1963].

———, 'What's left? It remains the mother tongue', RBB Online, 28 Oct. 1964, https://www.rbb-online.de/zurperson/interview_archiv/arendt_hannah.html, last accessed 18 Aug. 2018.

———, *The Origins of Totalitarianism* (7th ed.), Cleveland & New York: Meridian Books, 1962 [1951].

Aruch, O., 'The German commitment to Israel's security', MA dissertation, Oxford: University of Oxford, 2012.

Asmus, R. D., 'Germany after the Gulf War', *RAND Note*, 1992.

Asseburg, M. and J. Busse, *Der Nahostkonflikt: Geschichte, Positionen, Perspektiven*, München: C.H. Beck, 2016.

———, 'Deutschlands Politik gegenüber Israel' in T. Jäger, A. Höse and K. Oppermann (eds), *Deutsche Außenpolitik, Sicherheit, Wohlfahrt, Institutionen, Normen*, Wiesbaden: VS Verlag für Sozialwissenschaften, 2011, pp. 693-716.

Barkan, E., *The Guilt of Nations. Restitution and Negotiating Historical Injustices*, Baltimore & London: Johns Hopkins University Press, 2001.

Barkawi, T. and M. Laffey, 'The postcolonial moment in security studies', *Review of International Studies*, 32, 2 (2006), pp. 329-52.

BIBLIOGRAPHY

Bashīr, B. and A. Goldberg (eds), *The Holocaust and the Nakba: A New Grammar of Trauma and History*, New York: Columbia University Press, 2018.

Beljan, D. and M. N. Lorenz, 'Weizsäcker-Rede' in M. N. Lorenz and T. Fischer (eds), *Lexikon der 'Vergangenheitsbewältigung' in Deutschland*, Bielefeld: transcript, 2015, pp. 253-6.

Belkin, P., 'Germany's relations with Israel: Background and implications for German Middle East policy', CRS Report for Congress, Congressional Research Service, 2007.

Benz, W., *Was ist Antisemitismus*, Munich: C. H. Beck, 2004.

Bergmann, R. and H. Stark, 'Corruption allegations shake German-Israeli cooperation', *Die Zeit*, 13 Oct. 2017.

Blasius, R., "Völkerfreundschaft' am Nil: Ägypten und die DDR im Februar 1965. Stenographische Aufzeichnungen aus dem Ministerium für Auswärtige Angelegenheiten über den Ulbricht-Besuch bei Nasser', *Vierteljahrshefte für Zeitgeschichte*, 46 (1998), pp. 747-805.

Blumenau, Bernd, 'West Germany and the United States during the Middle East crisis of 1973: "Nothing but a semi-colony"?' in J. Hanhimäki, G.-H. Soutou and B. Germond (eds), *The Routledge Handbook of Transatlantic Security*, Milton Park & New York: Routledge, 2010, pp. 123-37.

Bohr, F., G. Latsch and W. Klaus, '1972 Olympics massacre: Germany's secret contacts to Palestinian terrorists', *Der Spiegel*, 28 Aug. 2012.

Borchard, M., L. Hänsel and M. Frings, *A Difficult Nexus of Relationships? A Comprehensive View of the USA, Germany, Israel and the Palestinian Territories*, Jerusalem: Konrad-Adenauer Foundation, 2016.

Braach-Maksvytis, M., 'Germany, Israel, Palestine and the (post)colonial imagination' in V. M. Langbehn and M. Salama (eds), *German Colonialism. Race, the Holocaust and Postwar Germany*, New York: Columbia University Press, 2011, pp. 294-315.

Breitman, R. and J. W. N. Goda, *Hitler's Shadow: Nazi War Criminals, U.S. Intelligence, and the Cold War*, Washington, DC: U.S. National Archives, 2010.

Brenner, M., 'In the shadow of the Holocaust: The changing image of German Jewry after 1945', Ina Levine Annual Lecture at the United States Holocaust Memorial Museum, Washington, 2010.

———, *Zionism: A Brief History*, Princeton: Markus Wiener Publishers, 2003.

Bundespräsident, 'Speech by President Richard von Weizsäcker during the Ceremony Commemorating the 40th Anniversary of the End of War in Europe and of National-Socialist Tyranny on 8 May 1985 at the Bundestag, Bonn', 2015, https://www.bundespraesident.de/SharedDocs/Downloads/DE/Reden/2015/02/150202-RvW-Rede-8-Mai-1985-englisch.pdf?__blob=publicationFile, last accessed 26 Aug. 2018.

——, 'Federal President Joachim Gauck on the Day of Remembrance of the Victims of National Socialism on 27 January 2015 in Berlin', http://www.bundespraesident.de/SharedDocs/Downloads/DE/Reden/2015/01/150127-Gedenken-Holocaust-englisch.pdf;jsessionid=0685A7397FAEF800D0CC4DE1BCE35811.1_cid378?__blob=publicationFile, last accessed 2 Dec. 2019.

Bundestag, '29th Sitting: Berlin, Thursday 26th April 2018', 26 Apr. 2018, http://dipbt.bundestag.de/doc/btp/19/19029.pdf, last accessed 16 July 2018.

——, 'Response of the Federal Government to the small question put by Mr Ulla Jelpke, Mr Jan van Aken, Eva Bulling-Schröter, another Member of Parliament and the DIE LINKE', 14 Aug. 2012, http://dipbt.bundestag.de/dip21/btd/17/104/1710482.pdf, last accessed 18 July 2018.

——, '3rd Sitting: Bonn, Tuesday 10th November 1998', 10 Nov. 1998, http://dipbt.bundestag.de/doc/btp/14/14003.pdf, last accessed 26 Apr. 2018.

——, '176th Sitting: Bonn, Thursday 12th November 1993', 12 Nov. 1993, http://dipbt.bundestag.de/doc/btp/12/12176.pdf, last accessed 26 Apr. 2018.

——, '111th Sitting: Bonn, 7th June 1967', 7 June 1967, http://dipbt.bundestag.de/doc/btp/05/05111.pdf, last accessed 19 July 2018.

——, '254th Sitting: Bonn, Wednesday 18th March 1953', 18 Mar. 1953, http://dipbt.bundestag.de/doc/btp/01/01254.pdf, last accessed 17 July 2018.

——, '252nd Sitting: Bonn, Wednesday 4th March 1953', 4 Mar. 1953, http://dipbt.bundestag.de/doc/btp/01/01252.pdf, last accessed 17 July 2018.

——, '228th Sitting: Bonn, Wednesday 10th September 1952', 17 June 1952, http://dipbt.bundestag.de/doc/btp/01/01228.pdf, last accessed 17 July 2018.

———, '204th Sitting: Bonn, Thursday 3rd April and Friday 4th April 1952', 26 Feb. 1952, http://dipbt.bundestag.de/doc/btp/01/01204.pdf, last accessed 17 July 2018.

Büttner, F., 'Germany's Middle East policy: The dilemmas of a 'policy of even-handedness' (politik der ausgewogenheit)' in H. Goren (ed.), *Germany and the Middle East: Past, Present, Future*, Jerusalem: Magnes Press, 2003, pp. 115-59.

———, 'German perceptions of the Middle East conflict: Images and identifications during the 1967 war', *Journal of Palestine Studies*, 6, 2 (1977), pp. 66-81.

Büttner, F. and P. Hünseler, 'Die politischen Beziehungen zwischen der Bundesrepublik Deutschland und den arabischen Staaten. Entwicklung, Stand und Perspektiven' in U. Steinbach and K. Karl (eds), *Deutsch-Arabische Beziehungen. Bestimmungsfaktoren und Probleme einer Neuorientierung*, Munich: Oldenbourg, 1981.

Büttner, F. and T. Scheffler, 'Die Nahostpolitik der sozial-liberalen Koalition' in R. Steinweg (ed.), *Hilfe + Handel=Frieden? Die Bundesrepublik in der Dritten Welt*, Frankfurt am Main: Suhrkamp, 1982, pp. 139-75.

Chesterman, S., 'Seating arrangements at the table of world morality. [Review of 'The Guilt of Nations: Restitution and Negotiating Historical Injustices' by Elazar Barkan]', *London Review of Books*, 22, 20 (2000), pp. 29-30. Available from https://www.lrb.co.uk/v22/n20/simon-chesterman/seating-arrangements-at-the-table-of-world-morality, last accessed 2 Dec. 2019.

Chomsky, N., *Fateful Triangle: The United States, Israel, and the Palestinians* (updated ed.), Cambridge, MA: South End Press, 1999.

Christian Democratic Union of Germany, 'A new departure for Europe. A new dynamic for Germany. A new cohesion for our country', 2018, https://www.cdu.de/system/tdf/media/dokumente/koalitionsvertrag_2018.pdf?file=1, last accessed 26 Apr. 2018.

Claussen, D., 'In the house of the hangman' in A. Rabinbach and J. Zipes (eds), *Germans and Jews since the Holocaust: The Changing Situation in West Germany*, New York: Holmes & Meier, 1986, pp. 50-64.

Conze, E., N. Frei, P. Hayes and M. Zimmermann, *Das Amt und die Vergangenheit: Deutsche Diplomaten im Dritten Reich und in der Bundesrepublik*, Munich: Karl Blessing Verlag, 2010.

Czollek, M., *Desintegriert Euch*, Munich: Carl Hanser Verlag, 2018.

Deligdisch, J., *Die Einstellung der Bundesrepublik Deutschland zum Staate Israel: Eine Zusammenfassung der Entwicklung seit 1949*, Bonn: Neue Gesellschaft, 1974.

Deutscher, I., 'On the Arab-Israeli war', *New Left Review*, 1, 44 (1967).

Deutschkron, I., *Bonn and Jerusalem: The Strange Coalition*, Philadelphia: Chilton, 1970.

Deutschlandfunk, 'Die Geschichte ist immer im Hintergrund', 10 Apr. 2002, http://www.deutschlandfunk.de/die-geschichte-ist-immer-im-hintergrund.724.de.html?dram:article_id=97329, last accessed 17 Apr. 2018.

Dietl, Ralph, 'Suez 1956: A European intervention?' *Journal of Contemporary History*, 43, 2 (2008), pp. 259-78.

Diner, D., 'Banished: Jews in Germany after the Holocaust' in M. Brenner (ed.), *A History of Jews in Germany since 1945: Politics, Culture, and Society*, Bloomington: Indiana University Press, 2018, pp. 7-55.

————, *Rituelle Distanz: Israels deutsche Frage* (1st ed.), Munich: Deutsche Verlags-Anstalt, 2015.

Ebeling, T., 'Bericht über die Durchführung des Abkommens zwischen der Bundesrepublik Deutschland und dem Staate Israel vom 10. September 1952' in Auftrage des Vorsitzenden der Deutschen Delegation in der Deutsch-Israelischen Gemischten Kommission, 1966.

Elias, N., *Was ist Soziologie?* (11th ed.), Weinheim: Juventa-Verlag, 2009 [1970].

EU Directorate-General for External Policies, 'Area C: More than 60% of the occupied West Bank threatened by Israeli annexation', 2013, http://www.europarl.europa.eu/RegData/etudes/briefing_note/join/2013/491495/EXPO-AFET_SP(2013)491495_EN.pdf, last accessed 26 Apr. 2018.

European Council, 'Venice Declaration – June 13, 1980', 1980, http://eeas.europa.eu/archives/docs/mepp/docs/venice_declaration_1980_en.pdf, last accessed 20 Dec. 2017.

European Parliament, 'Part IV - Other Declarations', 1999, http://www.europarl.europa.eu/summits/ber2_en.htm#partIV, last accessed 26 Apr. 2018.

Evans, R. J., *Rereading German History: From Unification to Reunification, 1800–1996*, London & New York: Routledge, 1997.

Fink, C., *West Germany and Israel: Foreign Relations, Domestic Politics and the Cold War, 1965–1974*, Cambridge: Cambridge University Press, 2019.

———, "The most difficult journey of all': Willy Brandt's trip to Israel in June 1973', *The International History Review*, 37, 3 (2015), pp. 503-18.

———, 'Ostpolitik and West German–Israeli relations' in C. Fink and B. Schäfer (eds), *Ostpolitik, 1969–1974. European and Global Responses*, Cambridge: Cambridge University Press, 2009, pp. 182-9.

———, 'Turning away from the past: West Germany and Israel, 1965–1967' in P. Gassert and A. E. Steinweis (eds), *Coping with the Nazi Past. West German Debates on Nazism and Generational Conflict, 1955–1975*, New York: Berghahn Books, 2006, pp. 176-94.

Finkelstein, N., *The Holocaust Industry* (2nd ed.), London: Verso, 2015.

Fischbach, M. R., *Records of Dispossession: Palestinian Refugee Property and the Arab–Israeli Conflict*, New York: Columbia University Press, 2003.

Fischer, L., 'Deciphering Germany's pro-Israel consensus', *Journal of Palestine Studies*, 48, 2 (2019), pp. 26-42.

Frangi, A., 'Germany and the Middle East peace process: The Palestinian perspective' in S. Harnisch and H. W. Maull (eds), *German Foreign Policy and the Middle East Conflict. German Foreign Policy in Dialogue. A Quarterly E-Newsletter on German Foreign Policy*, 3, 7 (2002), pp. 34-37.

Frei, N., *Adenauer's Germany and the Nazi Past: The Politics of Amnesty and Integration*, New York: Columbia University Press, 2002.

Frie, R., *Not in my Family: German Memory and Responsibility after the Holocaust*, New York: Oxford University Press, 2017.

Gardner-Feldman, L., *Germany's Foreign Policy of Reconciliation: From Enmity to Amity*, Lanham, MD: Rowman & Littlefield Publishers, 2012.

———, *The Special Relationship between West Germany and Israel*, London: Allen and Unwin, 1984.

Garfinkle, A. M., *Western Europe's Middle East Diplomacy and the United States*, Philadelphia: Foreign Policy Research Institute, 1983.

Gassert, P. and A. E. Steinweis (eds), *Coping with the Nazi Past: West German Debates on Nazism and Generational Conflict, 1955–1975*, New York: Berghahn Books, 2006.

Geisel, E., *Die Wiedergutwerdung der Deutschen: Essays & Polemiken*, Berlin: Edition Tiamat, 2015.

Gerlach, D., *Die Doppelte Front: Die Bundesrepublik Deutschland und der Nahostkonflikt 1967–1973*, Berlin: LIT Verlag, 2006.

German Federal Agency for Civic Education, 'Gesicherte Existenz Israels – Teil der deutschen Staatsräson – Essay', 4 Apr. 2005, http://www.bpb.de/apuz/29118/gesicherte-existenz-israels-teil-der-deutschen-staatsraeson-essay?p=all, last accessed 26 Apr. 2018.

German Federal Archives, '4. London Debt Agreement and Agreement with Israel', 1952a, http://www.bundesarchiv.de/cocoon/barch/0000/k/k1952k/kap1_1/para2_5.html, last accessed 2 July 2018.

———, 'Reparations negotiations with Israel', 1952b, https://www.bundesarchiv.de/cocoon/barch/0000/k/k1952k/kap1_2/kap2_46/para3_12.html, last accessed 27 July 2018.

German Ministry for Cooperation and Development, 'Situation and cooperation', 2016, http://www.bmz.de/de/laender_regionen/naher_osten_nordafrika/palaestinensische_gebiete/zusammenarbeit/index.html, last accessed 20 Apr. 2018.

Gidley, B. and J. Renton (eds), *Antisemitism and Islamophobia in Europe: A Shared Story?* London: Palgrave Macmillan, 2017.

Goldhagen, D. J., *Hitler's Willing Executioners: Ordinary Germans and the Holocaust*, London: Abacus, 1997.

Gordon, N. and S. Pardo, 'Normative power Europe meets the Israeli–Palestinian conflict', *Asia Europe Journal*, 13, 3 (2015), pp. 265-74.

Goschler, C., 'NS-Opfer: Das Ende der Wiedergutmachung', *Die Zeit*, 28 Jan. 2015.

———, *Schuld und Schulden: Die Politik der Wiedergutmachung für NS-Verfolgte seit 1945* (2nd ed.), Göttingen: Wallstein, 2008.

Gray, W. G., 'Hannfried von Hindenburg, Demonstrating reconciliation: State and society in West German foreign policy toward Israel, 1952–1965 (review)', *European History Quarterly*, 40, 1 (2010), pp. 145-6.

Greilsammer, I. and J. Weiler, *Europe's Middle East Dilemma: The Quest for a Unified Stance*, Boulder: Westview Press, 1987.

———, 'European political cooperation and the Palestinian–Israeli conflict: An Israeli perspective' in D. Allen and A. Pijpers (eds), *European Foreign Policy-Making and the Arab-Israeli Conflict*, The Hague & Lancaster: M. Nijhoff, 1984.

Haddad, T., *Palestine LTD.: Neoliberalism and Nationalism in the Occupied Territory*, London: I.B. Tauris, 2016.

Halevi, Nadav, 'A brief economic history of modern Israel', EH.Net Encyclopedia, http://eh.net/encyclopedia/a-brief-economic-history-of-modern-israel/, last accessed 18 Nov. 2019.

Hanieh, A., 'From state-led growth to globalization: The evolution of Israeli capitalism', *Journal of Palestine Studies*, 32, 4 (2003), pp. 5-21.

Hansen, N., *Aus dem Schatten der Katastrophe. Die deutsch-israelischen Beziehungen in der Ära Konrad Adenauer und David Ben Gurion. Ein dokumentierter Bericht*, Düsseldorf: Droste, 2002.

Hawel, M., *Die normalisierte Nation: Vergangenheitsbewältigung und Aussenpolitik in Deutschland*, Hannover: Offizin, 2007.

Herbert, U., 'Academic and public discourses on the Holocaust: The Goldhagen debate in Germany', *German Politics and Society*, 17, 3 (1999), pp. 35-53.

Herf, J., *Undeclared Wars with Israel. East Germany and the West German Far Left 1967-1989*, Cambridge: Cambridge University Press, 2016.

———, *Divided Memory. The Nazi Past in the Two Germanys*, Cambridge, MA: Harvard University Press, 1997.

Hestermann, J., *Inszenierte Versöhnung: Reisediplomatie und die deutsch-israelischen Beziehungen von 1957 bis 1984*, Frankfurt am Main: Campus, 2016.

———, 'Ein 'Tag der tiefen Trauer' – Israelische Reaktionen auf den Umbruch in der DDR und die deutsche Wiedervereinigung', Deutschland Archiv, www.bpb.de/189684, last accessed 18 Nov. 2019.

Hinnebusch, R., 'The Middle East in the world hierarchy: Imperialism and resistance', *Journal of International Relations and Development*, 14, 2 (2011), pp. 213-46.

Hobsbawm, E. J., *Nations and Nationalism since 1780: Programme, Myth, Reality*, Cambridge & New York: Cambridge University Press, 1990.

Hollis, R., 'The EU and the Israeli-Palestinian conflict, 1971-2013: In Pursuit of a Just Peace by Anders Persson (review)', *The Middle East Journal*, 69, 3 (2015), pp. 469-71.

———, 'The Israeli-Palestinian road block: Can Europeans make a difference?' *International Affairs*, 80, 2 (2004), pp. 191-201.

———, 'Europe and the Middle East: Power by stealth?' *International Affairs*, 73, 1 (1997), pp. 15-29.

Hubel, H., 'Cooperation and conflict in German and American policies towards regions outside Europe' in D. Junker, P. Gassert, W. Mausebach and D. B. Morris (eds), *The United States and Germany in the Era of the Cold War, 1945–1990, Vol. 2, 1968–1990: A Handbook*, Cambridge: Cambridge University Press, 2004, pp. 69-76.

Jäger, K., *Quadratur des Dreiecks: Die deutsch-israelischen Beziehungen und die Palästinenser*, Schwalbach: Wochenschau, 1997.

———, 'Die Bedeutung des Palästinenser-Problems für die deutsch-israelischen Beziehungen', *Aus Politik und Zeitgeschichte*, 16, 95 (1995), pp. 21-30.

Jander, M., 'Antisemitism and anti-Zionism in West Germany in the 1970s: Lessons for today', *Fathom Journal*, Summer (2017).

Jelinek, Y. A., *Deutschland und Israel 1945–1965. Ein neurotisches Verhältnis*, Munich: Oldenbourg, 2004.

———, *Zwischen Moral und Realpolitik. Deutsch-israelische Beziehungen 1945-1965. Eine Dokumentensammlung*, Schriftenreihe des Minerva Instituts für deutsche Geschichte Universität Tel Aviv, 16 (1997).

Jelinek, Y. A. and R. A. Blasius, 'Ben Gurion und Adenauer im Waldorf Astoria. Gesprächsaufzeichnungen vom israelisch-deutschen Gipfeltreffen in New York am 14. März 1960. Einführung von Rainer A. Blasius', *Vierteljahreshefte für Zeitgeschichte*, 45, 2 (1997), pp. 309-44.

Judt, Tony, *Postwar. A History of Europe since 1945*, London: Vintage, 2010.

Jureit, U. and Schneider, C., *Gefühlte Opfer. Illusionen der Vergangenheitsbewältigung*, Stuttgart: Klett-Cotta.

Kloke, Martin, 'Die Linke in Europa: Vereint gegen Israel?' *Tribüne. Zeitschrift zum Verständnis des Judentums*, 186, 47 (2008).

Kocka, J., 'German History before Hitler: The Debate about the German Sonderweg', *Journal of Contemporary History*, 23, 1 (1988), pp. 3-16.

Koerfer, D., 'Rezension Sachbuch: 'Jeder Deutsche ist ein Mörder'', *Frankfurter Allgemeine Zeitung*, 11 July 2002.

Könke, G., 'Wiedergutmachung und Modernisierung. Der Beitrag des Luxemburger Abkommens von 1952 zur wirtschaftlichen Entwicklung Israels', *Vierteljahrschrift für Sozial- und Wirtschaftsgeschichte*, 75, 4 (1988), pp. 503-48.

Krell, G., 'Schatten der Vergangenheit: Nazi-Deutschland, Holocaust und Nahost-Konflikt', HSFK-Report 7/2008, Frankfurt am Main: Hessische Stiftung Friedens- und Konfliktforschung, 2008.

Kyle, K., *Suez: Britain's End of Empire in the Middle East*, London: I.B. Tauris, 2003.

Large, D. C., *Munich 1972: Tragedy, Terror, and Triumph at the Olympic Games*, Lanham, MD: Rowman & Littlefield Publishers, 2012.

Lavy, G., *Germany and Israel: Moral Debt and National Interest*, London: Frank Cass, 1996.

Le More, A., *International Assistance to the Palestinians after Oslo: Political Guilt, Wasted Money*, London & New York: Routledge, 2008.

———, 'Killing with kindness: Funding the demise of a Palestinian state', *International Affairs*, 81, 5 (2005), pp. 981-99.

Leber, H., 'Chancellor Helmut Schmidt, his policy toward Israel, and the German responsibility for the Jewish people', *American Institute for Contemporary German Studies*, 14 Dec. 2015.

Leggewie, C. and E. Mayer, *Ein Ort, an den man gerne geht: Das Holocaust-Mahnmal und die deutsche Geschichtspolitik nach 1989*, Munich: Hanser, 2005.

Lewan, K. M., 'How West Germany helped to build Israel', *Journal of Palestine Studies*, 4, 4 (1975), pp. 41-64.

———, *Der Nahostkrieg in der westdeutschen Presse*, Cologne: Pahl-Rugenstein, 1970.

Lewy, M. and T. Newman, 'Germany and Israel in the 1990s and Beyond. Still a Special Relationship? (review)', *Israel Journal of Foreign Affairs*, 1, 2 (2007), pp. 137-43.

Lintl, P., 'Auswirkungen des ungelösten Konflikts auf israelische Machtkonstellationen und Akteursperspektiven' in *Akteure des israelisch- palästinensischen Konflikts: Interessen, Narrative und die Wechselwirkungen der Besatzung*, Berlin: SWP, 2018, pp. 9-31.

Litvak, M. and E. Webman, *From Empathy to Denial: Arab Responses to the Holocaust*, London: Hurst, 2011.

Lovatt, H., 'Occupation and sovereignty: Renewing EU policy in Israel-Palestine', *Policy Brief*, European Council on Foreign Relations & Foundation for European Progressive Studies, 2017.

Ludi, R., *Reparations for Nazi Victims in Postwar Europe*, Cambridge: Cambridge University Press, 2012.

Lustick, I., 'Negotiating truth: The Holocaust, Lehavdil and al-Nakba', *Journal of International Affairs*, 60, 1 (2006), pp. 51-77.

Maeke, L., *DDR und PLO*, Studien zur Zeitgeschichte, Bd. 92: Berlin, 2017.

Mark, S., H. Tsoref and L. Fischer, 'The Munich massacre, September 1972', Edited Document Collection, Jerusalem: Israel State Archives, 2012.

Merkel, Angela, 'Speech by Federal Chancellor Angela Merkel to the Knesset in Jerusalem on 18 March 2008', 18 Mar. 2008, https:// www.knesset.gov.il/description/eng/doc/speech_merkel_2008_eng. pdf, last accessed 16 July 2018.

Moeller, R. G., *War Stories. The Search for a Usable Past in the Federal Republic of Germany*, Berkeley, Los Angeles & London: University of California Press, 2001.

Mohr, M., *Waffen für Israel : Westdeutsche Rüstungshilfe vor dem Sechstagekrieg*, Berlin: Köster, 2003.

Morris, B., *Righteous Victims: A History of the Zionist–Arab Conflict, 1881– 1999* (1st ed.), New York: Vintage, 2001.

Müller, P., 'The Europeanization of Germany's foreign policy toward the Israeli–Palestinian conflict: Between adaptation to the EU and national projection', *Mediterranean Politics*, 16, 3 (2011), pp. 385-403.

Münkel, D., 'Große Koalition gegen Brandt. Wie Deutschlands Rechte und die Stasi den SPD-Politiker in den sechziger Jahren politisch vernichten wollten', *Die Zeit*, 13 Dec. 2013.

Musial, David, 'Wiedergutmachungs- und Entschädigungsgesetze', in M. N. Lorenz and T. Fischer (eds), *Lexikon der 'Vergangenheitsbewältigung' in Deutschland* (3rd ed.), Bielefeld: transcript, 2015.

Musu, C., *European Union Policy towards the Arab-Israeli Peace Process: The Quicksands of Politics*, Basingstoke: Palgrave Macmillan, 2010.

Nassauer, O., *Drei neue Dolphin-U-Boote für Israel*, Berlin: Berliner Informationszentrum für Transatlantische Sicherheit (BITS), 2017.

Nassauer, O. and C. Steinmetz, 'Rüstungskooperation zwischen Deutschland und Israel', research report 2003.1., Berlin: Berliner Informationszentrum für Transatlantische Sicherheit (BITS), 2003.

Nassauer, O., C. Steinmetz and Y. Pallade, 'Geheimnisumwittert: Die deutsch-israelische Rüstungszusammenarbeit', *Wissenschaft & Frieden*, 4 (2002).

Nicosia, F., *Zionism and Anti-Semitism in Nazi Germany*, Cambridge: Cambridge University Press, 2008.

Nitzan, J. and S. Bichler, *The Global Political Economy of Israel*, London & Sterling, VA: Pluto Press, 2002.

BIBLIOGRAPHY

Odlum, S., 'The U.S.-Israeli arms trade. It always takes two to tango', briefing note 2002.3., Berlin: Berliner Informationszentrum für Transatlantische Sicherheit (BITS), 2002.

Oz-Salzberger, F., *Israelis in Berlin*, Berlin: Jüdischer Verlag im Suhrkamp Verlag, 2016.

Pallade, Y., *Germany and Israel in the 1990s and Beyond: Still a 'Special Relationship'?* Frankfurt am Main: P. Lang, 2005.

Pamperrien, S., *Helmut Schmidt und der Scheisskrieg: Die Biografie 1918 bis 1945*, Munich: Piper, 2014.

Pardo, S. and J. Peters, *Uneasy Neighbours: Israel and the European Union*, Lanham, MD: Lexington Books, 2010.

Peres, S., *David's Sling*, London: Weidenfeld & Nicolson, 1970.

Persson, A., 'EU differentiation as a case of 'Normative Power Europe' (NPE) in the Israeli–Palestinian conflict', *Journal of European Integration*, 40, 2 (2018), pp. 193-208.

————, *The EU and the Israeli–Palestinian Conflict, 1971–2013: In Pursuit of a Just Peace*, Lanham, MD: Lexington Books, 2015.

Postone, M., 'Anti-semitism and National Socialism: Notes on the German reaction to 'Holocaust'', *New German Critique*, 19, 1 (1980), pp. 97-115.

Rabinbach, A., 'The Jewish question in the German question', *New German Critique*, 44 (1988), pp. 159-92.

Raz-Krakotzkin, A., 'Secularism, the Christian ambivalence towards the Jews, and the notion of exile' in A. Joskowitz and E. B. Katz (eds), *Secularism in Question. Jews and Judaism in Modern Times*, Philadelphia: University of Pennsylvania Press, 2015, pp. 276-99.

Rivlin, P., *The Israeli Economy from the Foundation of the State through the 21st Century*, Cambridge: Cambridge University Press, 2010.

Rose, J., *The Last Resistance*, London: Verso, 2017.

Roy, S. M., *The Gaza Strip: The Political Economy of De-Development* (3rd ed.), Washington, DC: Institute for Palestine Studies USA, Inc., 2016.

————, *Failing Peace: Gaza and the Palestinian-Israeli Conflict*, London & Ann Arbor: Pluto, 2007.

Rühle, H., 'Hat Deutschland Israels Atomwaffen finanziert?' *Die Welt*, 14 Apr. 2015.

Rybak, J., ''Unheilige Allianzen' und Projektionsbedürfnisse im Kontext der Gaza-Protestbewegung in Deutschland', *Chilufim: Zeitschrift für Jüdische Kulturgeschichte*, 18 (2015), pp. 151-200.

Sabrow, M., 'Höcke und Wir', *Zeitgeschichte-online*, Jan. 2017.

Sachar, H. M., *Israel and Europe: An Appraisal in History* (1st ed.), New York: Vintage, 1999.

Said, E., 'The morning after', *London Review of Books*, 15, 20 (1993), pp. 3-5.

Sand, S., *The Invention of the Jewish People*, London: Verso, 2009.

Scheffler, T., 'Die Normalisierung der Doppelmoral – 40 Jahre Deutsch-Israelische Beziehungen', *Prokla*, 73 (1988), pp. 76-96.

Schiller, K. and C. Young, *The 1972 Munich Olympics and the Making of Modern Germany*, Berkeley: University of California Press, 2010.

Schirrmacher, F., 'Eine Erläuterung. Was Grass uns sagen will', *Frankfurter Allgemeine Zeitung*, 4 Apr. 2012.

Schlichte, K. and A. Veit, 'Three arenas: The conflictive logic of external statebuilding' in B. Bliesemann de Guevara (ed.), *Statebuilding and State-Formation. The Political Sociology of Intervention*, London: Routledge, 2012, pp. 167-81.

Schmidl, Karin, "Vaterland' von Günther Schäfer Künstler entfernt antisemitische Schmierereien an der East Side Gallery', *Berliner Zeitung*, 2 Aug. 2015, https://www.berliner-zeitung.de/berlin/-vaterland – von-guenther-schaefer-kuenstler-entfernt-antisemitische-schmierereien-an-der-east-side-gallery-22401260, last accessed 16 July 2019.

Schmidt, W., 'From historical responsibility, moral obligation, and political conviction. German Chancellor Willy Brandt's efforts on behalf of Israel and peace in the Middle East', *Schriftenreihe der Bundeskanzler-Willy-Brandt-Stiftung*, 26 (2014).

Schölch, A., 'Die Gegenwart der Geschichte: Deutsche, Israelis, Palästinenser' in K. Schneider (eds), *20 Jahre Deutsch-Israelische Beziehungen*. Berlin: Deutsch-Israelischer Arbeitskreis (DIAK), Schriften, 1985, pp. 45-63.

Schwarz, H. P., *Konrad Adenauer: From the German Empire to the Federal Republic, 1876–1952*, London: Berghahn Books, 1997.

Segev, T., *The Seventh Million: The Israelis and the Holocaust*, New York: Hill and Wang, 1993.

Shafir, S., 'Helmut Schmidt: Seine Beziehungen zu Israel und den Juden', in *Jahrbuch für Antisemitismusforschung*, Berlin: Metropol, 2008.

Shalom, Z., 'Document: David Ben-Gurion and Chancellor Adenauer at the Waldorf Astoria on 14 March 1960', *Israel Studies*, 2, 1 (1997), pp. 50-71.

Shiek, D. and Pedatzur, R., 'Naval power and its importance for Israel's future security', 2002, http://www.msf-13.com/pdf/paper_01.pdf, last accessed 2 Dec. 2019.

Shpiro, S., 'Shadowy interests: West German-Israeli intelligence and military cooperation, 1957–82', in C. Jones and T. T. Petersen (eds), *Israel's Clandestine Diplomacies*, London: Hurst, 2013, pp. 169-88.

———, 'Communicating interests across history: German–Israeli security cooperation' in H. Goren (ed.), *Germany and the Middle East: Past, Present, Future*, Jerusalem: Magnes Press, 2003, pp. 305-30.

———, 'Intelligence services and foreign policy: German–Israeli intelligence and military', *German Politics*, 11, 1 (2002), pp. 23-42.

Slobodian, Quinn, 'The borders of the Rechtsstaat in the Arab Autumn: Deportation and law in West Germany, 1972/73', *German History*, 31, 2 (2013), pp. 204-24.

Slyomovics, S., *How to Accept German Reparations*, Philadelphia: University of Pennsylvania Press, 2014.

Sontheimer, M., 'Ausstellung über Verleger Axel Springer. Fluchtpunkt Jerusalem,' *taz*, 12 Mar. 2012.

Der Spiegel, 'ISRAELS BLITZKRIEG', 12 June 1967, https://www.spiegel.de/spiegel/print/d-46394367.html, last accessed 2 Dec. 2019.

———, 'FESTAKT – Tempo 60', 10 Feb. 1960, http://www.spiegel.de/spiegel/print/d-43063250.html, last accessed 22 Jan. 2016.

Stauber, R., 'The impact of the Sinai campaign on relations between Israel and West Germany', *Modern Judaism*, 33, 3 (2013), pp. 235-59.

———, 'Between realpolitik and the burden of the past: Israel's diplomats and the 'Other Germany'', *Israel Studies*, 8, 3 (2003), pp. 100-22.

Sterling, E., 'Judenfreunde - Judenfeinde. Fragwürdiger Philosemitismus in der Bundesrepublik', *Die Zeit*, 10 Dec. 1965.

Stern, F., *The Whitewashing of the Yellow Badge: Antisemitism and Philosemitism in Postwar Germany*, Oxford : Pergamon, 1992.

Taylor, F., *Exorcising Hitler: The Occupation and Denazification of Germany*, London: Bloomsbury, 2012.

Tempel, S., *Legenden von der Allmacht: Die Beziehungen zwischen amerikanisch-jüdischen Organisationen und der Bundesrepublik Deutschland seit 1945*, Frankfurt am Main: P. Lang, 1995.

Thrall, N., *The Only Language They Understand: Forcing Compromise in Israel and Palestine*, New York: Metropolitan, 2017.

Thünemann, H., 'Mehr Denkmäler – weniger Gedenken?' *Public History Weekly*, 8 (2013). doi: https://doi.org/10.1515/phw-2013-416.

Times of Israel, 'Far-right leader: Nazi era a 'speck of bird poop' in glorious German history', 2 June 2018, https://www.timesofisrael.com/far-right-leader-nazi-era-a-speck-of-bird-poop-in-german-history/, last accessed 16 July 2018.

Timm, Angelika, 'Ideology and realpolitik: East German attitudes towards Zionism and Israel', *Journal of Israeli History Politics, Society, Culture*, 25, 1 (2006), pp. 203-22.

———, *Hammer, Zirkel, Davidstern: Das gestörte Verhältnis der DDR zu Zionismus und Staat Israel*, Bonn: Bouvier, 1997.

Tooze, A., 'Reassessing the moral economy of post-war reconstruction: The terms of the West German settlement in 1952', *Past & Present*, 210 (2011), pp. 47-70.

Tovy, J., 'Talking after Auschwitz? The public-political struggle in Israel over the negotiation of a reparations agreement with West Germany, 1951–1952', *Holocaust Studies*, 23, 4 (2017), pp. 483-504.

Trimbur, D., 'American influence on the Federal Republic of Germany's Israel Policy, 1951–1956' in H. Goren (ed.), *Germany and the Middle East: Past, Present, Future*, Jerusalem: Magnes Press, 2003, pp. 263-91.

———, *De la Shoah à la Réconciliation? La Question des Relations RFA-Israël, 1949–1956*, Paris: CNRS, 2000.

Tsoref, H. and M. Wolffsohn, 'Wie Willy Brandt den Nahost-Frieden verspielte', *Die Welt*, 9 June 2013.

Turner, M. and O. Shweiki (eds), *Decolonizing Palestinian Political Economy: De-Development and Beyond*, Basingstoke: Palgrave Macmillan, 2014.

Ullrich, Peter, 'Linke, Nahostkonflikt, Antisemitismus. Wegweiser durch eine Debatte. Eine kommentierte Bibliographie', *Analysen*, Rosa-Luxemburg Stiftung, 2014.

———, *Die Linke, Israel und Palästina: Nahostdiskurse in Großbritannien und Deutschland*, Berlin: Dietz, 2008.

UN News, 'Living conditions in Gaza 'more and more wretched' over past decade, UN finds', 11 July 2017, https://news.un.org/en/story/2017/07/561302-living-conditions-gaza-more-and-more-wretched-over-past-decade-un-finds, last accessed 11 Sep. 2018.

Unabhängiger Expertenkreises Antisemitismus, 'Unterrichtung durch die Bundesregierung. Bericht des Unabhängigen Expertenkreises Antisemitismus', Deutscher Bundestag, 18. Wahlperiode, 7 Apr. 2017.

Vogel, R., *The German Path to Israel: A Documentation*, London: Wolff, 1969.

Vogt, S., *Subalterne Positionierungen. Der deutsche Zionismus im Feld des Nationalismus in Deutschland 1890–1933*, Göttingen: Wallstein, 2016.

Voigt, S. (2008). 'Das Verhältnis der DDR zu Israel', Bundesamt für Politische Bildung, http://www.bpb.de/internationales/asien/israel/45014/ddr-israel?p=0, last accessed 18 Nov. 2019.

von Hindenburg, H., *Demonstrating Reconciliation: State and Society in West German Foreign Policy Toward Israel, 1952-1965*, New York: Berghahn Books, 2007.

von Jena, Kai, 'Versöhnung mit Israel? Die deutsch-israelischen Verhandlungen bis zum Wiedergutmachungsabkommen von 1952', *Vierteljahreshefte für Zeitgeschichte*, 75, 4 (1986), pp. 457-80.

Vowinckel, A., 'Der kurze Weg nach Entebbe oder die Verlängerung der deutschen Geschichte in den Nahen Osten', *Zeithistorische Forschungen/Studies in Contemporary History*, 2 (2004), pp. 236-54.

Walser, M., 'Rede anlässlich der Verleihung des Friedenspreises des Deutschen Buchhandels', 11 Oct. 1998, https://www.friedenspreis-des-deutschen-buchhandels.de/sixcms/media.php/1290/1998_walser_mit_nachtrag_2017.pdf, last accessed 2 Dec. 2019.

Weingardt, M., *Deutsche Israel- und Nahostpolitik. Die Geschichte einer Gratwanderung seit 1949*, Frankfurt am Main: Campus, 2002.

Weiss, V., '"Volksklassenkampf" - Die antizionistische Rezeption des Nahostkonflikts in der militanten Linken der BRD', *Tel Aviver Jahrbuch für Deutsche Geschichte*, 33 (2005), pp. 214-38.

Weiss, Y., *A Confiscated Memory: Wadi Salib and Haifa's Lost Heritage*, New York: Columbia University Press, 2011.

Weitz, Yechiam, 'Ben Gurions Weg zum 'Anderen Deutschland"', *Vierteljahreshefte für Zeitgeschichte*, 48, 2 (2000), pp. 255-79.

Welzer, H., S. Möller and K. Tschuggnall, *Opa war kein Nazi: Nationalsozialismus und Holocaust im Familiengedächtnis* (3rd ed.), Frankfurt am Main: Fischer, 2002.

Wetzel, D. (ed.), *Die Verlängerung von Geschichte: Deutsche, Juden und der Palästinakonflikt*, Frankfurt am Main: Verlag Neue Kritik, 1983.

Wiegrefe, Klaus, 'Der Fluch der bösen Tat. Die Angst vor Adolf Eichmann', *Der Spiegel*, 11 Apr. 2011.

———, 'Germany's unlikely diplomatic triumph: An inside look at the reunification negotiations', *Der Spiegel*, 29 Sep. 2010.

Wildangel, R., 'Die Europäische Union und der israelisch-palästinensische Konflikt: Von der Deklaration zur Aktion?' in P. Lintl (ed.), *Akteure des israelisch- palästinensischen Konflikts: Interessen, Narrative und die Wechselwirkungen der Besatzung*, Berlin: SWP, 2018, pp. 48-66.

Winkler, W., 'Adolf Eichmann und seine Unterstützer. Ein kleiner Nachtrag zu einem bekannten Rechtsfall' in W. Renz (ed.), *Interessen um Eichmann: Israelische Justiz, deutsche Strafverfolgung und alte Kameradschaften*, Frankfurt am Main: Campus, 2012, pp. 289-319.

Wolffsohn, M., *Eternal Guilt?* New York: Columbia University Press, 1993.

————, 'Das deutsch-israelische Wiedergutmachungsabkommen von 1952 im internationalen Zusammenhang', *Vierteljahreshefte für Zeitgeschichte*, 36, 4 (1988), pp. 691-731.

————, *Friedenskanzler? Willy Brandt zwischen Krieg und Terror*, Munich: dtv, 2018.

Yablonka, H., *The State of Israel vs. Adolf Eichmann*, New York: Schocken Books, 2004.

Yergin, Daniel, *The Prize. The Epic Quest for Oil, Money and Power*, New York: Simon & Schuster, 1991.

Zertal, Idith, *Israel's Holocaust and the Politics of Nationhood*, Cambridge: Cambridge University Press, 2005.

Zimmermann, M., 'The Arab-Israeli conflict as a challenge to German–Israeli relations' in A. Wittstock (ed.), *Rapprochement, Change, Perception and Shaping the Future: 50 Years of German-Israeli and Israeli-German Diplomatic Relations*, Berlin: Frank & Timme, 2016, pp. 43-55.

Zuckermann, M., *Zweierlei Holocaust: Der Holocaust in den politischen Kulturen Israels und Deutschlands* (3rd ed.), Göttingen: Wallstein, 2004.

INDEX